Journal of International  Business

Management International Review

David M. Brock/Julian Birkinshaw (Guest Editors)
Contemporary Issues in Multinational Strategy and Structure

Note from the Guest Editors

David M. Brock/Julian Birkinshaw
**Multinational Strategy and Structure:
A Review and Research Agenda**

Sunil Venaik/David F. Midgley/Timothy M. Devinney
Integration-Responsiveness Pressures

Tony Edwards/Anthony Ferner
Reverse Diffusion in Multinationals

Brent B. Allred/K. Scott Swan
**Global Versus Multidomestic:
Culture's Consequences on Innovation**

Stephen B. Tallman/J. Michael Geringer/David M. Olsen
**Resources, Strategy, Structure and Performance
among Japanese MNE's**

Mark V. Cannice/Roger (Rongxin) Chen/John D. Daniels
Managing International Technology Transfer Risk

D 21247

ISBN 978-3-409-12544-4   ISBN 978-3-322-90999-2 (eBook)

DOI 10.1007/978-3-322-90999-2

EDITORIAL BOARD

Professor Raj Aggarwal, Kent State University, Kent – U.S.A.
Professor Jeffrey S. Arpan, University of South Carolina, Columbia – U.S.A.
Professor Daniel van Den Bulcke, Universiteit Antwerpen – Belgium
Professor John A. Cantwell, Rutgers University, Newark – U.S.A.
Professor S. Tamer Cavusgil, Michigan State University, East Lansing – U.S.A.
Professor Frederick D.S. Choi, New York University – U.S.A.
Professor Farok Contractor, Rutgers University, Newark – U.S.A.
Professor John D. Daniels, University of Miami, Coral Gables – U.S.A.
Professor Peter J. Dowling, University of Canberra – Australia
Professor Santiago García Echevarría, Universidad de Alcála de Henares, Madrid – Spain
Professor Lawrence A. Gordon, University of Maryland, College Park – U.S.A.
Professor Sidney J. Gray, University of Sydney – Australia
Professor Geir Gripsrud, Norwegian School of Management, Sandvika – Norway
Professor Jean-François Hennart, Tilburg University – The Netherlands
Professor Georges Hirsch, Centre Franco-Vietnamien de Formation à la gestion, Paris – France
Professor Andrew Inkpen, Thunderbird, The American Graduate School of International Management, Glendale – U.S.A.
Professor Eugene D. Jaffe, Bar-Ilan University, Ramat-Gan – Israel
Professor Erdener Kaynak, Pennsylvania State University, Middletown – U.S.A.
Professor Yui Kimura, University of Tsukuba, Tokyo – Japan
Professor Michael Kutschker, Katholische Universität Eichstätt, Ingolstadt – Germany
Professor Reijo Luostarinen, Helsinki School of Economics – Finland
Professor Klaus Macharzina, Universität Hohenheim, Stuttgart – Germany
Professor Roger Mansfield, Cardiff Business School – United Kingdom
Professor Mark Mendenhall, University of Tennessee, Chattanooga – U.S.A.
Professor Rolf Mirus, University of Alberta, Edmonton – Canada
Professor Michael H. Moffett, American Graduate School, Phoenix – U.S.A.
Professor Krzysztof Y. Obloj, University of Warsaw – Poland
Professor Lars Oxelheim, Lund University – Sweden
Professor Ki-An Park, Kyung Hee University, Seoul – Korea
Professor Robert D. Pearce, University of Reading – United Kingdom
Professor Lee Radebaugh, Brigham Young University, Provo – U.S.A.
Professor Edwin Rühli, Universität Zürich – Switzerland
Professor Alan M. Rugman, Indiana University, Bloomington, U.S.A.
Professor Rakesh B. Sambharya, Rutgers University, Camden, U.S.A.
Professor Reinhart Schmidt, Universität Halle-Wittenberg – Germany
Professor Hans Schöllhammer, University of California, Los Angeles – U.S.A.
Professor Oded Shenkar, The Ohio State University, Columbus – U.S.A.
Professor Vitor Corado Simoes, Universidade Técnica de Lisboa – Portugal
Professor John Stopford, 6 Chalcot Square, London NW1 8YB – United Kingdom
Professor Daniel P. Sullivan, University of Delaware, Newark – U.S.A.
Professor Norihiko Suzuki, International Christian University, Tokyo – Japan
Professor Stephen Bruce Tallmann, University of Utah, Salt Lake City – U.S.A.
Professor George Tesar, Umeå University, Umeå – Sweden
Professor José de la Torre, Florida International University, Miami – U.S.A.
Professor Rosalie L. Tung, Simon Fraser University, Burnaby, BC – Canada
Professor Jean-Claude Usunier, University of Lousanne, Lousanne – Dorigny – Switzerland
Professor Alain Charles Verbeke, Vrije Universiteit Brussel – Belgium
Professor Lawrence S. Welch, Mt Eliza Business School, Melbourne, Australia
Professor Martin K. Welge, Universität Dortmund – Germany
Professor Bernard Yin Yeung, New York University – U.S.A.
Professor Masaru Yoshimori, Yokohama National University – Japan

BOOK REVIEW EDITOR

Professor Dr. Johann Engelhard, Universität Bamberg – Germany

EDITOR

MANAGEMENT INTERNATIONAL REVIEW, *Professor Dr. Profs. h.c. Dr. h.c. Klaus Macharzina, Universität Hohenheim (510 E), Schloss-Osthof-Ost, D-70599 Stuttgart, Germany, Tel. (0711) 4 59-29 08, Fax (0711) 459-3288, E-mail: klausmac@uni-hohenheim.de, Internet: http://www.uni-hohenheim.de/~mir Assistant Editors: Professor Dr. Michael-Jörg Oesterle, Universität Bremen, Germany, Professor Dr. Joachim Wolf, Universität Kiel, Germany, Editorial office: Mrs. Sylvia Ludwig*

Management International Review
© Gabler Verlag 2004

VOLUME 44 SPECIAL ISSUE 2004/1

CONTENTS

Note from the Guest Editors 3

David M. Brock/Julian Birkinshaw

Multinational Strategy and Structure: A Review and Research Agenda 5

Sunil Venaik/David F. Midgley/Timothy M. Devinney

A New Perspective on the Integration-Responsiveness Pressures Confronting Multinational Firms 15

Tony Edwards/Anthony Ferner

Multinationals, Reverse Diffusion and National Business Systems 49

Brent B. Allred/K. Scott Swan

Global Versus Multidomestic: Culture's Consequences on Innovation .. 81

Stephen B. Tallman/J. Michael Geringer/David M. Olsen

Contextual Moderating Effects and the Relationship of Firm-Specific Resources, Strategy, Structure and Performance among Japanese Multinational Enterprises 107

Mark V. Cannice/ Roger (Rongxin) Chen/John D. Daniels

Managing International Technology Transfer Risk: Alternatives and Complements to Ownership Structure 129

GUIDELINE FOR AUTHORS

mir welcomes articles on original theoretical contributions, empirical research, state-of-the-art surveys or reports on recent developments in the areas of

a) International Business b) Transnational Corporations c) Intercultural Management d) Strategic Management e) Business Policy.

Manuscripts are reviewed with the understanding that they are substantially new, have not been previously published in whole (including book chapters) or in part (including exhibits), have not been previously accepted for publication, are not under consideration by any other publisher, and will not be submitted elsewhere until a decision is reached regarding their publication in **mir**. The only exception is papers in conference proceedings, which we treat as work-in-progress.

Contributions should be submitted in English language in a Microsoft or compatible format by e-mail to the Editor at klausmac@uni-hohenheim.de. The complete text including the references, tables and figures should as a rule not exceed 25 pages in a usual setting (approximately *7000 words*). Reply papers should normally not exceed 1500 words. The title page should include the following elements: Author(s) name, Heading of the article, Abstract (two sections of about 30 words each), Key Results (20 words), Author's line (author's name, academic title, position and affiliation) and on the bottom a proposal for an abbreviated heading on the front cover of the journal.

Submitted papers must be written according to mir's formal guidelines. Only those manuscripts can enter the reviewing process which adhere to our guidelines. Authors are requested to

– use *endnotes* for clarification sparingly. References to the literature are indicated in the text by author's name and year of publication in parentheses, e.g. (Reitsperger/Daniel 1990, p. 210, Eiteman 1989). The references should be listed in alphabetical order at the end of the text. They should include full bibliographical details and be cited in the following manner: e.g.

> Reitsperger, W. D./Daniel, S. J., Dynamic Manufacturing: A Comparison of Attitudes in the U.S. and Japan, *Management International Review*, 30, 1990, pp. 203–216.
>
> Eiteman, D. K., Financial Sourcing, in Macharzina, K./Welge, M. K. (eds.), *Handwörterbuch Export und Internationale Unternehmung*, Stuttgart: Poeschel 1989, pp. 602–621.
>
> Stopford, J. M./Wells, L. T. Jr., *Managing the Multinational Enterprise*, New York: Basic Books 1972.

– avoid *terms* that may be interpreted denigrating to ethnic or other groups.

– be especially careful in dealing with gender. Traditional customs such as "... the manager wishes that **his** interest ..." can favor the acceptance of inequality were none exist. The use of plural pronouns is preferred. If this is impossible, the term "he or she" or "he/she" can be used.

In the case of publication authors are supplied one complimentary copy of the issue and 30 off-prints free of charge. Additional copies may be ordered *prior to printing*. Overseas shipment is by boat; air-delivery will be charged extra.

The author agrees, that his/her article is published not only in this journal but that it can also be reproduced by the publisher and his licensees through license agreement in other journals (also in translated versions), through reprint in omnibus volumes (i.e. for anniversary editions of the journal or the publisher or in subject volumes), through longer extracts in books of the publisher also for advertising purposes, through multiplication and distribution on CD ROM or other data media, through storage on data bases, their transmission and retrieval, during the time span of the copyright laws on the article at home and abroad.

© Gabler Verlag 2004

Note from the Guest Editors

Like all multinational enterprises, this special issue took substantial amounts of integration and responsiveness. As editors our job was to integrate the work of the authors and reviewers. Our job would not have been possible, however, were it not for the responsiveness of the authors – to the Call for papers and later to reviews – and of the many dedicated reviewers upon whom we called. This note is mainly to reflect on the processes we followed in editing this edition, divulge the usual acceptance-rate statistics, and finally – but most importantly – to acknowledge the reviewers.

The Call for this special issue went out in mid-2001, with a submission deadline of 28 February 2002. We received 23 manuscripts, 18 of which were sent out to reviewers. The other five were considered unsuitable relative to the Call for the Special issue which specified empirical work within the areas of Strategy and Structure of Multinational Enterprises. After the first review round eight of the 18 were invited to resubmit, nine were rejected, and one was withdrawn by the authors. In the second round two papers were accepted, two rejected, and the remaining four invited to undergo a further revision. Three of these four were subsequently accepted. Thus five papers are being published here, giving a net acceptance rate of 22 percent.

All submissions, reviews, and letters back and forth among editors, authors and reviewers were sent by e-mailed Word files. Most papers were sent to two reviewers, but in six of the 18 cases we called upon a third reviewer's input to help clarify a decision or to provide authors with additional guidance. Reviewers were usually asked to respond within one month, and we undertook to turn each submission around within three months. We stayed within this three-month limit in 100% of cases, with most decision letters going back to authors closer to the two-month mark. The Special Issue context demands relatively fast processing of reviews and revisions. On several occasions we sincerely apologized to authors for the fact that we could not persevere with their papers under these relatively tight deadlines, but expressed the confidence that their work would be published in due course in 'regular' journal issues.

Note from the Guest Editors

Thirty scholars were kind enough to review papers for this Issue. We were truly impressed by the dedication and professionalism of so many busy people. In particular, we risk the inevitability of offending those who we forget to mention, but convey special appreciation for going a lot further than the proverbial extra mile to Cyril Bouquet, Nicole Coviello, Andrew Delios, Gary Jones, Janet Murray, Lilach Nachum, and Heather Wilson. The full list of reviewers is appended, with our appreciation for giving their valuable time and insights. Thanks also to Rudolf Hastenteufel of the mir Editorial Office; and to Klaus Macharzina and Joachim Wolf, editors of this wonderful journal, for the opportunity to work on this project.

DAVID BROCK
JULIAN BIRKINSHAW

List of Reviewers for this Special Issue

Yair Aharoni	Tel Aviv University
Tamar Almor	College of Management
Brent Allred	College of William & Mary
Henrik Bresman	Massachusetts Institute of Technology
Cyril Bouquet	University of Western Ontario
Mark Casson	University of Reading
Nicole Coviello	University of Calgary and University of Auckland
Doren Chadee	University of Auckland
Wade Danis	Marquette University
Andrew Delios	National University of Singapore
Anthony Ferner	De Montfort University
Anne-Wil Harzing	University of Melbourne
Susan Hill	London Business School
Johny Johansson	Georgetown University
Stewart Johnston	University of Melbourne
Gary K. Jones	American University
Stefan Jonsson	Stockholm School of Economics
Mark Lehrer	University of Rhode Island
Michael Mol	Nijmegen University
Janet Murray	Saint Louis University
Lilach Nachum	University of Cambridge and Baruch College
Rajneesh Narula	Copenhagen Business School
Elisabeth Rose	University of Auckland
Tagi Sagafi-nejad	Loyola College in Maryland
Jay Sankaran	University of Auckland
Joanna Scott-Kennel	Victoria University of Wellington
Sully Taylor	Portland State University
David C. Thomas	Simon Fraser University
Heather Wilson	University of Auckland
Ivo Zander	Stockholm School of Economics

David M. Brock/Julian Birkinshaw

Multinational Strategy and Structure: A Review and Research Agenda[1]

Abstract

- A review essay, including a background to the Special Issue. We sketch out the major changes that we see underway in the strategies and structures of MNEs. Some of these are developed in the papers that follow; others are based on extant literature and empirical observation. The five papers in the special issue are introduced in context of an integration-responsiveness framework, and we delineate some of the contributions of each paper.

Key Results

- The major changes in strategy and structure in MNEs discussed are increasing levels of global integration, innovation by design, new network structures, outsourcing of major value-chain activities, E-commerce, and the backlash against globalization.

- A brief overview of the integration-responsiveness framework, the papers in the Special Issue, and how each paper relates to the framework.

Authors

David Brock, Senior Lecturer, Department of Business Administration, Ben-Gurion University, Beer-Sheva, Israel.
Julian Birkinshaw, Associate Professor, Strategic and International Management, London Business School, UK.

From the PricewaterhouseCoopers building in Auckland to the Nationale Nederlanden in Warsaw, Nissan in Amsterdam and Esso in Paris, to Tokyo's Marriott and Vancouver's HSBC, impressive architectural structures around the globe remind us of the dominance of multinationals over the contemporary organizational landscape. But the apparent stasis and permanence of corporate office blocks belie the state of flux in both the strategies and structures of multinational enterprises (MNEs) as well as the academic literature focused on understanding and explaining their activities.

There are enormous changes underway in the make-up of large MNEs – from the emergence of new organisation structures to the outsourcing of major parts of the value chain to the development of new mindsets. However, the academic literature has struggled to do justice to the magnitude of the changes that are underway. The prevailing view of the multinational corporation in the literature is either dated, with its basis in the structures identified by Stopford and Wells thirty years ago, or it is driven by theoretical abstractions such as networks, isomorphic fields, or transaction costs.

This special issue of **mir** focuses on updating and rethinking our knowledge of strategy and structure in MNEs. We began with the aim of promoting more phenomenon-based research. What is *actually* happening in MNEs? And what light can we as academics shed on these phenomena? We called for fresh data, new perspectives, and hopefully some surprising conclusions. Thanks to the effort and ingenuity of the authors and reviewers of the 23 papers received in response to the Call, we now have all three. And we have a far clearer understanding of several key contemporary issues in the management strategy and structure.

The 23 papers submitted reflected a wide variety of topics, with surprisingly few overlaps. Three papers dealt with some aspect of global sourcing. Three proposed some form of theory development, but were not considered within the scope of this Special Issue. The issues of HR management, technology, and integration processes each featured twice. Topics that appeared only once but we had hoped to see more of included innovation, regional headquarter roles, coordination mechanisms, ownership structures, and international joint ventures.

We have two objectives in this introductory essay. First, we would like to sketch out the major changes that we see underway in the strategies and structures of MNEs. Some of these are developed in the papers that follow; others are based on our own observations. But they are all high visible and, we would argue, highly important trends that deserve considerably greater research attention than they currently receive. The second purpose of this essay is to introduce the five papers in the special issue, and to delineate some of the commonalities and differences between them.

Major Changes in Strategy and Structure in MNEs

What are the major strategic challenges facing executives in large MNEs today? Many of the top-of-mind concerns are specific to today's economic situation: surviving the economic downturn, the threat of terrorism or war, and regulatory concerns following the collapse of Enron and Worldcom. But over and above these specific concerns, there are a number of broad issues that tend to recur – the need to find new sources of growth, the challenge of generating profits in big emerging economies like China and India, the demands for greater global coordination from major customers, and so on. It is this latter set of issues that we are interested in here. Rarely today does one hear executives worrying about how to enter a foreign market, or how to structure their international operations. That is not to suggest these are unimportant issues. Rather, the implication is that these issues have been given considerable attention over the last decade and are now "under control". Attention, instead, turns to new challenges that the executives in question have little experience in dealing with. And without trying to claim it is comprehensive, here is our list of these new challenges and changes:

Increasing Levels of Global Integration

Integrative structures often in unexpected areas. On the supply-side, MNEs are sourcing more products and services on a global basis, often from less developed parts of the world. And on the demand side, MNEs are seeking out new ways of coordinating their activities to deliver increased value to their global customers. One trend is towards "global account managers" to coordinate activities worldwide to important customers. A related trend is towards shifting the emphasis from selling products to providing "services and solutions" to big global customers.

Innovation by Design

Most large MNEs are not good at innovation. They are often good at managing systematised innovation processes such as drug development, but they struggle with out-of-the-box thinking and truly innovative ideas. Aware of this shortcoming, many MNEs including Royal Dutch/Shell, Roche and Intel are experimenting with new designs for innovation, such as corporate venturing units, incubators, and idea-generation programs. Others, including 3M, HP and Sara Lee, are focusing on creating a more innovative and/or entrepreneurial culture. Research suggests that there are no silver bullets to the problem of innovation, and that most structured efforts fail, but that is not preventing a great deal of energy going into this issue.

New Network Structures

There is a common feeling among many MNEs that matrix structures have created complexity and inertia, and that the *Transnational* model, in all its variations, has been hard to implement effectively. As a result, many are now experimenting with simpler structures – spinning off businesses and activities that do not fit, and using more market-like coordination systems.

Outsourcing of Major Value-chain Activities

Large, global players are emerging as specialists in each and every step of the value chain. The most well known examples are in the field of IT services (EDS, Accenture, IBM Global Services) and contracting manufacturing (Flextronics, Solectron, Celestica), but the same phenomenon can also be seen in R&D services, logistics, catering and facilities management. And often these new specialists are located in lower-cost parts of the world.

E-commerce and the Internet

While e-commerce has not lived up to the hype of the late 1990s, its impact on the MNE's strategy and structure is still substantial. E-commerce has speeded up fulfilment, and it has facilitated many of the outsourcing trends identified above. It has also facilitated more rapid international growth. Amazon.com, for example, has a Canadian business without a single employee – it runs its software out of the US, and all fulfilment and distribution activities are subcontracted to Canada post. There are also internal coordination benefits from the Internet, in terms of knowledge and information sharing.

The Backlash against Globalization

MNEs have attracted the brunt of the criticism from so called "anti-globalization" protestors during WTO meetings in Seattle, Genoa and elsewhere. The anti-globalisation movement is a diverse mix of groups without a coherent agenda, but it has forced MNEs to rethink their more contentious policies, and it has encouraged them to better articulate the benefits they bring to less developed countries. Corporate imperialism may be dead, but we are not yet sure what is going to replace it.

While these points are concerned with new trends and un-charted research phenomena, there is also a great deal of terrain that remains unchanged. In particular, many of the conceptual tools that were developed during the 1980s continue to serve us well. We would argue, for example, that we understand the economic logic for the existence of MNEs, the processes through which they move overseas, and the key trade-offs and tensions that MNE executives have to manage on an ongoing basis. This is not to suggest that the field of international business has reached a state of maturity. Rather, we would suggest that the potential for generating additional insights from our established theoretical frames is limited, so rather than invest energy in another study based on transaction cost economics, we would encourage researchers to seek out new ways of looking at the world. It is beyond the scope of this essay – and perhaps beyond our capabilities as well – to provide much insight into the nature of these new theoretical lenses, but if history is any guide the advances will come from the application of some of the cutting-edge ideas in cognate disciplines such as economics, sociology and economic geography.

Overview of Papers in the Special Issue

The five papers that follow in this special issue address a variety of themes. To give them some coherence, we have reverted to one of the most enduring conceptual frameworks in the field of international business, the so-called Integration-Responsiveness grid, first introduced to the field by C. K. Prahalad in 1976, and then elaborated by Chris Bartlett in 1979.

Integration and Responsiveness

It is well established that MNEs face competing pressures for local responsiveness (LR) and for global integration (GI). Bartlett and Ghoshal (1988), for example, point out that "retaining local flexibility while achieving global integration" is a feature of transnational organizations (1988, p. 66). Rosenzweig and Singh (1991), focusing on the subsidiary unit, make a related observation, namely: "subsidiaries of MNEs face dual pressures: They are pulled to achieve isomorphism with the local institutional environment, and they also face an imperative for consistency within the organization" (1991, p. 340).

However, we can already note differing views of GI and LR in these sources: Some see GI/LR as environmental contingencies, perhaps akin to industry structural forces (Yip 2003). This view is exemplified in the above quote from Rosenzweig and Singh (1991). The fiercer the local competition, the more complex the operating environment, and the more fragmented the global marketplace, the more important it will be for the business to have the autonomy to respond locally. On the other hand, the more globalized the industry, the more the competitors and bases for competition in a country are similar to those in other countries, the less the need for LR and the greater the rewards of global integration (Westney 1993, Yip 2003). Alternately, GI and LR can be seen as some organizational-level strategic or structural design parameters. The Bartlett and Ghoshal (1988) quote above reflects this view.

This lack of consensus as to the basis realm of the integration-responsiveness (IR) framework is the motivation for *"A New Perspective on the Integration-Responsiveness Pressures Confronting Multinational Firms"*, by Sunil Venaik, David Midgley and Timothy Devinney. Their review of the literature and empirical analysis of the domain raise important concerns about the way in which IR ideas have been operationalized. For example, more prior work concentrates on the consequences of integration-responsiveness pressures rather than the pressures themselves. And they find that some researchers have measured pressures whereas others measure managerial responses to pressures, confounding external pressures with firm heterogeneity. Their empirical findings indicate that IR pressures have a greater number of dimensions than previously thought and that they are better conceptualized as formative rather than reflective in nature. They conclude that investigators need to conceptualize and measure the environmental pressures facing multinationals at a more fundamental level.

Responsiveness Pressures

Who can resist the arguments for responsiveness? Who would begrudge the management of multinational businesses around the world the flexibility to tailor their product and service offerings, their incentive packages, their inventory control policies, their planning systems and their cash management protocols to the local task environment? In all the dozens of interviews we've had with managers, all the debates with students, and in a steady flow of scholarly journal articles these themes of local adaptation, autonomy, and responsiveness prove popular.

Hard, empirical evidence for these themes, however, is relatively scarce. Patterson and Brock (2002) use word counts on a small sample of articles to indicate that contemporary authors – particularly those in the 'Subsidiary Development' research stream (e.g., Birkinshaw/Hood/Johnson 1998) – seem to indicate a trend toward concepts related to autonomy rather than control. Further, there continues to be research on subsidiary specific advantages and centres of excellence (Moore 2001). And we are also reminded that even in this world of global strategies, some local adaptation is needed (Kanter/Dretler 1998, Macharzina 2001).

The ultimate in responsiveness in an organizational structure would be a true bottom-up flow of ideas, information, and – ultimately – managerial decision making. In *Multinationals, Reverse Diffusion and National Business Systems*, Tony Edwards and Anthony Ferner discuss Reverse Diffusion (RD) – the phenomenon whereby managerial practices are transferred from foreign subsidiaries to the home-country operations. Pulling together the limited relevant findings from previous research, and drawing on prior case study evidence, they provides a set of structured arguments about the logic, determinants and mechanisms of RD – specifically concerning diffusion of HRM practices. Although these practices are clearly rare, their findings shed light on the sort of multinational in which reverse diffusion is most likely to occur, its potential consequences, and the processes through which it occurs.

Another classic factor that generally requires responsiveness on the part of the MNE is national culture. In *Global versus multidomestic: Culture's consequences on innovation*, Brent Allred and Scott Swan examine the relationship of national culture to firm innovation. Hypotheses are developed and tested using data from 536 companies across ten countries competing in four global and four multidomestic industries. Using the Hofstede cultural framework they find that individualism, low power distance, and low uncertainty avoidance are more positively related to innovation within multidomestic industries; while Confucian dynamism is more positively related to innovation within global industries. On the other hand the relationship between masculinity/femininity and innovation does not seem to vary across industry type.

However, while illustrating fascinating aspects of responsiveness, both the above articles also reflect aspects of integration. For a multinational to avail itself of the benefits of reverse diffusion, integrative mechanisms are needed to link subsidiaries with the rest of the firm; and specifically to identify and transfer the relevant managerial practices. In fact Edwards and Ferner conclude that one of the main requirements for successful RD is "an 'infrastructure' of mechanisms of diffusion". And Robins, Tallman and Fladmoe-Lindquist (2002) suggest that while international cooperative ventures need to become autonomous, aspects of strategic integration seem to be a key success factor. In the following section we discuss these integration forces in some more detail.

Integration Pressures

More than simply being a portfolio of unconnected businesses around the world, Multinationals generally try to create value by realizing synergies among their component parts. Indeed, to compensate for the costs and complexities of doing business across national borders the MNE needs a structure and strategy "that integrates and manages for worldwide business leverage and competitive advantage" (Yip 2003, pp. 5–6). Global integration refers to an exchange resources within country units of an MNE, and is a key element of international competition (Mauri/Phatak 2001). Recent research on integrating mechanisms includes studies of global account management (Birkinshaw/Toulan/Arnold 2001, Montgomery/Yip 2000), global purchasing (Mol/van Tulder/Beije 2002), corporate political activity (Blumentritt/Nigh 2002), perceived individual career benefits (Newburry 2001), and human resource practices (Ghoshal/Gratton 2002). Malnight (2001) finds evidence of global knowledge sharing, global data sharing, and global facilities sharing. Luo (2002) finds that integration is positively related to resource distinctiveness – an apparent effort to build protective layers around proprietary assets in foreign markets.

A key factor in enabling MNEs to realize and enhance their value is their ability to leverage firm-specific resources. Thus *Contextual moderating effects and the relationship of firm-specific resources, strategy, structure and performance among Japanese multinational enterprises* by Stephen Tallman, Michael Geringer and David Olsen develops and tests a path analytic model of resource value-strategy-structure-performance relationships for MNEs in which resource and strategic variables are interdependent. The model is tested using multi-year data from a sample of large Japanese industrial MNEs in order to examine the effects of *keiretsu* membership on hypothesized relationships. Their results suggest that resource value, strategy, and structure have significant interdependencies and simultaneously impact performance. Interestingly – and also within the scope of integrating mechanisms – *Keiretsu* membership has significant moderating effects under some circumstances.

Integrating mechanisms can also be used for defensive purposes – for example to protect proprietary technology against misappropriation (Luo 2002). Mark Cannice, Roger Chen and John Daniels's paper on *Managing International Technology Transfer Risk: Alternatives and Complements to Ownership Structure* uses transaction cost theory to predict and assess firms' methods of managing international technology transfer risks. This exploratory study builds propositions for protecting technology when exploiting it through foreign production. The method includes a comparative case analysis of nine US high-tech manufacturers in four Asian countries. They propose that companies rely not only on ownership structure (e.g. entry mode selection) to protect against technology misappropriation, but also on making transferred technologies more tacit and headquarters-dependent. Finally, viewing technology transfer from the transferee's perspective, they develop a theoretical framework on managing international technology transfer risks. They find that firms not only rely on their transferred technologies' tacitness to increase the difficulty of misappropriation, but also that internationally transferred technologies' are dependent on headquarters-controlled technology to decrease the value of those technologies to potential misappropriators, thus decreasing the motivation to misappropriate. They also conclude that firms use more technology protection levers for core technologies than for peripheral technologies.

Concluding Comments

While the five papers in this special issue offer some important insights into the structural and strategic challenges facing MNEs, there is considerable scope for further research in any and all of the areas described earlier. In fact, we would go further. Despite (or perhaps because of) the burgeoning volume of academic literature, there are relatively few studies that actually put the spotlight on the leading-edge trends and phenomena in the world of business. We would like to see more of this sort of research – studies that immerse themselves in the complex realities of decision making in large MNEs, or that seek out the new and unexplored frontiers of international business practice. To be sure, this is difficult research to conduct, but it is exhilarating work and the payoffs are substantial.

Acknowledgement

1 Thanks to Shlomit Baruch, Cyril Bouquet, and Robert-Jan Bulter.

References

Bartlett, C. A./Ghoshal, S., Organizing for Worldwide Effectiveness: The Transnational Solution, *California Management Review*, 31, 1, 1988, pp. 54–74.
Birkinshaw, J./Hood, N./Johnson, S., Building Firm-specific Advantages in Multinational Corporations: The Role of The Subsidiary Initiative, *Strategic Management Journal*, 19, 3, 1998, pp. 221–241.
Birkinshaw, J. M./Toulan, O./Arnold, D., Global Account Management in Multinational Corporations: Theory and Evidence, *Journal of International Business Studies*, 32, 2, 2001, pp. 321–348.
Blumentritt, T. P./ Nigh, D., The Integration of Subsidiary Political Activities in Multinational Corporations, *Journal of International Business Studies*, 31, 1, 2002, pp. 57–77.
Ghoshal, S./Gratton, L., Integrating the Enterprise, *Sloan Management Review*, 44, 1, 2002, pp. 31–38.
Harzing, A., *Managing the Multinationals: An International Study of M*, Northampton, MA: E. Elgar 1999.
Harzing, A., An Empirical Analysis and Extension of the Bartlett and Ghoshal Typology of Multinational Companies, *Journal of International Business Studies*, 31, 1, 2000, pp. 101–120.
Kanter, R. M./Dretler, T., "Global Strategy" and Its Impact on Local Operations: Lessons from Gillette Singapore, *Academy of Management Executive*, 12, 4, 1998, pp. 60–68.
Luo, Y., Organizational Dynamics and Global Integration: A Perspective from Subsidiary Managers, *Journal of International Management*, 8, 2002, pp. 189–215.
Macharzina, K., The End of Pure Global Strategies?, *Management International Review*, 41, 2001, pp. 105–108.

Malnight, T. W., Emergent Structural Patterns within Multinational Corporations: Toward Process-based Structures, *Academy of Management Journal*, 44, 6, 2001, pp. 1187–1210.

Mauri, A. J./Phatak, A. V., Global Integration as Inter-area Product Flows: The Internalization of Ownership and Location Factors Influencing Product Flows Across MNC Units, *Management International Review*, 41, 2001, pp. 233–249.

Montgomery, D. B./Yip, G. S., The Challenge of Global Customer Management, *Marketing Management*, 9, 4, 2000, pp. 22–29.

Mol, M./van Tulder, R. J. M./Beije, P. R., Global Outsourcing: Antecedents and Performance Consequences, Working Paper, University of Rotterdam 2002.

Moore, K. J., A Strategy for Subsidiaries: Centres of Excellence to Build Subsidiary Specific Advantages, *Management International Review*, 41, 2001, pp. 275–290.

Newburry, W., MNC Interdependence and Local Embeddedness Influences on Perceptions of Career Benefits From Global Integration, *Journal of International Business Studies*, 32, 3, 2001, pp. 497–507.

Patterson, S. L./Brock, D. M., The Development of Subsidiary Management Research: Review and Theoretical Analysis, *International Business Review*, 11, 2, 2002, pp. 139–163.

Robins, J. A./Tallman, S./Fladmoe-Lindquist, K., Autonomy and Dependence of International Co-operative Ventures: An Exploration of the Strategic Performance of U.S. Ventures in Mexico, *Strategic Management Journal*, 23, 2002, pp. 881–901.

Rosenzweig P./Singh, J., Organizational Environments and the Multinational Enterprise, *Academy of Management Review*, 16, 2, 1991, pp. 340–361.

Westney, D. E., Institutionalization Theory and the Multinational Corporation, in Ghoshal S., Westney D. E. (eds.), *Organization Theory and the Multinational Corporation*, New York: St Martin's Press 1993.

Yip, G. S., *Total Global Strategy II*, Upper Saddle River, NJ: Prentice Hall 2003.

Sunil Venaik/David F. Midgley/Timothy M. Devinney

A New Perspective on the Integration-Responsiveness Pressures Confronting Multinational Firms[1]

Abstract

- The integration-responsiveness (IR) framework has been used extensively in the literature and has proven useful in describing the issues facing managers in multinational organisations. In a review of the literature and empirical analysis of the domain of IR we raise important concerns about the way in which the ideas of Prahalad and Doz have been operationalised.

Key Results

- Our literature review indicates little consensus as to the definition of the domain of IR, and that some investigators measure pressures whereas others measure managerial responses to pressures, confounding external pressures with firm heterogeneity. Our empirical findings indicate that IR pressures have a greater number of dimensions than previously thought and that they are better conceptualised as formative rather than reflective in nature. We conclude that investigators need to conceptualise and measure the environmental pressures facing multinationals at a more fundamental level.

Authors

Sunil Venaik, Assistant Professor, Indan Institute of Management, Ahmedabad, Gujarat, India and Senior Lecturer, Enterprise & Intenational Business, University of Queensland Business School, University of Queensland, Brisbane, QLD, Australia.
David F. Midgley, Professor of Marketing, INSEAD, Fontainebleau, Cedex, France.
Timothy M. Devinney, Professor and Director, Centre for Corporate Change, Australian Graduate School of Management, Sydney, NSW, Australia.

Introduction

"*Pressure:* from the Latin pressura – the action of pressing" (Webster's Dictionary).

The *Integration-Responsiveness* framework of Prahalad and Doz (1987) has been used extensively in the international business literature to typify the diverse and often-conflicting environmental *pressures* confronting firms as they expand worldwide (Bartlett/Ghoshal 1989, Birkinshaw/Morrison/Hulland 1995, Harzing 2000, Johansson/Yip 1994, Kobrin 1994, Martinez/Jarillo 1991, Murtha/Lenway/ Bagozzi 1998, Roth/Morrison 1990, Taggart 1998). Stated simply, firms come under pressure to take an integrated approach to their global activities – that is, to coordinate their business units and strategies to attain maximum efficiency and competitive advantage. These pressures for *Global Integration* might lead to responses such as producing parts in a single location for global use at efficient scale, or mandating global consistency in brand positioning. Concurrently, firms face a countervailing set of pressures to adapt their activities to the unique circumstances of the countries in which they operate. These pressures for *Local Responsiveness* may prompt responses such as producing parts locally to obtain tax incentives or adapting brand positioning to local market circumstances. These combined pressures form the *Integration-Responsiveness* (hereafter, IR) framework.

Although the IR framework has been successfully applied for over a decade, many theoretical and empirical studies have focused on the *consequences* of these pressures rather than the pressures themselves. Where scholars have sought to evaluate IR pressures, these have often been inferred from the firm's choice of strategy and structure; in other words, from the *firm response* to these pressures. Hence, far less attention has been paid to the underlying nature of the IR pressures or to measuring them directly; leaving their scope, nature and form less than fully articulated in the literature.

Does this matter? We believe so for both conceptual and methodological reasons. First, the strategy literature suggests that different firms may react differently to the same pressures (Bartlett/Ghoshal 1989). This heterogeneity confounds the relationship between firm response and underlying pressures – making it difficult to test the IR framework from observations of response alone. It is important to measure the IR pressures as separate constructs and to show how they and other factors impact on managerial choices of strategy and structure. Second, such measures of IR pressures as have been employed in the literature are potentially problematic because of a failure in all cases to distinguish between firm responses and environmental pressures. Furthermore, many approaches are relatively undeveloped from a methodological perspective, tapping different domains of pressures and assuming simple, one-dimensional reflective latent constructs of integration and responsiveness. They overlook the complexity of measurement including additional dimensions, higher-order structures and formative rather than reflective constructs. Imperfect measurement runs the risk of producing misleading or contradictory results. Our paper thus underlines the need to put the measurement of IR pressures on a firmer footing.

Important questions remain about the scope, nature and measurement of IR pressures:

- What component pressures should be included in the IR domain?
- How many dimensions are needed to accurately represent this domain?
- Is the dimensional structure best represented as one level or is it higher-order?
- Are these dimensions best conceptualised as *reflecting* latent constructs of integration and responsiveness or as *forming* them?
- How might component pressures and/or dimensions best be modelled to study their impact on the managerial responses of strategy and structure?

While not attempting to resolve all these issues in this exploratory study, we hope to demonstrate the need for greater vigilance in the conceptualisation and measurement of IR pressures, and indicate fruitful avenues for future research. Similarly, although this study is based on measures derived from the literature, considerable scope exists to develop new measures and methodologies.

The remainder of our paper divides into three sections. First, drawing upon new literature in the areas of strategy and construct measurement, we begin with a survey of the extensive literature on the IR framework, identifying possible alternative answers to the above questions. This survey also provides us with the item measures for our study. Next, we explain our methodology, including the procedure for data collection and analysis. We conclude with a discussion of our findings and directions for future research, speculating as to the appropriate definition of the domain of IR pressures and the criteria we might use to validate measures of these.

The Integration-Responsiveness Framework

The Development of the Framework

The IR framework grew out of earlier evolutionary theories of the development of multinational enterprises (MNEs) (Perlmutter 1969, Stopford/Wells 1972, Vernon 1966). Although popular, these models did not encompass the new technological, market, competitive and governmental factors that were beginning to impact on multinationals (Bartlett 1986). To incorporate these factors, authors – beginning with Fayerweather (1969), Prahalad (1975) and Doz (1976), followed by Prahalad and Doz – reformulated the classic differentiation and integration approach of Lawrence and Lorsch (1967) into the IR framework of today.

Prahalad and Doz identified the economic, technological, political, customer and competitive factors that create the global integration and local responsiveness pressures on the diverse businesses and functions in MNEs. Initially, they identified three environmental pressures: the need for (1) global integration of activities, (2) global strategic coordination, and (3) local responsiveness. Given the high correlation between (1) and (2), they combined them to create two essential dimensions – global integration and local responsiveness. Prahalad and Doz's work is of undoubted scholarly value and practical significance and two aspects of this work are particularly germane to our arguments.

First, Prahalad and Doz had a rich and diverse view of the underlying pressures, listing seven component domains for their "pressures for global strategic coordination" and five for "pressures for local responsiveness" (1987, pp.18–21) with each component a complex area in its own right. Arguably much of the later – particularly survey-based – literature has tended to reduce these to simple questionnaire items. Moreover, it has focused on Prahalad and Doz's 12 domains without questioning whether these are exhaustive or reflect the current business environment.

Second, Prahalad and Doz conceptualised these pressures largely in terms of the firm's response (e.g., the need for *global integration of activities*, the need for *local responsiveness [in activities]*). Domains are referred to as "criteria" (p. 18) and pressures in each domain are rated as "high", "medium" or "low" in their early case examples. The pressures themselves are discussed briefly and the majority of chapters (3–12) focus on managerial and firm response to them, culminating in a prescription for the "ideal" diversified, multinational corporation. This conceptualisation has influenced much of the work on the IR framework, generating valuable studies of firm response and managerial decision-making in the areas of organisation structure, coordination and product adaptation. Indeed, the IR framework has proved useful for classifying MNEs and their international strategy and organisation (Bartlett/Ghoshal 1989) and is represented in the popular literature by the phrase *"Think global, act local"* – itself suggesting firm and managerial responses, not the pressures underlying them. Although valuable, the study of firm response has meant that less attention has been paid to the nature of the pressures themselves. Furthermore, it carries an implicit assumption at odds with current thinking in the strategy literature.

Pressures, Firm Response and Firm Heterogeneity

The IR framework as originally advanced by Prahalad and Doz (1987) and Bartlett and Ghoshal (1989) belongs to the alignment school of strategic thought, dominant at that time, which asserted that the "fit" between strategy and environment mattered most to firm performance (Burns/Stalker 1961, Miles/Snow 1978). Hence there is no great need to distinguish between pressures and firm response because the firm chooses the *single* most appropriate response to the pressures it faces. For example, a firm faced by *low* pressures for global integration and *high* pressures for local responsiveness would choose a multi-domestic strategy and structure. Assuming firms make correct choices, we can legitimately infer the underlying pressures from the observed response and Prahalad and Doz's focus on firm response would be entirely appropriate. However, the "fit" school has been subsequently criticised as overly deterministic and other schools of thought have emerged; namely, distinctive competences (e.g. Teece/Pisano/Shuen 1997), managerial cognition (e.g. Burgeois 1984) and neo-institutional (e.g. Carson et al. 1999), each, in their own way, breaking the deterministic link between environment and firm strategy. The distinctive competences school suggests that firms compete through differentiated skills, complementary assets and routines that may prompt them to deploy different strategies within the same environment. Similarly, the managerial cognition school argues that managerial preferences, beliefs, perceptions, ideologies and power, directly influence strategic choice – again leading to different strategies being selected in similar circumstances. Finally, the neo-institutional school argues that the firm's arrangements with its value-chain make some forms of strategic and organizational change more open to some firms than others. In short, current strategic thinking emphasizes heterogeneity of firm choice – making it increasingly difficult to infer environmental pressures from firm responses, and suggesting that it would be better to measure pressures and responses as distinct and different constructs.

The Measurement of Constructs

Just as the literature on strategy has evolved since 1987, so too has that on the measurement of theoretical constructs. Conventionally, latent constructs were regarded as *one-dimensional* entities to be measured with a battery of highly correlated questionnaire items, termed *reflective* indicators. Despite the origins of this approach in the development of personality batteries, most researchers concentrate on first-order constructs using scale development techniques – factor analysis in particular – to identify a small number of indicators to measure one construct of interest. They have seldom looked for higher-order structures across large numbers of first-order constructs. In contrast, the well-known 5-factor model of personality emerged from further analyses of earlier studies with a greater number of first-order constructs, each in turn measured with a number of questionnaire items (Digman 1997). This is important because the environmental pressures facing a multinational enterprise cover a domain of *greater* breadth, diversity and complexity than personality. According to Rossiter (2002), the key to construct validity is *content* validity. Given the breadth and diversity of IR pressures, we must have a large enough number of items to tap this domain adequately and an appropriate analysis to understand it.

A related issue is dimensionality. In psychology, considerable effort has been devoted to determining how many dimensions are necessary to describe a domain – a key issue because under-extraction (i.e., assuming there are fewer dimensions than in reality) has been shown to result in dramatically poor estimation of constructs (Fava/Velicer 1996). This occurs through misattribution of the relationship between item measures and the dimensions. As demonstrated subsequently, the IR literature often embodies an implicit or explicit assumption that two dimensions are adequate to describe the domain, without questioning whether this assumption is indeed appropriate.

Beyond the issues of order and dimensionality, increasingly the literature has recognised that not all constructs are necessarily best considered as *reflective* in the way described above (Bollen/Lennox 1991, Edwards/Bagozzi 2000, Fornell/Bookstein 1982). It is equally plausible to define a construct formed with a number of uncorrelated entities – termed a *formative index*. A classic example is an index of socio-economic status formed from, say, education, income and dwelling value. In contrast to reflective measures, a change in one of these implies a change in socio-economic status without the requirement that the others also change in a correlated way.

One could make a similar argument for the pressures facing firms. For example, integration pressures may underlie the firm's need to integrate its activities worldwide – "the importance of multinational customers", "the presence of multinational competitors", "investment intensity", etc. (Prahalad/Doz 1987, pp.18–19). There is little reason to believe that these pressures will be highly correlated as required by the reflective viewpoint, or that they will necessarily correlate with one dimension as required by this conventional approach to measuring constructs. Why, for example, would a set of items designed to measure the "importance of multinational customers" necessarily correlate with one designed to measure the "presence of multinational competitors" or "investment intensity", particularly across such diverse industries as software, capital equipment or food products. Indeed, the diversity of phenomena that need to be considered under the heading of "environmental pressures" suggests at least a *prima facie* theoretical and methodological case for the formative viewpoint. Thus this distinction between formative and reflective indicators needs to be resolved to ensure that researchers use appropriate methods for measuring, modelling and validating the IR framework empirically. A hybrid approach may also be an alternative, whereby pressures such as the "presence of multinational customers" are measured by a set of reflective indicators as a first-order construct, and then the various first-order pressures are analysed within a higher-order, formative framework.

Figure 1. Possible Structures for the Domain of Integration-Responsiveness

(a) A First-Order Reflective Structure

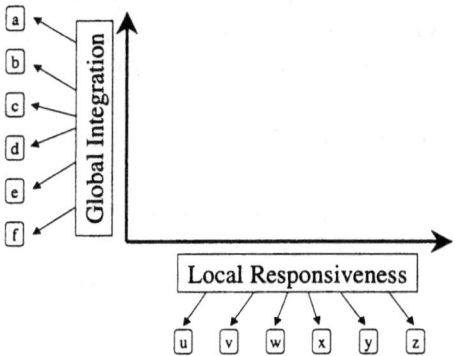

(b) A First-Order Formative Structure

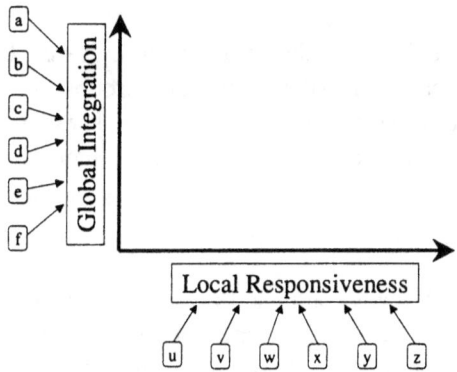

(c) Second-Order Hybrid Structure

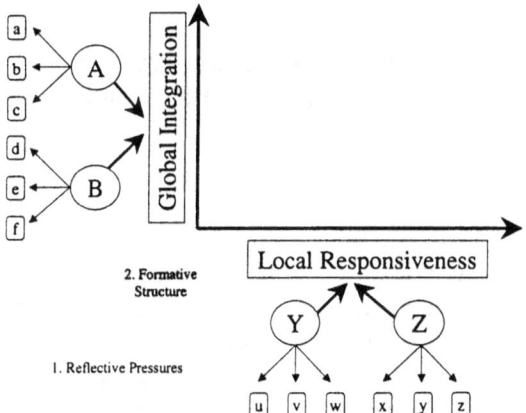

Three perspectives on measurement are summarized in Figure 1. (a) A simple first-order reflective structure with correlated sets of items measuring each of the two dimensions (a–f measuring integration and u–z measuring responsiveness).[2] (b) The same structure stated in formative terms where the reversal of the arrows removes the assumption of correlated items. (c) A second-order, hybrid structure where individual pressures are measured reflectively (pressure A by items a–c, Z by x–z, etc.) but the second order framework is generated in a formative manner – that is, there is no requirement for A to be highly correlated with B, only that both correlate with integration and not with responsiveness. Other possibilities exist (including second-order reflective models and correlations between major dimensions) but space precludes their discussion here.

How Have Pressures Been Conceptualised and Measured?

There is an extensive literature on the environmental pressures faced by multinational enterprises that can be broadly classified into three groups as illustrated by Table 1, which outlines the key papers in each category. These papers are illustrative of the major work in the area and not meant to be exhaustive.

Early Studies

A group of early studies examines the environmental pressures that influence the decisions and performance of global firms (e.g., Bartlett/Ghoshal 1989). Pressures are typically identified either from descriptive case studies or inferred from firm decisions rather than measured in a formal manner.

Studies Outside the Paradigm

A second group examines environmental pressures in a formal manner but are not explicitly within the IR paradigm (e.g., Carpano/Chrisman/Roth 1995) and hence will not be considered here.

Formal IR Studies

Finally, a number of studies have examined the IR framework proposed by Prahalad and Doz in a more formal manner, such as by examining a part – rather than the whole – of the domain of environmental pressures, in particular focusing on aspects of global integration (e.g., Birkinshaw et al. 1995). They also include studies examining both integration and responsiveness pressures (e.g.,

Table 1. Examples of the IR literature

Group 1: Early studies
  A. Bartlett and Ghoshal 1989
  B. Cvar 1986
  C. Doz 1986
  D. Flaherty 1986
  E. Ghemawat and Spence 1986
  F. Jain 1989
  G. Mahini and Wells 1986
  H. Porter 1986
  I. Takeuchi and Porter 1986

Group 2: Studies outside the paradigm
  J. Carpano, Chrisman, and Roth 1994
  K. Ghoshal and Nohria 1989

Group 3: Formal IR studies

  (a) **Studies measuring aspects of global integration**
      L. Birkinshaw, Morrison, and Hulland 1995
      M. Johansson and Yip 1994
      N. Kobrin 1991
      O. Kobrin 1994

  (b) **Studies measuring integration-responsiveness pressures**
      P. Ghoshal and Nohria 1993
      Q. Johnson 1995
      R. Prahalad and Doz 1987
      S. Roth and Morrison 1990

  (c) **Studies measuring firm response to pressures**
      T. Harzing 2000
      U. Jarillo and Martinez 1990
      V. Martinez and Jarillo 1991
      W. Murtha, Lenway, and Bagozzi 1998
      X. Taggart 1997, 1998

Note: full citations in references.

Roth/Morrison 1990) and studies that focus on measuring firm strategy and structure and infer environmental pressures from firm decisions rather than measure them directly (e.g., Jarillo/Martinez 1990). Since this group is most relevant to our purposes we will review them in depth.

Formal Measurement of IR Pressures

Studies Measuring Aspects of Global Integration

Birkinshaw et al. (1995) measure the drivers of global integration with four factors, providing support for Prahalad and Doz's multidimensional view of global integration pressures. They are "(1) standardization of market demands, (2) evidence of competitive action within the industry, (3) economies of scale and (4) differences in comparative advantage across countries" (1995, p. 645). Johansson and Yip (1994) use an overall environmental pressures construct called "industry drivers" formed with two measures, overall cost drivers and overall market drivers, each formed with a number of items. Theirs is one of the few studies to use the formative rather than reflective approach. Kobrin (1991) takes a different approach, using an index of global integration based on intra-firm trade, which, "rests on the assumption that intra-firm flows of products across industries correlate with all important intra-firm flows of resources and information" (p. 20). Kobrin (1994) developed an index of "geo-centric managerial mindset", which he correlated with firm strategy and structure. By reporting a coefficient alpha he is implicitly assuming that this construct is one-dimensional and reflective (Rossiter 2002). Although the above studies offer valuable insights into global integration, clearly they have made very different assumptions as to conceptualization, dimensionality and measurement. Birkinshaw et al. (1995) and Johansson and Yip (1994) conceptualize their constructs as pressures (i.e., distinct and different from firm response). Kobrin (1991) conceptualizes a firm response, but later conceptualizes a managerial cognition (Kobrin 1994). Kobrin (1994) and Johansson and Yip (1994) view their constructs as one-dimensional, Birkinshaw et al. (1995) as multidimensional. Kobrin (1991, 1994) and Birkinshaw et al. (1995) measure their constructs as reflective and first-order, Johansson and Yip (1994) as formative and second-order.

Studies Measuring Integration-Responsiveness Pressures

In their empirical analysis of the IR framework, Roth and Morrison (1990) and Johnson (1995) identify three strategic groups of globally integrated, locally responsive and multi-focal firms in international industries. Both studies measure the industry pressures with the same 14 items. However, these are neither classified nor validated as representing separate integration and responsiveness dimensions, and by reporting a coefficient alpha for this scale they implicitly regard industry pressures as one-dimensional and reflective. Another issue is whether 14 items are adequate to capture the broad domain of integration pressures. Prahalad and Doz originally suggested 12 pressures and others have argued there are more (Devinney/Midgley/Venaik 2000). The measurement literature would suggest several items per pressure and hence a large battery of items for reliable measurement of broad and diverse domains (Marsh et al. 1998). In this respect, Ghoshal and Nohria (1993) measure pressures rather sparsely, with one measure for integration and two measures for responsiveness, which they then use to classify multinational firms into the four strategic groups. All three studies add to our understanding of multinational firms by taking a broader perspective on pressures than previous studies, by conceptualisng them as distinct from firm response and by questioning whether the observed strategic groups fit the IR framework. Nonetheless, differing approaches to the dimensionality and measurement of the IR pressures are apparent: Roth and Morrison (1990) and Johnson (1995) view pressures as one-dimensional and reflective, Ghoshal and Nohria (1993) as two-dimensional but with sparse measurement.

Studies Measuring Firm Response to Pressures

Jarillo and Martinez (1990) and Martinez and Jarillo (1991) examine the roles of MNE subsidiaries using a hybrid of Porter's (1986) configuration/coordination framework and the IR framework. In particular, they look for two dimensions in subsidiary activities: (1) integration with the activities of other subsidiaries and (2) geographical localisation of activities within the host country. They use principal component analysis to produce two factors: "integration of the subsidiary with the parent" and "amount of localization of the strategy of the subsidiary." By using principal component analysis rather than common factor analysis they are adopting a formative approach (Diamantopoulos/Winklhofer 2001), and their arguments for the adequacy of two dimensions in their data are essentially qualitative. Clearly their study is of firm response rather than pressures per se. In their later paper (1991) they apply cluster analysis to these dimensions to find only three of four strategic groups of subsidiaries; namely, integrated, autonomous and "active" subsidiaries attempting to balance both pressures.

Taggart (1997, 1998) followed up and "critically reviewed" the work of Jarillo and Martinez (Jarillo/Martinez 1990, Martinez/Jarillo 1991). He is more faithful to the IR framework, measuring integration and responsiveness. However, his items are phrased in terms of firm decisions such as "centralization of production planning" or "market area served" with the responsiveness items answered in terms of subsidiary autonomy to make decisions. Like Jarillo and Martinez, he uses factor analysis (method unspecified) and cluster analysis to identify strategic groups. By reporting Cronbach alpha, Taggart implicitly assumes that his dimensions are reflective and his factor analyses demonstrate each to be one-dimensional. However, the two-dimensional IR structure itself is assumed on the basis of the literature and not subsequently validated.

Harzing (2000) provides an empirical analysis of the Bartlett and Ghoshal (1989) typology again using a sample of subsidiaries. She collected data measuring corporate strategy, organisational design, interdependence amongst subsidiaries and local responsiveness. As the appendix to her paper indicates, these measures are of firm responses to pressures rather than pressures; e.g., "Give your best estimate of the % of marketing for company products sold by this subsidiary that is consciously adapted to local circumstances." Cluster analysis is then used on the corporate strategy measures with the assumption of three groups – multi-domestic, global and transnational – that are validated through tests on the other variables. As Harzing applies cluster analysis directly to the four items on corporate strategy, then tests the differences of means on the other variables, it is unclear what assumptions are made as to the nature of the measures. However, by adding corporate strategy and organisational design to integration and responsiveness, she is potentially adding dimensions beyond the original two.

Murtha, Lenway and Bagozzi (1998) provide a final, distinctive study in this section, conducting an empirical test of the constructs of integration, responsiveness and coordination (IRC – the original three-dimensional formulation of Prahalad and Doz 1987). They follow a more formal scale development and testing process than many scholars, progressively purifying their measures from 168 to 24 items for the final analysis, of which 12 measure IRC. They assume one-dimensional, reflective scales for each dimension and use confirmatory factor analysis to validate these. However, they focus on "attitudes that underlie international strategy processes" resulting in a set of measures referred to as "mind-set variables". These show that the authors are measuring managerial beliefs and cognition rather than pressures or firm response (p. 101).

Although each of these studies has its own unique, valuable aspects, there is a common thread. By and large those authors studying firm response to environmental pressures follow the literature on the number of IR dimensions. Only Murtha et al. (1998) take a broader view and subject their mind-set scales to confirmation. There is less agreement on the nature of these dimensions, particularly the scope of their domain. Jarillo and Martinez (Jarillo/Martinez 1990, Martinez/Jarillo 1991) seek to blend Porter (1986) and Prahalad and Doz (1987) whereas Taggart (1997, 1998) and Murtha et al. (1998) take a more pure IR view. Harzing (2000) also follows from the IR literature but she adds further dimensions. These authors also differ in their form of measurement: Jarillo and Martinez (Jarillo/Martinez 1990, Martinez/Jarillo 1991) use a formative approach, as, in essence, does Harzing (2000). Taggart (1997, 1998) and Murtha et al. (1998) use the traditional reflective approach.

Looking at our third group and its sub-categories, we see an astonishing diversity of approaches. Some researchers focus purely on global integration, some on both pressures. Some measure pressures, others firm response including the managerial mind-set that is partially a determinant of that response. Some use formative measures others reflective. Some researchers seek to validate the dimensionality and specification of their constructs; others make assumptions following the literature in asserting two – or at most three – dimensions.

An equally important issue is the definition of the relevant domain of pressures and/or responses. As indicated by Table 2 – which lists the various measures in the literature – there is little agreement as to this domain, with the consequence

Integration-Responsiveness Pressures

Table 2. Sources for Individual Measures

#	Measures	Type (PS/FR)	GI/LR
1	R & D investment required	PS	GI
2	Production investment required	PS	GI
3	Rate of product innovation	PS	GI
4	Rate of process innovation	PS	GI
5	Technological complexity	PS	GI
6	Rate of technological change	PS	GI
7	Competitors are mostly global	PS	GI
8	Competitors sell globally standardized products	PS	GI
9	The nature of competition is global	PS	GI
10	Sharing of sales force resources	FR	GI
11	Sharing of distribution channel resources	FR	GI
12	Sharing of production resources	FR	GI
13	Sharing of R & D resources	FR	GI
14	Sharing of management services	FR	GI
15	Co-ordination of marketing	FR	GI
16	Co-ordination of production	FR	GI
17	Co-ordination of procurement	FR	GI
18	Co-ordination of R & D	FR	GI
19	Subsidiary sales as proportion of parent's worldwide sales	FR	GI
20	Strategic importance of local market to parent	FR	GI
21	Proportion parent company's sales that are global	FR	GI
22	Proportion of business unit managers that are expatriate	FR	GI
23	Advertising investment required	PS	GI
24	Extent of global dispersion of production facilities	FR	GI
25	Transport costs relative to sales value	PS	LR
26	Extent of production cost differences between countries	FR	LR
27	Degree of competition in local markets	PS	LR
28	Number of competitors in local markets	PS	LR
29	Customers served are mostly local	FR	LR
30	Customers served are mostly government	FR	LR
31	Customer needs vary across countries	PS	LR
32	Customer segments served vary across countries	FR	LR
33	Demand in the local market is expanding	PS	LR
34	Product decisions influenced by government	FR	LR
35	Price decisions influenced by government	FR	LR
36	Advertising decisions influenced by government	FR	LR
37	Promotion decisions influenced by government	FR	LR
38	Sourcing decisions influenced by government	FR	LR
39	R & D decisions influenced by government	FR	LR
40	Entry decisions influenced by government	FR	LR
41	Quality of local infrastructure: logistics	PS	LR
42	Quality of local infrastructure: channels	PS	LR
43	Quality of local infrastructure: advertising	PS	LR
44	Quality of local infrastructure: personnel	PS	LR
45	Quality of local infrastructure: suppliers	PS	LR
46	Strategic importance of subsidiary to local government	FR	LR
47	Level of tariff barriers against importing	PS	LR
48	Level of non-tariff barriers against importing	PS	LR

Note: Letters that correspond to the references in Table 1 indicate the 'Sources' of the measures. * Type is indicated as {GI = Global Integration; LR = Local Responsiveness} and {PS = Pressure; FR = Firm Response} that many studies include items tapping different domains. It is also telling to note how little correspondence there is between studies, implying that we have little cross-validity from a measurement testing perspective.

Our earlier discussion, and this detailed review of the literature formally measuring IR pressures, leads us to three speculative propositions.

Proposition 1. The domain of pressures impacting on multinational firms requires more than two dimensions for adequate description. This can be argued from a theoretical perspective (Devinney/Midgley/Venaik 2000), by reference to the diversity of measures shown in Table 2, and from recourse to measurement theory (the content of the domain likely being too broad for two factor solutions).

Proposition 2. Pressure dimensions will be better measured as formative rather than reflective indicators. The main argument here would be that within each dimension there is no compelling reason that the item measures should be inter-correlated. Why, for example, should investment intensity correlate with the presence of multinational competitors? Yet both may go together to form a pressure for global integration of activities.

Proposition 3. For the purposes of building models of multinational firm structure and strategy, pressure dimensions will be better measured as environmental pressures and not as firm response to these pressures. The latter confounds managerial choices and other factors with the underlying pressures.

In the next section we will subject these propositions to an empirical test and we will also develop and test two further propositions specific to our research setting.

Methodology

In this section we will discuss our measures, our unit of analysis, the sample we obtained (and potential biases) and our approach to analysing these data.

Measures

To ensure reasonable coverage of the domain of IR pressures, we used all 48 measures from the literature listed in Table 2. Initially 23 items were considered as pressures and 25 as firm responses to pressures. Common heuristics for factor analysis suggest a minimum of 3 relevant variables per factor extracted, hence these numbers are adequate for extracting more than the two or three dimensions most scholars envisage for IR pressures. All items were measured with 7-point scales with each end anchored by a verbal description. For example:

Pressure

In our business, *customer needs* are (*please circle appropriate number*):

    Similar worldwide   1 2 3 4 5 6 7   **Vary** across countries

Firm Response

In our business, the strategic importance of the local subsidiary market to the parent company is (*please circle appropriate number*):

    Low 1 2 3 4 5 6 7 **High**

Where appropriate, each section explained whether the respondent was to answer with respect to *environmental pressures* or *firm responses to these pressures*. For validation purposes, measures were also included for business-unit autonomy, as discussed shortly.

Unit of Analysis

Prahalad and Doz (1987) argued persuasively that IR pressures should be different for different divisions of the MNE (p. 22). Equally, many studies focus on the subsidiary in the local country as the point at which the pressures for integration and responsiveness intersect. Integrating these two views, we chose to focus on a business unit within the subsidiary as our unit of analysis and the head of the unit as our key informant.

Sample

A stratified random sample of MNE subsidiaries was selected from the Dun and Bradstreet WorldBase. To ensure sufficient variance, this included manufacturing and services, consumer and industrial products, and subsidiaries in industrialised and developing countries.

Questionnaires were mailed to 728 subsidiaries with a separate questionnaire for each of the business units in the firm. The responses represented 191 business units from 126 subsidiaries of 119 parent MNEs. 84 were engaged in man-

Table 3. Descriptive Statistics

No.	Item Measures	Mean	Std. Dev.
1	R&D investment required	4.1	2.0
2	Production investment required	4.9	1.9
3	Rate of product innovation	4.4	1.7
4	Rate of process innovation	3.9	1.5
5	Technological complexity	4.8	1.6
6	Rate of technological change	4.4	1.7
7	Competitors are mostly global	5.0	2.0
8	Competitors sell globally standardized products	4.4	1.7
9	The nature of competition is global	4.4	1.9
10	Sharing of sales force resources	2.7	2.2
11	Sharing of distribution channel resources	3.5	2.2
12	Sharing of production resources	3.4	2.3
13	Sharing of R&D resources	3.8	2.3
14	Sharing of management services	4.4	2.0
15	Co-ordination of marketing	2.7	1.6
16	Co-ordination of production	3.8	2.2
17	Co-ordination of procurement	3.5	2.1
18	Co-ordination of R&D	4.8	2.1
19	Subsidiary sales as proportion of parent's worldwide sales	10.2	14.1
20	Strategic importance of local market to parent	4.8	1.7
21	Proportion parent company's sales that are global	44.9	21.5
22	Proportion of business unit managers that are expatriate	13.4	17.0
23	Advertising investment required	3.9	1.9
24	Extent of global dispersion of production facilities	3.9	2.2
25	Transport costs relative to sales value	4.9	1.5
26	Extent of production cost differences between countries	3.9	1.5
27	Degree of competition in local markets	5.7	1.3
28	Number of competitors in local markets	5.2	1.7
29	Customers served are mostly local	5.2	1.8
30	Customers served are mostly government	2.5	1.7
31	Customer needs vary across countries	3.4	1.7
32	Customer segments served vary across countries	3.2	1.5
33	Demand in the local market is expanding	4.5	1.5
34	Product decisions influenced by government	4.1	2.0
35	Price decisions influenced by government	3.9	2.1
36	Advertising decisions influenced by government	3.7	2.0
37	Promotion decisions influenced by government	3.6	2.0
38	Sourcing decisions influenced by government	3.5	1.9
39	R&D decisions influenced by government	3.0	1.8
40	Entry decisions influenced by government	3.9	2.0
41	Quality of local infrastructure: logistics	2.9	1.4
42	Quality of local infrastructure: channels	2.8	1.4
43	Quality of local infrastructure: advertising	2.8	1.4
44	Quality of local infrastructure: personnel	2.9	1.4
45	Quality of local infrastructure: suppliers	3.2	1.4
46	Strategic importance of subsidiary to local government	3.3	1.8
47	Level of tariff barriers against importing	3.0	1.7
48	Level of non-tariff barriers against importing	2.4	1.5

Note: All items on seven-point scales, except numbers 19, 21 and 22. Questions 19 and 21 relate to the markets served by the business unit.

ufacturing sectors and 24 in service sectors. Nearly equal numbers operated in consumer and industrial markets. Although the subsidiaries are located in 36 countries, their parent companies are mainly large Japanese, UK and American MNEs with a median of 22,000 employees worldwide, and 325 employees in the subsidiary. Respondents had an average of ten years experience. The descriptive statistics of the measures are shown in Table 3 and indicate adequate variance for our analyses.[3]

Potential Biases

Questionnaire-based surveys inevitably raise concerns about potential bias. Before analysing our data we examined three such biases, namely, measure equivalence, common method bias and non-response bias.

Measure Equivalence

Whether the same measures can be applied across respondents from different countries would be debatable were we interviewing consumers in less-developed countries. However, as our respondents were senior managers, mostly university educated, speak English, travel widely and have been exposed to the business concepts incorporated in our measures, this issue was of less concern. Nonetheless, we did check the equivalence of our measures. First, for each subsidiary we computed Kogut and Singh's (1988) cultural distance measure. Second, we ranked our subsidiaries by cultural distance (low, medium and high distance) and compared the means for our measures between the high and low groups. After correcting for the known bias in multiple comparisons, there are no significant differences between these means. Scale equivalence problems in these data are unlikely to have biased our analyses.

Common Method Bias

Using a common 7-point scale across all measures can create a response bias. However, the factor analyses that we report subsequently demonstrate that there is no common factor loading on all measures (the *ex post* one-factor test, Podsakoff/Organ 1986). Hence there is unlikely to be any common method bias.

Non-response Bias

To test for a non-response bias, the original sample drawn from Dun and Bradstreet and those subsidiaries who eventually responded were compared on three criteria: the number of countries, how long the subsidiary has operated and the number of employees. We received responses from subsidiaries in 60% (36 out of 60) of the countries we sampled so any bias due to the countries included or excluded is likely to be small. These data also covered all the continents. However, the responding subsidiaries were older and larger than non-respondents. The median age and size of the subsidiaries responding was 30 years and 325 employees versus 21 years and 250 employees for the non-respondents. Our sample therefore under-weights smaller and newer subsidiaries to some extent. However, despite these slight biases the final dataset is more than adequate for our analyses, especially in terms of the heterogeneity of environments that it covers.

Analysis Techniques

Analysis techniques that might be used on our data, which feature in the IR literature, include principal component analysis, common factor analysis, confirmatory factor analysis and cluster analysis. By and large, principal component analysis and common factor analysis have been used to construct IR dimensions, whereas confirmatory factor analysis has been used in one paper – Murtha et al. (1998) – to validate these dimensions. Cluster analysis has been used to identify strategic subsidiary groups.

To test the number of dimensions and the traditional reflective perspective, and to group our item measures for subsequent analysis, we apply the common factor model through maximum likelihood factor analysis. Maximum likelihood factor analysis has the advantage that it allows the choice of the number of factors to be made using Schwartz's Bayesian Information Criterion. Kass and Raftery (1995) show this criterion to be one of the better ways of making such choices and avoiding under-extraction. We perform an oblique rotation on the obtained factors (PROMAX) as there seems no compelling reason to assume these pressures to be orthogonal and the oblique model is more general. This procedure is essentially exploratory as the prior literature focuses on two dimensions and provides little guidance on additional dimensions or which items might load on any new dimension. This made the application of confirmatory factor analysis problematic and is our reason for choosing an exploratory procedure.[4] Next, we apply partial least squares (PLS) to test formative and hybrid models and to compare reflective with formative indicators.

Comparing reflective and formative indicators raises important theoretical, methodological and empirical issues.[5] Fornell and Cha (1994) argue that the primary criterion for choice of indicator model should be the "substantive theory behind the model" (p. 61), although they note that this choice has implications for the predictive power of the chosen indicator. A reflective index can never outperform a formative one in terms of prediction. This is because reflective indicators minimise the trace of the residual errors in the "outer" (measurement) model whereas formative indicators minimise the trace of the residual variance in the "inner" (structural) model (Fornell/Rhee/Yi 1991). Using predictive power as the second criterion for comparing measurement models requires that we state the question in terms of the magnitude by which the reflective model under-performs the formative. For example, where theory gives inadequate guidance as to choice of model, but this magnitude is small, we might still prefer the better-known reflective model.

The issue of predictive power causes debate in the structural equation modelling literature, a debate that derives, in part, from the differing objectives of the two major methodologies, LISREL and PLS. LISREL endeavours to replicate the observed *covariance* between all the indicators in the model on the basis of some hypothesised inner and outer model. This leads to an emphasis on parameter estimation and the degree of fit between the hypothesised and observed covariance matrix. The emphasis on fit seen in papers using LISREL has been argued to be over-stated and to ignore effect sizes (Chin 1998b). Fit is certainly one criterion but even with LISREL we need predictive power if our models are to be useful (Meehl 1990). In contrast, PLS emphasises prediction of the *variance* in the latent constructs. Indeed, there is no analogy between the chi-square comparisons of fit between hypothesised model and data seen in LISREL and the residuals of a hypothesised PLS model estimated directly from the data. In the absence of fit indices, PLS models are judged on R^2, path magnitudes and the standard errors of their parameter estimates – similar to ordinary least squares regression. This makes comparison between models sometimes difficult as different model structures may lead to similar "reduced form" equations. Hence, one normally is required to look at the mix of indicators beyond R^2 – path coefficients, standard errors, effect sizes and so forth – and their consistency with posited theory to choose amongst different models.

It is also difficult to incorporate formative indices within LISREL. They run counter to its objective of explaining covariance, as there is no theoretical requirement to explain any covariance between the individual items that make up a formative index. It is possible to incorporate them but only at a cost. One way, is by forming them externally to the analysis and importing them into LISREL as a single item variable. However, this may not be efficient from an estimation perspective and requires some additional reflective measures for the construct in order to estimate the weights for each indicator (Diamantopoulos/Winklhofer 2001). Such additional measures do not always make theoretical sense or may be difficult to obtain. It can also be done within LISREL when it is possible to identify the formative model correctly within the covariance structure. However, the circumstances in which this is possible are rather limited (MacCallum/Browne 1993). PLS is much more flexible in this regard, allowing both reflective and formative indices within its framework, and this is the reason we chose to use it. However, this discussion of contrasting objectives is useful as it suggests we should consider theory, predictive power, parameter estimates and their standard errors when comparing reflective and formative models.

Finally, we should consider the results of the test for comparing reflective and formative models developed by Bollen and Ting (2000). This test uses the 'nested' vanishing tetrads that are implied by comparing the two measurement models and derives from the work of Spearman (e.g., Spearman/Holzinger 1924). A vanishing tetrad is where the theoretical model implies that the product of a pair of covariances should equal the product of another pair, a hypothesis that can be tested statistically. The tetrad test is a confirmatory – rather than exploratory – procedure because it requires the researcher to specify which tetrads should vanish, which is only possible once they have "narrowed down their plausible structures to a limited number of alternatives" (p. 5). However, Bollen and Ting note that their test does not stand on its own because, for one example, vanishing tetrads can emerge from formative indicators with near zero covariance, leading to an incorrect choice of the reflective model. Thus the results from this test have to be placed alongside the more conventional assessment of parameters that we suggest above.

For PLS analysis of formative indicators we include the additional reflective construct of *Autonomy* which is required to identify these (Diamantopoulos/ Winklhofer 2001) and the choice of this construct requires justification. The locus of decision-making – that is, whether decisions are taken at headquarters (i.e., centralised) or in the country subsidiaries (i.e., autonomous) – is a critical issue in multinational firms (Dunning 1988, Hedlund 1986). Further, the way in which decisions are implemented within the global network of subsidiaries is likely to impact on the performance of the MNC (Kashani 1989). According to Prahalad and Doz (1987, p.181), "the power to allocate resources must be vested in managers in such a way that it reinforces the (firm's) strategic posture and hence the world-view. For example, relative power to allocate resources should reside with product managers if a global orientation is desired, and with area managers if a locally responsive strategy is desired." Thus, pressures for global integration are likely to result in centralisation of decisions in the headquarters whereas pressures for local responsiveness are likely to result in autonomous decision-making in the subsidiaries. Hence, including *Autonomy* not only allows us to identify pressures measured by formative indicators but it also allows us to make a theoretical proposition, empirical support for which would increase our confidence in these measures.

Proposition 4. Pressures for global integration will tend to reduce, whereas pressures for local responsiveness will tend to increase, business unit *Autonomy.*

This construct is derived from responses as to the degree of business unit *Autonomy* in six key business decision-making areas of product, price, place, promotion, and positioning and organisational processes. The construct is one-dimensional and measured reliably ($\alpha = 0.86$). *Autonomy* can be considered a firm *response* to the environment in which it operateol – a response that involves a number of complex management choices. Because of this we would not expect any pressures measured as firm responses to impact on *Autonomy*, their effect should be already incorporated into the construct. This leads to our final proposition.

Proposition 5. (A more specific version of Proposition Three) Pressures measured through firm responses should have no impact on *Autonomy*.

A series of controls are also included on *Autonomy*, including business or consumer markets, products or services, durable or non-durable goods, and country of parent, subsidiary sizes and ages. These provide us with greater confidence that observed effects are not spurious results of industry and firm heterogeneity.

Results

Reflective Models of Integration-Responsiveness Pressures

After removing 23 questionnaires with missing responses and three that were outliers there are 165 complete questionnaires for analysis. We ran maximum likelihood factor analysis on three domains or sets of items: (1) all items; (2) measures of environmental pressures; and (3) measures of firm responses to these pressures. These follow from our initial classification in Table 2. We checked the empirical support for our classification by Kaiser's measure of sampling adequacy – which tests whether the items belong to the same domain and are appropriate for factor analysis. For all three sets, Kaiser's measure is adequate (0.68, 0.70 and 0.69 respectively), although not high enough to provide clear support for the common factor model. Comparisons between these sets provide good support for our initial classification, with only 4 of 48 items wrongly classified according to the empirical correlations.

The Bayesian criterion indicates that five factors are appropriate for describing the overall domain of pressures and firm responses, four for the domain of pressures and three for the domain of firm responses. On the basis of extensive simulation studies, Velicer and Fava (1987) suggest that applied researchers should only interpret factors with four or more high item loadings (≥ 0.60). For the five-factor overall model, the first four factors are well identified with 6, 5, 5 and 4 high loadings. The fifth factor is less well identified with 3 such loadings. For the four-factor model of pressures, the first two factors are well identified (5 and 4 high loadings) but the third and fourth are less well identified (3 and 2 high loadings). For the three-factor model of firm response to pressures, the first factor is well identified (6 high loadings) but the other two less so (3 high loadings each). As one might expect there is a good degree of similarity between these three factor analyses. Two of the factors found in the pressures domain are identical to those found in the overall analysis, and a third is similar. The fourth factor is different but not well identified. Two of the factors in the firm response domain are also the same as the overall analysis; the third is different but not well identified. As a consequence of similarity and identification issues, we only report the overall analysis here. Table 4 presents the rotated factor pattern; only items with high loadings are shown.

Factor ONE interprets as *"the influence of local regulations on firm decisions"*, Factor TWO as *"pressures from the local business infrastructure"*, Factor THREE as *"the impact of global competition"*, Factor FOUR as *"pressures from technological change"*, and Factor FIVE as *"intra-firm sharing of resources"*.

Table 4. Rotated Factor Pattern, Overall Analysis, Loadings ≥ 0.60

No. Item Measures	Type	ONE	TWO	THREE	FOUR	FIVE
3 Rate of product innovation	PS				0.75	
4 Rate of process innovation	PS				0.65	
5 Technological complexity	PS				0.70	
6 Rate of technological change	PS				0.88	
7 Competitors are mostly global	PS			0.60		
8 Competitors sell globally standardised products	PS			0.63		
9 The nature of competition is global	PS			0.60		
12 Sharing of production resources	FR					0.81
13 Sharing of R & D resources	FR					0.81
14 Sharing of management services	FR					0.62
16 Co-ordination of production	FR			0.72		
17 Co-ordination of procurement	FR			0.66		
34 Product decisions influenced by government	FR	0.60				
35 Price decisions influenced by government	FR	0.84				
36 Advertising decisions influenced by government	FR	0.87				
37 Promotion decisions influenced by government	FR	0.87				
38 Sourcing decisions influenced by government	FR	0.68				
40 R&D decisions influenced by government	FR	0.74				
41 Quality of local infrastructure: logistics	PS		0.86			
42 Quality of local infrastructure: channels	PS		0.91			
43 Quality of local infrastructure: advertising	PS		0.67			
44 Quality of local infrastructure: personnel	PS		0.74			
45 Quality of local infrastructure: suppliers	PS		0.64			

Note: PS = Pressure, FR = Firm Response.

Factors TWO and FOUR are clearly *pressures*, whereas Factors ONE and FIVE are clearly *firm response to pressures*. Factor THREE is a hybrid, linking three global competitive pressures and firm coordination of production and procurement (supporting the original insight of Prahalad and Doz). Factor TWO is correlated with Factors THREE (−0.22), FOUR (−0.19) and FIVE (−0.16) while Factor THREE is correlated with Factors FOUR (0.30) and FIVE (0.31). The factors for the other two domains also show similar inter-correlations. Overall, these analyses provide good support for Proposition One. Two dimensions are not adequate to describe the domain of the pressures impacting on multinational firms. Environmental pressures and firm responses to these pressures are also probably better thought of as different types of constructs, since they are, in the main, empirically distinct in these data, only the hybrid Factor THREE clouds the issue.

Comparing Reflective and Formative Models of Integration-Responsiveness Pressures

A formative model was generated through PLS by examining the impact of pressures and firm responses on the independent reflective construct of *Autonomy*. For the sake of consistency of comparison with the factor analysis, we ran three models with the same three domains and we kept the item measures grouped together in the same way as suggested by the factor analysis. Other modelling strategies are clearly possible – such as searching for a grouping or including items that do not load heavily in the reflective analysis – but would generate results that would be difficult to compare. Instead, here we compare models with the same overall structure, the only difference being whether the five IR dimensions are generated reflectively or formatively. Diamantopoulos and Siguaw (2002) point out that most comparisons in the literature follow the same strategy.

Again the five-factor model of both pressures and responses outperforms either the pressure or response domain models. As shown in Figure 2, the five formative dimensions explain approximately 26% of the variance in *Autonomy*. This compares with approximately 20% for the pressure model and 15% for the firm response model. Due to its superiority we will only comment further on the five-factor model, particularly on how this formative model compares with reflective equivalents.

We have already outlined our theoretical case for why the pressures on multinational firms are better measured by formative indicators. This case is summarised in *Proposition 2*. In this section we will focus on an empirical comparison of reflective and formative indices for these pressures. We will use predictive power (variance in *Autonomy* explained by the five dimensions and the magnitude of their paths), the standard errors of the inner and outer coefficients (t statistics) and the tetrad test to make this comparison.

Figure 2. First-Level Formative Model

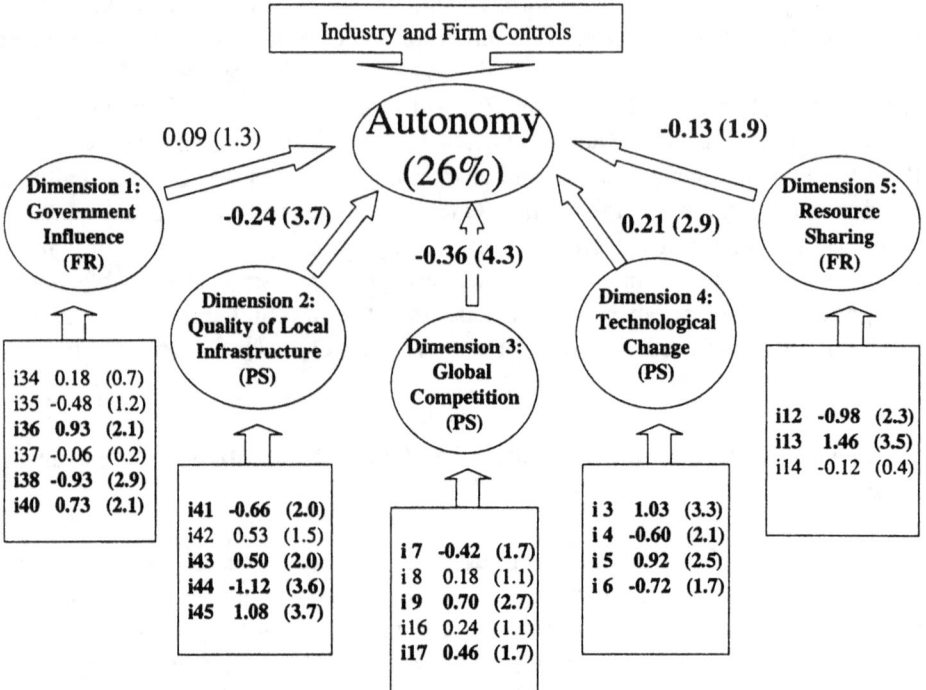

Note: Boxes contain outer item coefficients; inner paths are next to arrows (absolute values of the bootstrap t-statistic in parenthesis). Figure under the independent, reflective construct of *Autonomy* is the R^2.

Dimension 1, Dimension 2, etc. refers to the same sets of item measures as identified in Table 4. PS = Pressure; FR = Firm Response.

Predictive Power

As Figure 2 shows, formative indicators explain *Autonomy* reasonably well with an R^2 of 26%, of which 23% is explained by the five dimensions and only 3% by the firm and industry controls. Three of the dimensions also have significant and meaningful inner paths – those from the three dimensions measured as pressures (D2, D3 and D4) – whereas the two dimensions measured as managerial responses do not explain *Autonomy* to any meaningful degree. D1 has an insignificant and small coefficient and D5, although significant, has a coefficient of magnitude well below the 0.20 recommended for minimum effects (Meehl 1990). These results support Proposition 5.

The paths for the three dimensions measured as pressures also provide some support for Proposition 4. Increasing values of D3: *Global Competition* decreases *Autonomy* as predicted (four of five item weights being positive, with the "nature of competition is global" having the largest weight). Interestingly, "competitors are mostly global" has a negative weight, which is not predicted. In these circumstances, MNEs may possibly allow local managers some tactical autonomy to compete. The path from D4: *Technological Change* is also plausible in terms of recent studies. For example, Birkinshaw and Hood (2001) show that MNEs increasingly use their subsidiaries as the sources of innovations that the parent can leverage on a global basis. To achieve this, it is necessary to provide autonomy to the subsidiary managers in order to motivate them to take the entrepreneurial risks. Interestingly, the item weights for D4 suggest a subtler story. Increasing technological complexity or higher rates of product innovation increases *Autonomy*, whereas a higher rate of process innovation or rapid rates of technological change decreases it. It is possible that product innovation benefits from local market input, whereas the firm may centralize process innovation to gain scale and consistency. The final path from D2: *Quality of Local Infrastructure* to *Autonomy* also requires a subtler interpretation. First, we need to note that "poor" infrastructure was coded as 7 on the 1 to 7 questionnaire scales. Hence, from the weights in Figure 2, poor distribution channels, advertising media and material suppliers decrease *Autonomy*, whereas poor logistics and poor availability of skilled personnel increase it (as would be predicted by earlier theories). MNEs might be more likely to centralize critical marketing and supply decisions where they had concerns about the local situation, whereas decisions on personnel recruitment and logistics might require more local knowledge in difficult circumstances.

To generate a reflective model for comparison we followed two approaches. First, we simply reversed the direction of the paths between item measures and dimensions and reran the same model in PLS. As expected, this model underperforms its formative counterpart, explaining only 21% of the variance in *Autonomy*, of which the five dimensions explain 14% and the remainder determined by the firm and industry controls. While there is no statistical test of this under-performance (the models having identical degrees of freedom) this is a sizeable difference – the reflective dimensions only explaining 14% as opposed to the formative dimensions 23%. Moreover, there is only one path that is both significant and meaningful, that between D3 and *Autonomy* (with a coefficient of −0.42). This, in itself, casts doubt as to whether a reflective formulation is useful for explaining integration and responsiveness. Second, as PLS generates reflective constructs in a different manner to maximum likelihood factor analysis used for Table 4, we imported the factor scores from that analysis into PLS and ran an equivalent model. The results were essentially the same implying that the results are not an artefact of the particular factoring algorithm. These reflective, common factors explain only 9% of the variance in *Autonomy* with the firm and industry controls explaining 7% (for a total of 16% variance explained). Again only D3 had a significant and meaningful coefficient value (−0.40). Overall, we conclude that formative indicators have substantially better predictive power than reflective ones.

Parameter Estimates

Predictive power is only one criterion for assessment; we must also examine the robustness of our parameter estimates and the degree to which they support our theoretical propositions. We examined the outer model coefficients for the formative and reflective models. For the reflective model we examined the item loadings and for formative model the item weights (Chin 1998a).[6] Bootstrapping was used to generate standard errors and t-statistics. For the reflective model, the dimensions are all well measured, with high loadings (20 of the items having loadings above the recommended 0.60 level and only 3 marginally below this) and highly significant t-values ranging from 2.4 to 10.3. This result is to be expected; it is essentially a replication of the earlier factor analysis, this time through the reflective algorithm of PLS. It does, however, demonstrate that the substantial under-performance of the reflective model is not a result of measurement problems – in a reflective sense these dimensions are well measured. For the formative model, all the dimensions have an adequate number of significant weights but a few coefficients are not well estimated. For example D1 has three out of six items with significant weights ($p < 0.05$, two tail), D2 four out of five, D3 only one out of five (but three at $p < 0.10$), D4 three out of four (and all four at $p < 0.10$) and D5 two out of three. In part, this derives from using the reflective analysis to group items. As noted earlier, other strategies might be better. However, these formative dimensions are certainly more than adequate to the purpose at hand.

Tetrad Test

We ran the vanishing tetrad test on each of our five dimensions. The test rejects the reflective model for the first four dimensions ($p < 0.01$) but not for the fifth. Thus the tetrad test supports the conclusions we made above on the basis of predictive power and parameter estimates: namely, these dimensions are better conceptualised as formative. The one exception is D5: *Resource Sharing*. Interestingly, when we re-ran the Figure 2 model with D5 specified as reflective its path became non-significant and small, further supporting Proposition 5. Other effects remained the same.

Overall, the tests of predictive power, parameter estimates and tetrads, provide good support for the formative approach, particularly for measuring pressures. For measuring firm responses to pressures, on some occasions formative models are indicated, whereas on others reflective models may be better.

Higher-Level and Hybrid Models

We also examined a number of higher level and hybrid models. In particular, a hybrid model where the first level is a reflective formulation and the second level composed of two formatively constructed dimensions (*Integration* – formed from Factors THREE, FOUR and FIVE and *Responsiveness* – formed from Factors ONE and TWO). This and other hybrid models do not perform well, explaining only 6% of the variance in *Autonomy*. Finally, we sought a second level or order solution in the reflective perspective, by factor analysing our factor solutions from the initial analyses. Again these solutions are not compelling, although this result is clouded by only having five first-order factors as input.

Conclusions

We examined how IR pressures might best be conceptualised, described and measured using literature review, exploratory factor analysis and PLS modelling. The exploratory nature of these analyses precludes us from making definitive statements; however, they do highlight several inter-related issues with the IR framework.

Lack of Consensus as to Construct Definition

There is little agreement in the literature as to how the IR pressures should be defined, conceptualised and measured. Some authors see them as environmental pressures and some as firm responses, some assume two dimensions and others more, some measure reflectively, far fewer formatively. An equally critical issue is the definition of the domain – on which there is no consensus either. Yet, as Rossiter (2002) points out, content validity is the most essential aspect of construct validity.

To this might be added a concern over whether the original 12 pressures of Prahalad and Doz are themselves a broad enough expression of the domain. For example, Devinney et al. (2000) argue that global firms face pressures in a third area of their environment, namely their nexus of contracts. They suggest that the "pressures for transactional completeness" be accorded equal status to the IR pressures of Prahalad and Doz. What is clear is that we will never understand the domain of organisational pressures by limiting our search *ex ante*.

Under-extraction, Alternative Models and Under-sampling of the Domain

Our exploratory analyses took a broad definition of this domain, including pressures and firm responses totalling 48 item measures from the literature. We will subsequently argue that even this is inadequate, but our definition is broader than that of many previous studies. The results suggest that more than two dimensions are required to describe this domain – either three pressures plus two firm response dimensions (overall analysis) or four pressures and three firm response dimensions (other analyses). Indeed, two-dimensional solutions are firmly ruled out by the Bayes criterion and by statistical tests on the maximum likelihood function. Moreover, correlations between these dimensions suggest that IR pressures are not likely to be orthogonal as is generally assumed both normatively and empirically.

The models and comparisons we conducted using PLS also suggest that formative approaches may outperform traditional reflective ones. It is not hard to see why, they allow each item to be optimally weighted in its predictive impact on the construct, rather than forced into the straitjacket of commonality. Rossiter (2002) has also argued that many constructs are better conceived as formative. This distinction is particularly important when our item measures cover such a broad domain as the IR pressures. To insist that an item such as "scale economies" be highly correlated with "global competition" in a reflective construct of "integration" is unnecessarily restrictive. Furthermore, in much of the IR literature, and in our work, a pressure such as "scale economies" is measured with a single question. From another perspective, say that of an economics paper, several items might measure such a pressure. For that reason, we need to be cautious about our results for higher-order and hybrid models. These do not appear to perform well, suggesting that a first-order formative model is best. On the other hand, 48 items is a relatively small number on which to base these analyses. IR researchers, including us, may have under-sampled the universe of items – having possibly already defined this universe too narrowly as suggested above. This conclusion must remain speculative, however, until studies are conducted with more extensive batteries of items.

We would like to emphasise that although empirical results help us to validate our measurement models, the choice between formative and reflective models must be driven fundamentally by theory, not empirical testing.[7] In this paper, we have started to build theoretical support for the formative model as more appropriate to the study of pressures, but we readily admit there is much work to be done to fully articulate this position. In addition, even though there is no definitive test for choosing between a formative and a reflective model, as we have shown above, PLS and tetrad tests provide a number of criteria on which a more informed judgment can be made about the relative superiority of the two measurement models, and in particular, the appropriateness of a formative structure in situations that the literature considers, perhaps without questioning, to be reflective.[8]

The Way Forward

Our attempts in this paper were modest and represent only a call and guide for future research. As such, we have provided useful speculation that will hopefully engender future work that concentrates on the development of parsimonious measures and techniques for the understanding of international strategy, structure and environment. It is our viewpoint that the IR framework is an area that is so critical to international business thinking that it behoves us to get it right. In doing so we need to concentrate on:

1. The development of scales and measures that represent more clearly and accurately the environmental pressures facing firms operating in the international arena.
2. A simultaneous development of measures that can tap the underlying mental models of managers that allow for an understanding of how organisations react to pressures and decide on specific strategic orientations.
3. Moving beyond simple reflective and multivariate modelling techniques that are limited in application and have built into them implicit assumptions about the nature of the phenomenon being investigated.

Point (1) directs us toward a research program that requires greater refinement and clarity about what we mean by a "pressure" and a "response" and the domain of each. In addition, our review of the literature points out a rather serious problem of scale comparability across studies. Until there is greater emphasis on scales and measurement and repeated usage of identical scales our ability to falsify some of the basic precepts in the field will be limited.

Point (2) requires us to come to grips with a less than rational model of the world where we cannot assume that the cognitive models used by managers are optimal for the environment in which they operate. Techniques exist that allow for the direct examination of mental models (e.g., choice modelling techniques (Louviere/Henscher/Swait 2000)), however, these have yet to be applied in international business research. This is critical because the path from pressures to strategy and structure goes through the institutional structures of firms and the mental models of their managers. Until we have an understanding of this path, our ability to make substantive prescriptions will be severely limited.

Point (3) follows on from this idea. To date modelling in international business has limited itself somewhat unfairly. In the case of the IR framework, the assumption has been that firms choose different paths based upon their reactions to underlying pressures. However, this is a limited viewpoint as we noted earlier.

It does not address exactly what determines what a "good" response is, nor does it deal with how firms compete across strategies and structures. Devinney et al. (2000), in an attempt to address this issue, argue that a frontier specification is more appropriate than cluster based techniques since it implies that alternative structures can coexist even in a rational world. Our results show some likelihood that this may indeed be the case. The correlation structure of our factors shows positive correlations within the groupings of Integration and Responsiveness but negative correlations between these groupings, suggesting that a trade-off between integration and responsiveness exists. Econometric techniques (Bauer 1991) exist that allow for such analysis but the data collection requirements and theoretical assumptions are different than those traditionally applied.

Similarly, there is a tendency to boil the IR framework down to generic structures, which was not the intent of Prahalad and Doz and certainly is not the intent of Bartlett and Ghoshal. However, none of the techniques used in the research cited here deal with the issue of heterogeneity except to assume that it is picked up in the error terms of the model applied. If we believe that heterogeneity is as important as similarity one needs different modelling techniques from standard cluster analysis. One such avenue to pursue is the application of mixture models (e.g., Wedel/Kamakura 2000) – put simply, simultaneous estimation of clusters and linear models – that fit more appropriately into dynamic capabilities world where heterogeneity of strategy and structure rather than convergence is the norm.

To date, we have tended to apply models we know rather than models that are appropriate and ignore the extent to which these models have embedded assumptions about the theories being tested. If the international business field is to advance we need to develop more parsimonious approaches to testing theories and to apply those consistently across a host of studies to improve not only their validity but also their value to managers. It is one thing to argue that a framework is meant to characterise issues for managers but quite another to show that that framework makes a substantive difference to performance when applied by managers. This distinction is seen most starkly in textbooks that present a structure that is two-dimensional, with simple and orthogonal dimensions, whereas the reality of the multinational is potentially at least three-dimensional, with complex and correlated dimensions. Academic validity and managerial application must go hand in hand.

The implications of this research go beyond the IR framework alone and touch many areas of interest to international business researchers. The methods and tests utilized in this study show how a model can benefit in terms of both fit and insight from using formative rather than reflective indicators, and by separating environmental pressures from firm response to those pressures. In addition, our results show that reliance solely on reliability measures to determine whether a construct is appropriately measured – as in many of the studies we cite – is completely inadequate. We must have a deeper understanding of the likely dimensionality and possible covariance structures. Hence, it is important when developing and testing theory to ensure that the measurement domain is sufficiently broad to ensure validity and that more concern is shown for the nature of the measures employed to tap the theoretical constructs. The agenda for the field of international business should include greater debate on the definition of this domain, willingness to consider additional dimensionality and more theoretical debate and empirical comparisons on the merits of formative versus the reflective indicators. Above all, there should be greater discussion of how environmental pressures might best be measured and conceptualised. This debate should include issues of sampling both the domain and the universe of firms and subsidiaries, and possible methodologies for separating exogenous from endogenous phenomena. In this way we can move to a more articulate theory of the MNE: one that recognises the diversity and subtlety of the environmental pressures faced by these firms, and that clearly separates these pressures from the many innovative ways in which MNEs adapt to the pressures they face.

Endnotes

1 We would like to thank Erin Anderson, the participants at the 2002 AIB Conference, the 2000 EIBA Conference, seminar participants at the University of Illinois and the AGSM, as well as the reviewers and editors of the *Management International Review* for their helpful comments. The Australian Research Council, INSEAD, and The Centre for Corporate Change at the AGSM supported this research. The authors are listed in reverse alphabetical order with each having contributed equally to the project.
2 In accordance with convention, for the reflective structure the arrows are shown pointing outward e.g. the item values reflect (are a consequence of) the construct value. For a formative structure, the inward pointing arrows imply that the construct value is formed from (is a consequence of) the item values.
3 More details on the sample are available from the authors. These have been excluded due to space limitations.
4 We are grateful to a reviewer for providing this point.
5 Again, we are grateful to a second reviewer for making this point.
6 Multicollinearity can result in poor estimates for the coefficients of a *formative* outer model. However, in our data none of the matrix condition indices gave any concern, all falling well below accepted limits.
7 We are thankful to the editors for this point.
8 Again, we are thankful to the editors for this point.

References

Bartlett, C. A., Building and Managing the Transnational: The New Organizational Challenge, in Porter, M. E. (ed.), *Competition in Global Industries*, Boston: Harvard Business School Press 1986, pp. 367–401.

Bartlett, C. A./Ghoshal, S., *Managing Across Borders: The Transnational Solution*, Boston: Harvard Business School Press 1989.

Bauer, P., Recent Developments in the Econometric Estimation of Frontiers, *Journal of Econometrics*, 46, 2, 1991, pp. 39–56.

Birkinshaw, J./Morrison, A./Hulland, J., Structural and Competitive Determinants of Global Integration Strategy, *Strategic Management Journal*, 16, 8, 1995, pp. 637–655.

Birkinshaw, J./Hood, N., Unleash Innovation in Foreign Subsidiaries, *Harvard Business Review*, March 2001, pp. 131–137.

Bollen, K. A./Lennox, R., Conventional Wisdom on Measurement: A Structural Equation Perspective, *Psychological Bulletin*, 110, 2, 1991, pp. 305–314.

Bollen, K. A./Ting, K.-F., A Tetrad Test for Causal Indicators, *Psychological Methods*, 5, 1, 2000, pp. 3–22.

Burgeois, L. J., Strategic Management and Determinism, *Academy of Management Review*, 9, 4, 1984, pp. 586–597.

Burns, T./Stalker, G. M., *The Management of Innovation*, London: Travistock 1961.

Carpano, C./Chrisman, J. J./Roth, K., International Strategy and Environment: An Assessment of the Performance Relationship, *Journal of International Business Studies*, 25, 3, 1994, pp. 639–656.

Carson, S./Devinney, T./Dowling, G./John, G., Understanding Institutional Designs Within Marketing Value Systems. *Journal of Marketing*, 63, Special Issue 1999, pp. 115–130.

Chin, W. W., The Partial Least Squares Approach for Structural Equation Modeling, in Marcoulides, G. A. (ed.), *Modern Methods for Business Research*, Mahwah, NJ: Erlbaum 1998a.

Chin, W. W., Issues and Opinion on Structural Equation Modeling, *MIS Quarterly*, March 1998b, vii–xvi.

Cvar, M. R., Case Studies in Global Competition: Patterns of Success and Failure, in Porter, M. E. (ed.), *Competition in Global Industries*, Boston: Harvard Business School Press 1986, pp. 483–515.

Devinney, T./Midgley, D./Venaik, S., The Optimal Performance of the Global Firm: Formalising and Extending the Integration – Responsiveness Framework, *Organization Science*, 11, 6, 2000, pp. 674–695.

Diamantopoulos, A./Winklhofer, H. M., Index Construction with Formative Indicators: An Alternative to Scale Development, *Journal of Marketing Research*, 38, 2, 2001, pp. 269–277.

Diamantopoulos, A./Siguaw, J.A., Reflective vs. Formative Indicators in Measure Development: Does the Choice of Indicators Matter?, in Tynan, A. C. et al. (eds.), *Proceedings Annual Conference of the Academy of Marketing*, Nottingham, July 2002.

Digman, J. M., Higher Order Factors of the Big Five, *Journal of Personality and Social Psychology*, 73, 6, 1997, pp. 1246–1256.

Doz, Y., *National Policies and Multinational Management*, Unpublished Doctoral Dissertation, Harvard Business School 1976.

Doz, Y., Government Policies and Global Industries, in Porter, M. E. (ed.), *Competition in Global Industries*, Boston: Harvard Business School Press 1986, pp. 225–266.

Dunning, J. H., *Explaining International Production*, London: Unwin Hyman 1988.

Edwards, J./Bagozzi, R., On the Nature and Direction of Relationships Between Constructs and Measures, *Psychological Methods*, 5, 2, 2000, pp. 155–174.

Fayerweather, J., *International Business Management: Conceptual Framework*, New York: McGraw-Hill 1969.

Fava, J. L./Velicer, W. F., The Effects of Underextraction in Factor and Component Analysis, *Educational and Psychological Measurement*, 56, 6, 1996, pp. 907–929.

Flaherty, M. T., Coordinating International Manufacturing and Technology, in Porter, M. E. (ed.), *Competition in Global Industries*, Boston: Harvard Business School Press 1986, pp. 83–109.

Fornell, C./Cha, J., Partial Least Squares, in Bagozzi, R. (ed.), *Advanced Methods of Marketing Research*, Cambridge, MA: Basil Blackwell 1994.

Fornell, C./Bookstein, F. L., Two Structural Equation Models: LISREL and PLS Applied to Consumer Exit – voice Theory, *Journal of Marketing Research*, 19, 4, 1982, pp. 440–452.

Fornell, C./Rhee B.-D./Yi, Y., Direct Regression, Reverse Regression, and Covariance Structure Analysis, *Marketing Letters*, 2, 3, 1991, pp. 309–320.

Ghemawat, P./Spence, A. M., Modeling Global Competition, in Porter, M. E. (ed.), *Competition in Global Industries*, Boston: Harvard Business School Press 1986, pp. 61–79.

Ghoshal, S./Nohria, N., Horses for Courses: Organizational Forms for Multinational Corporations, *Sloan Management Review*, 34, 2, 1993, pp. 23–35.

Ghoshal, S./Nohria, N., Internal Differentiation Within Multinational Corporations, *Strategic Management Journal*, 10, 4, 1989, pp. 323–337.

Harzing, A., An Empirical Analysis and Extension of the Bartlett and Ghoshal Typology of Multinational Companies, *Journal of International Business Studies*, 31, 1, 2000, pp. 101–120.

Hedlund, G., The Hypermodern MNC – A Heterarchy? *Human Resource Management*, 25, 1, Spring 1986, pp. 9–35.

Jain, S. C., Standardization of International Marketing Strategy: Some Research Hypotheses, *Journal of Marketing*, 53, 1, 1989, pp. 70–79.

Jarillo, J. C./Martinez, J. I., Different Roles for Subsidiaries: The Case of Multinational Corporations, *Strategic Management Journal*, 11, 7, 1990, pp. 501–512.

Johansson, J./Yip, G., Exploiting Globalisation Potential: U.S. and Japanese Strategies, *Strategic Management Journal*, 158, 1994, pp. 579–601.

Johnson, J. Jr., An Empirical Analysis of the Integration – Responsiveness Framework: U.S. Construction Equipment Industry Firms in Global Competition, *Journal of International Business Studies*, 26, 3, 1995, pp. 621–635.

Kashani, K., Beware the Pitfalls of Global Marketing, *Harvard Business Review*, 67, 5, 1989, pp. 91–98.

Kass, R. E./Raftery, A. E., Bayes Factors, *Journal of the American Statistical Association*, 90, 430, 1995, pp. 773–795.

Kobrin, S. J., An Empirical Analysis of the Determinants of Global Integration, *Strategic Management Journal*, 12, Special Issue 1991, pp. 17–31.

Kobrin, S. J., Is There a Relationship Between a Geocentric Mind – Set and Multinational Strategy? *Journal of International Business Studies*, 25, 3, 1994, pp. 493–511.

Kogut, B./Singh, H., The Effects of National Culture on the Choice of Entry Mode, *Journal of International Business Studies*, 19, 3, 1988, pp. 411–432.

Lawrence, P./Lorsch, J., *Organization and Environment*, Boston: Harvard Business School 1967.

Louviere, J. J./Henscher, D. A./Swait, J. D., *Stated Choice Models: Analysis and Applications*, Cambridge: Cambridge University Press 2000.

MacCallum, R. C./Browne, M. C., The Use of Causal Indicators in Covariance Structure Models: Some Practical Issues, *Psychological Bulletin*, 114, 3, 1993, pp. 533–541.

Mahini, A./Wells, L. T. Jr., Government Relations in the Global Firm, in Porter, M. E. (ed.)., *Competition in Global Industries*, Boston: Harvard Business School Press 1986, pp. 291–312.

Marsh, H. W./Hau K-T./Balla, J. R./Grayson, D., Is More Ever Too Much? The Number of Indicators per Factor in Confirmatory Factor Analysis, *Multivariate Behavioral Research*, 33, 2, 1998, pp. 181–220.

Martinez, J./Jarillo, J., Coordination Demands of International Strategies, *Journal of International Business Studies*, 22, 3, 1991, pp. 429–444.

Miles, R. E./Snow, C. C., *Organizational Strategy, Structure and Process*, New York: McGraw-Hill 1978.

Meehl, P. E., Why Summaries of Research on Psychological Theories are Often Uninterpretable, *Psychological Reports*, 66, 1990, pp. 195–244.

Murtha, T./Lenway, S./Bagozzi, R., Global Mind – sets and Cognitive Shift in a Complex Multinational Corporation, *Strategic Management Journal*, 19, 2, 1998, pp. 97–114.

Perlmutter, H., The Tortuous Evolution of the Multinational Corporation, *Columbia Journal of World Business*, January–February 1969, pp. 9–18.

Porter, M. E., Competition in Global Industries: A Conceptual Framework, in Porter, M. E. (ed.), *Competition in Global Industries*, Boston: Harvard Business School Press 1986, pp. 15–60.

Podsakoff, P./Organ, D., Self Reports in Organizational Research: Problems and Prospects, *Journal of Management*, 12, 4, 1986, pp. 531–544.

Prahalad, C., The Strategic Process in a Multinational Corporation, Unpublished Doctoral Dissertation, Graduate School of Business Administration, Harvard University 1975.

Prahalad, C./Doz, Y., *The Multinational Mission: Balancing Local Demand and Global Vision*, New York: Free Press 1987.

Rossiter, J. R., The C-OAR-SE Procedure for Scale Development in Marketing, *International Journal of Research in Marketing*, 19, 4, 2002, pp. 1-31.

Roth, K./Morrison, A., An Empirical Analysis of the Integration – Responsiveness Framework in Global Industries, *Journal of International Business Studies*, 21, 4, 1990, pp. 541-564.

Spearman, C./Holzinger, K., The Sampling Error in the Theory of Two Factors, *British Journal of Psychology*, 15, 1924, pp. 17-19.

Stopford, J./Wells, C. Jr., *Managing the Multinational Enterprise: Organisation of the Firm and Ownership of the Subsidiaries*, New York: Basic Books 1972.

Taggart, J. H., An Evaluation of the Integration–Responsiveness Framework, *Management International Review*, 37, 4, 1997, pp. 295-318.

Taggart, J. H., Strategic Shifts in MNC Subsidiaries, *Strategic Management Journal*, 19, 7, 1998, pp. 663-681.

Takeuchi, H./Porter, M. E., Three Roles of International Marketing in Global Strategy, in Porter, M. E. (ed.), *Competition in Global Industries*, Boston: Harvard Business School Press 1986, pp. 111-146.

Teece, D./Pisano, G./Shuen, A., Dynamic Capabilities and Strategic Management, *Strategic Management Journal*, 18, 7, 1997, pp. 509-533.

Velicer, W. F./Fava, J. L., An Evaluation of the Effects of Variable Sampling on Component, Image and Factor Analysis, *Multivariate Behavioral Research*, 25, 1987, pp. 97-114.

Wedel M./Kamakura, W., *Market Segmentation*, London: Kluwer 2000.

Vernon, R., International Investment and International Trade in the Product Cycle, *Quarterly Journal of Economics*, 80, May 1966, pp. 190-207.

Tony Edwards/Anthony Ferner

Multinationals, Reverse Diffusion and National Business Systems[1]

Abstract

■ The paper addresses the issue of 'reverse diffusion' in the field of HRM, defined as the transfer of practices from foreign subsidiaries to the domestic operations. Pulling together the limited relevant findings from previous research, and drawing on our own case study evidence, it provides a set of structured arguments about the logic, determinants and mechanisms of reverse diffusion.

Key Results

■ The findings shed light on the sort of multinational in which reverse diffusion is most likely to occur, the impact it brings and the processes through which it occurs.

Authors

Tony Edwards, Lecturer in International HRM, The Management Centre at King's College, University of London, London, UK.
Anthony Ferner, Professor of International Human Resource Management, Leicester Business School, De Montfort University, Leicester, UK.

Introduction

In recent years an extensive literature has emerged concerned with the diffusion of human resource management (HRM) practices in multinational companies (MNCs), reflecting the growing size and scope of MNCs. The literature is primarily concerned with the diffusion of practices from the home country to plants in other countries, which can be termed 'forward diffusion'. In recent work (Edwards 1998, 2000, Ferner/Varul 1999, 2000) both authors of this paper have investigated a different form of diffusion, one in which practices are transferred from foreign subsidiaries to operations in the country of origin. We have termed this process 'reverse diffusion' (RD). RD can occur either as part of a wider process of diffusion in which a practice originates in a foreign subsidiary and flows across the organization to other foreign subsidiaries as well as to the domestic plants, which we term 'flow' diffusion, or as part of a narrower process where a practice is diffused from one foreign plant to the domestic plant(s) only, which we term 'strict' RD.

RD is an important phenomenon for three main reasons. First, a growing number of MNCs are undertaking internal restructuring, which in many cases has taken the form of greater international integration. This often involves production or service provision becoming more standardised across borders, raising the scope for the diffusion of practices across sites. Greater international integration can also take the form of generating inter-unit linkages in which plants in different countries buy and sell components or services from one another, something which is commonplace in automotive firms. In some firms, international integration has encouraged the development of specialised knowledge in MNCs beyond the domestic operations, based on exploiting knowledge within host environments (e.g. Rugman/Verbeke 2001, Zanfei 2000), and writers have pointed to the emergence of 'federal' or 'heterarchic' organisational forms (e.g. Hedlund 1986) in which the authority and influence of the centre is weakened and the role of the subsidiaries in generating new practices is enhanced. Therefore, greater international integration facilitates the diffusion of practices across borders in general and RD in particular.

Second, engaging in RD may affect the competitive position of a multinational. Indeed, Bartlett and Ghoshal (1998) refer to the organisational form in which information is diffused across the MNC from wherever it originates as the 'solution' to managing across borders. Tapping the diverse range of practices in plants in different countries can lead managers in domestic plants to initiatives which enhance efficiency. RD can also be a key way in which MNCs learn about structures and mechanisms appropriate for serving international markets. This is particularly the case in MNCs in the early stages of internationalisation and in which structures and systems characteristic of the home country do not appear to be well suited for international operations. MNCs from countries which have been relatively 'closed' to patterns of foreign direct investment, such as Germany, fall into this category, as do MNCs from many newly industrialising countries, such as China. However, RD can also harm a multinational's competitive position; this is particularly likely where crude attempts are made to simply 'bolt on' a new practice to pre-existing employment relations practices in the hope that it will operate in the same way as in the donor unit.

Third, RD can have a significant impact on the national business system of the home country. One aspect of this is the impact on employees: despite talk of the emergence of 'global' firms, over half of the people who work for MNCs are based in domestic plants (United Nations 2001). Thus RD has the potential to affect more employees than does 'forward' diffusion. More generally, RD is a mechanism through which national business systems evolve. As new practices characteristic of other systems are implemented in the domestic operations of MNCs they may subsequently be diffused to other local firms, particularly those supplying the multinational. In this way, practices which were once seen as being 'foreign' cease to be so, becoming established in the new business system and acting as a force for change.

The paper aims to develop the concept of RD of HR practices by examining three of its fundamental aspects. First, we consider the factors that promote it, distinguishing between the influence of the characteristics of subsidiaries, companies and countries, so as to establish the sort of multinational in which RD is most likely to occur. Second, we explore the impact of RD on the way multinationals operate in order to assess the extent to which RD alters the *modus operandi* of MNCs themselves and the knock-on impact on the parent business systems. Third, we investigate the processes through which RD occurs, considering the crucial role of power in these processes. In addressing these questions our intention is to provide a set of structured arguments about the logic, determinants and mechanisms of reverse diffusion, pulling together the limited relevant findings of previous research and building on these by drawing for illustrative material on our own empirical research. The paper is structured as follows: a brief review of the main aspects of the literature on the diffusion of practices is provided in section two; this is followed by a description of the methods employed in data collection; the following three sections are organised around the three key aspects of RD discussed above; and in the final section we conclude and provide pointers towards a future research agenda.

Patterns and Weaknesses in the Literature

The literature on the diffusion of HRM practices in MNCs has told us much about a number of key aspects of this phenomenon. For instance, it has indicated that MNCs from some countries are more likely to adopt a centralised, ethnocentric approach to diffusing practices than those from other countries (see Ferner 1997, for a review). The literature has also revealed much about the way in which expatriate employees are sent to the foreign subsidiaries by the HQ with a brief of implementing practices used in the home country (e.g. Kopp 1994). However, in considering the reverse diffusion of HR practices, three key weaknesses in the literature are evident.

First, it is overwhelmingly concerned with forward diffusion. One strand to this literature, particularly evident in the 1970s and early 1980s, examined the nature of HR practices in the subsidiaries of American MNCs, and the transfer of policies such as union avoidance and innovative pay systems (e.g. Hamill 1984). A second strand, prominent in the late 1980s and early 1990s, centered on the attempts by many Japanese firms to implement new forms of work organization in their overseas plants (e.g. Oliver/Wilkinson 1992). While these issues are important, the reverse diffusion of HR practices has been neglected.

Second, many models of international HRM make explicit conceptual allowance for the possibility of reverse diffusion. For example, Taylor et al.'s model of strategic international HRM considers that the transfer of HRM policies and practices 'can go in any direction' (1996, pp. 996–997). However, while these models are of some value in highlighting broad conditions under which RD is likely to occur, there is a dearth of *empirical* evidence, particularly in the field of HRM. There is considerable evidence concerning the reverse diffusion of technological innovations (e.g. Andersson et al. 2001, Archibugi/Michie 1997, Bartlett/Ghoshal 1998, ch. 7, Tasi 2001, Zanfei 2000) as a consequence of the increasing tendency for MNCs to create 'centres of excellence' outside their home country. A full discussion of this literature is well beyond the scope of the paper, but it is worth noting that some of its key themes – for example, the explicit and tacit barriers to transfer represented by different national institutional arrangements for managing technological innovation (see esp. Hall/Soskice 2001) – apply at a general level to the reverse diffusion of HRM; these themes are returned to below.

A third weakness of the literature is that where RD is considered explicitly it is dealt with predominantly in terms of models of flows of information and practices between different units of MNCs (e.g. Gupta/Govindarajan 1991, 2000, Taylor et al. 1996), a tendency naturally promoted by the increasing focus in the literature on the move towards 'knowledge-based' economic activity (for a review see Child/McGrath 2001). The problem with this approach is that the *power* dimension of diffusion is usually glossed over, despite the crucial role of power in promoting or impeding the flow of practices between different parts of a multinational. The ability of one actor to overcome the potential resistance of other actors to achieve their aims is central to any process of organisational change, of course, and so power relations between actors must form a central part of analysis of reverse diffusion.

Thus, in general, the issue of RD of HR practices has been covered in only a patchy way, with a dearth of empirical studies in particular. In developing our arguments we add to the literature by drawing on two sources of data which explicitly address the issue of RD. These are described in the following section.

Methodology

The paper draws on evidence from two research projects, on British and German MNCs respectively. Both studies examined the ways in which multinationals use plants outside the home country as sites for generating new practices that can be transferred across their operations. The firms selected for the projects varied by sector, size, stage of internationalisation, method of growth, and so on, in order to assess the impact of these variables on the extent and nature of reverse diffusion. The primary research instrument in each project was the in-depth, semi-structured interview. Respondents were drawn from a number of locations and levels within the corporate hierarchy, predominantly within the HR or industrial relations functions. Interviews were tape-recorded and transcribed, except in a very small number of cases where recording was not possible. The line of questioning in all of the cases covered a common set of areas of HR practice, notably pay and performance, training and development and work organisation, as well as the co-ordination of HR policies across sites. While this commonality was important for making comparisons across the firms, a significant strength of the semi-structured interview technique was that the questioning was sufficiently open-ended to allow respondents to identify where RD occurs.

The study of British MNCs consisted of mini-case studies of ten firms. In all ten cases, interviews were conducted in a workplace in Britain and in the corporate HQ, and in most cases at divisional level too. These data provided the primary basis for assessing the extent to which the multinationals looked to their sites outside the UK for practices that could be spread across their international operations, including those in the UK. They also allowed an investigation of the impact on the British sites of this process, and the mechanisms through which it occurred. In the two firms in which there was clear evidence of RD, further interviews were conducted in their American subsidiaries. In total, thirty-two interviews were carried out during 1995 and 1996.

In the project examining German MNCs some three dozen firms were examined. Where possible, interviews were carried out both in the British operations and at German headquarters[2]. Eighty interviews were conducted between 1996 and 1998 (see Ferner/Varul 1999 for further details) with a range of senior management respondents. A major research question that emerged in the early stages of this project concerned how far German MNCs were coming to exhibit the characteristics of many British and American MNCs that internationalised much earlier, and this entailed examining the sources and mechanisms of 'Anglo-Saxon' influence in HRM.

A key methodological problem in assessing the existence or otherwise of reverse diffusion concerns what constitutes convincing evidence that it has occurred. Two key criteria were used to establish the existence of RD in the case studies. First, and more importantly, was it possible to identify a practice in the domestic plants that had originated in a specific overseas plant? Second, were there channels and mechanisms in place through which such practices could have been reverse diffused? In order to assess these issues, a series of questions were put to multiple respondents in order to shed light on the origins of new practices in the domestic plants. Where the resulting data indicated that a practice had been transferred from subsidiaries or plants in other countries, respondents were asked a further series of questions relating to the process through which they were diffused and the impact they had had on employment practice in the domestic plants. The questioning focused on such mechanisms as international committees, task forces and working groups as well as the extent of transfer of staff across sites (see Appendix 1). As we will show, respondents in two of the British and five of the German MNCs were able to trace in detail the precise path of reverse-diffused practices.

Where there was convincing evidence of RD, we subsequently attempted to make a categorisation of reverse diffused practices according to their impact on the companies in which they occurred. Thus RD can either be *evolutionary* or *transformative* in its effects. RD which is evolutionary is directed towards an optimal mix of practices within an existing *modus operandi*. That is, the multinational maintains a set of assumptions concerning the way it operates but seeks to fine-tune this through learning from its plants in different countries, making incremental improvements to operations. Transformative RD, in contrast, exerts a much more significant impact since it seeks to move the firm towards a new *modus operandi*. This type of RD is most likely where senior managers perceive the firm to be at a disadvantage in relation to other MNCs and to seek to catch up by diffusing sources of competitive advantage from its foreign subsidiaries. The responses to a series of questions concerned with the nature of the impact of reverse diffusion on the policies and practices within the MNCs were used as the basis for assessing whether the impact was evolutionary or transformative. In particular, we sought to assess whether RD had challenged the fundamental characteristics of the organisation.

In practice, making a neat distinction between those instances of RD that were evolutionary and those that were transformative was not always easy, so that the categorisation was more a matter of degree than an absolute judgement. However, we believe that the distinction has important heuristic and analytical value (see below), and that one of the aims of future research should be to develop more precise and focused operational measures of the impact of RD practices on the modus operandi of a company. A further analytical issue relating to the distinction is that the transformative impact of reverse-diffused HR practices was often part of a far wider process of business transformations within firms, involving a general restructuring of corporate strategies and structures. As a 'downstream' activity, HRM was often subordinated to these broader changes, and its impact could not easily be seen in isolation from them. Most notably, some of the German companies were undergoing a significant if partial process of 'Anglo-saxonisation' along a series of dimensions, including a move to an organisational structure based on international business divisions with 'bottom-line' responsibilities, the opening up of shareholding to outsiders and in several cases quotation on the New York Stock exchange, a move to international accounting conventions, the appointment of senior execs with Anglo-American business experience, and so on (see Ferner/Varul 1999). Such changes represented a very significant departure from the premises on which German companies had traditionally operated in their domestic business system and reflected their (partial) absorption of 'Anglo-Saxon' practices as a form of adaptation to the imperatives of international operation within the global economy.

The data have limitations. The case study method necessarily means that the scope for generalisations across MNCs is limited. A further weakness is that the two projects were designed independently, so they are not fully comparable; the extent of fieldwork in the foreign subsidiaries was much greater in the German MNCs project than the project examining British MNCs; and the level of access, and hence the amount of data collected, varied to some extent across the firms within each project.

Nevertheless, the two projects are comparable in important ways. Crucially, they both relied on in-depth, semi-structured interviews carried out at multiple levels within the companies. The sample of mini-case studies in both projects reflects a range of key characteristics. A major strength of comparing the data from the two projects is that this allows consideration to be given to the similarities and differences between the extent and nature of RD in MNCs of more than one nationality. Indeed, the Anglo-German comparison presents a number of interesting points of difference. The German system of employment is regulated to a greater extent than the British system, for example, and FDI from Germany has increased sharply only relatively recently whereas British MNCs have tended to internationalise earlier in their development.

Moreover, a major strength of the data is that they were drawn from multiple levels of the same company. Hence, the assessments both of whether RD has occurred and, if it has, whether it is transformative or evolutionary in its impact are based on the perspectives of actors at both HQ and plant level. Relying only on plant level data is not ideal for assessing the role of HQ in the process of

RD; as we go on to demonstrate, the HQ is often influential both in establishing mechanisms through which RD can occur and in overcoming resistance at plant level. A further limitation of plant level data is that they are not well suited for evaluating the impact that RD has on the wider company. On the other hand, using only data drawn only from the HQ would not form a strong basis with which to evaluate the operation and impact of diffused practices at plant level. Crucially, a sole focus on the HQ would risk failing to pick up on those instances of RD in which the HQ is not directly involved; as we will see, in some MNCs the HQ does not initiate, and may not even be aware of, the occurrence of RD.

Both studies have served as data sources for previous publications (e.g. Edwards 1998, 2000, Ferner/Varul 1999, 2000). Therefore, it is not our intention to present all of the key findings from each project. Rather, we use the data in an illustrative way to address a range of arguments concerning RD that could usefully be assessed in future research. In addition, a third, small-scale study of a Swedish MNC, *Swedco* (Hayden/Edwards 2001), is drawn on as appropriate.

Factors Stimulating the Growth of RD

Whilst there are grounds for believing that RD is an important phenomenon, it is not likely to be found in all MNCs. Rather, existing literature suggests that it is most likely to occur in MNCs with certain characteristics. In this section we distinguish between those characteristics which relate to aspects of the subsidiaries, of the wider company and of the national business systems in which the MNC operates, and we demonstrate how these sets of characteristics are interrelated.

Headquarter-subsidiary Relations and RD

One strand of work has looked at the nature of relationship between HQ and subsidiaries, stressing structural relationships as well as more cultural issues of corporate socialisation and integration. Gupta and Govindarajan (1991) consider how the nature of corporate control within MNCs varies across four types of subsidiary. Two of these are likely to be providers of practices that can be reverse diffused: the Global Innovator, which 'serves as the fountainhead of knowledge for other units' (1991, p. 773); and the Integrated Player, which similarly provides knowledge for other subsidiaries but is also the recipient of knowledge from other subsidiaries. These two types of subsidiary are both likely to enjoy considerable autonomy from the centre, especially the Global Innovators; to be subject to 'behavioural' rather than 'outcome' control; and to be evaluated 'flexibly' against budgetary targets. These types of subsidiary would appear to be the most likely sources of reverse-diffused innovations for the wider MNC.

This points to an important current in the literature: the analysis of the varying functions of different subsidiaries within the overall corporate division of labour (e.g. Ghoshal/Nohria 1993). The term 'world mandate' has been used to refer to a phenomenon in which a subsidiary has responsibilities beyond its national market and contributes to the development of corporate strategy (Birkinshaw 1996). In the field of HRM, subsidiaries with a 'mandate' are those most likely to be providing new practices to the rest of the group in the areas of, for example, payment systems and work organisation, and hence to be a source of reverse diffusion. Birkinshaw and colleagues argue that these subsidiaries tend to have a high degree of strategic autonomy vis-à-vis HQ; substantial 'overseas linkages' in terms of sales, both to sister plants and to external customers; an entrepreneurial culture; and a low level of competition in their domestic market (Birkinshaw et al. 1998).

The study of German MNCs demonstrates the ways in which some UK subsidiaries had taken on an entrepreneurial role, thereby promoting the RD of HR practices (for a detailed analysis, see Ferner/Varul 2000). British subsidiaries played active, in some cases leading, roles in the introduction of new HR policies in relation to performance management and payment systems, international management development, and an explicit corporate 'culture'. As a result, German parent firms were adopting many of the key features characterising longer established MNCs from the USA and the UK. British sites served as an attractive location from which to gain experience of such practices: British MNCs have been at the forefront of internationalization in many industries such as telecommunications and business services; the UK has been very open to FDI, and as such has been influenced by HR innovations by MNCs more than most countries; and the deregulated nature of the British labour market makes it an attractive 'test-bed' in which to experiment with new practices. Accordingly, many of the British sites had taken on the role of 'vanguard' subsidiaries, developing an innovative role – sometimes without the prompting or even knowledge of HQ – in supplying new practices to the rest of the group.

In some cases, HQ played an active role in identifying innovative subsidiaries and in encouraging them to spread practices that they had developed to other sites. This was evident in one of the British MNCs, *Engineering Products*. Regular site visits by corporate managers resulted in certain plants receiving a mandate to transfer their innovation to the other sites: the Spanish plant transferred a form of cellular assembly; the French plant a system of reorganising production to create 'internal customers' for each unit; and the American plant a set of competencies for engineers. While RD can occur without the plants being accorded formal roles in this way, these instances demonstrate that the HQ is often influential in promoting RD through the allocation of mandates to subsidiaries.

The Characteristics of the Wider Company and RD

The ability of subsidiaries to develop strategic functions is related to the orientation of the wider company. Bird et al. (1998) delineate four organisational forms amongst Japanese MNCs, one of which is the 'Open Hybrid' in which 'the firm is open to adopting innovations and good ideas regardless of where they originate in the firm' (1998, p 166). These companies, which have much in common with 'transnational' (Bartlett/Ghoshal 1989) and 'geocentric' (Perlmutter 1969) firms, engage in a high level of diffusion of HR practices, including diffusion from foreign subsidiaries to domestic plants. The extent to which subsidiaries create and diffuse innovations varies considerably even within the same company (e.g. Bartlett/Ghoshal 1998).

The study of British MNCs can be used to identify particular organisational characteristics which promote RD. In particular, the existence of international management structures such as business divisions, rather than geographically-based units, deepens managerial contact across sites, facilitating diffusion between domestic and foreign plants. The study suggests that RD is also most likely in MNCs with single or related businesses rather than conglomerates, and in MNCs which have sought to achieve synergies between sites in different countries through standardising production or service provision. Moreover, MNCs which have a high proportion of their operations located abroad and have operated internationally for some time are those most likely to engage in RD because they have the greatest scope to observe practices of other national business systems and have had the time to develop mechanisms for identifying and diffusing practices across their sites. Finally, MNCs which have grown through acquisition rather than through greenfield sites are more likely to engage in RD because they acquire new practices as they expand. These six characteristics of MNCs – international management structures, a low level of diversification, integrated production or service provision, a high proportion of activities located abroad, 'maturity' and growth through acquisition – promote RD. The key findings from the ten UK firms are presented in table 1. An assessment of the existence of RD was made using the two key criteria set out in the methodology, namely whether there were channels and mechanisms in place through which practices could be reverse diffused and whether it was possible to identify a practice in the UK plants that had originated in a specific overseas plant. The evidence of RD was strong in *ChemCo* and very strong in *Engineering Products*. Crucially for the argument above, these two companies were those in which the 'facilitating characteristics' identified above were most prevalent.

Table 1. British MNCs; the Corporate Characteristics that Promote Reverse Diffusion

Company	Int'l structure	Extent of diversi-fication	Integrated	% outside home country	Maturity	Main method of growth	Evidence of RD
Rotate	Multi-domestic	Conglomerate	Low/moderate	10%	10 years	Organic	None
HoldingCo	Multi-domestic	Conglomerate	Low	15%	20+ years	Acquisition	None
Devolve	Multi-domestic	Conglomerate	Low	50%	20+ years	Acquisition	None
StopFast	Matrix	Single	Moderate	45%	20+ years	Acquisition	Very weak
PowerCo	Matrix	Related	Moderate	20%	10 years	Acquisition	Very weak
GlobalChoc	Matrix	Related	Moderate	60%	20+ years	Mixed	Weak
StrongBrew	Matrix	Related	Moderate	50%	20+ years	Acquisition	Weak
Pack&Print	Matrix	Related	Moderate	60%	20+ years	Acquisition	Weak
Chemco	Global	Related	Moderate/high	55%	20+ years	Acquisition	Strong
Engineering Products	Global	Related	High	50%	20+ years	Mixed	Very strong

Source: Data from the British MNCs project. See Edwards (2000) for a fuller discussion.

This is confirmed by the German study. The five firms in which RD was most evident, particularly in the chemicals and electrical engineering sectors, were those in which these characteristics were largely present (see Table 2). All of the firms had a global aspect to their structure, operated in a range of product areas but with these being related to each other, were integrated internationally, had a fairly high proportion of their operations outside the home country and had operated internationally for some time. Four of the five companies had expanded internationally at least in part through acquisition, though the case of Chem3 illustrates that RD can also occur in MNCs which have grown organically, particularly where the international operations have been part of the company for some time. The data from Swedco provides further supportive evidence that these characteristics promote the incidence of RD. The company is organised principally around international divisions, is diversified into related lines of business, is highly integrated, has around 80% of employees outside Sweden, is mature in that it has operated internationally for several decades, and has grown partly through acquisitions. Generally, therefore, it appears that the data from the German MNCs and the Swedish MNC provide further support for the contention that these characteristics promote RD.

Table 2. Selected German Case-studies Companies; Characteristics Promoting Reverse Diffusion

Company	Int'l structure	Extent of diversification	Integrated	% outside home country	Maturity	Main method of growth	Evidence of RD
Chem1	Matrix	Related	Moderate – high	40%	30+ years	Mixed	Moderate
Chem2	Matrix	Related	Moderate – high	47%	30+ years	Acquisition	Moderate – strong
Chem3	Global	Related	High	64%	30+ years	Organic	Strong
Chem5	Matrix	Related	Moderate – high	64%	20+ years	Acquisition	Moderate – strong
Elec6	Matrix	Related	Moderate – high	43%	30+ years	Mixed	Moderate – strong

Source: selected data from the German MNCs project (figures on% employment abroad are for mid-1990s). See Appendix 2 for a full list of companies from this project.

National Business System Characteristics and RD

A further set of factors promoting or impeding RD relates to characteristics of the national business systems in which MNCs operate. Key here is what Smith and Meiskins (1995) term the hierarchy of economies within the international economic system; they argue that firms from countries low down the hierarchy have an interest in emulating practices from those higher up, something they term 'dominance effects'. Despite criticisms of the notion of dominance effects (e.g. the implied homogeneity within national economies), it does capture the interest amongst organisational actors, particularly senior managers, in emulating practices originating in economically successful countries. RD is one mechanism through which MNCs can draw on such practices and, therefore, is likely to be most commonly found in MNCs from countries which are not dominant. For example, the case study of Engineering Products, one of the British MNCs, found RD flowed from those subsidiaries which had pioneered the use of practices associated with systems then seen as dominant, such as 'lean' production, although these subsidiaries were located in countries (France and Spain) which were not the original 'home' for these practices. A further illustration is Hayden and Edwards' (2001) study of a Swedish multinational which revealed the way the firm had used its British and American operations to adopt 'variable' forms of compensation and 'Anglo-Saxon' management development practices, apparently reflecting a perception amongst senior managers that the UK and the USA were more advanced in these areas. Data from the German MNCs project likewise produced a number of examples of the adoption of such Anglo-Saxon practices, notably in systems for the management of performance, that were strongly perceived as the way forward for companies in the process of becoming more international. For instance, in one chemicals-pharmaceutical firm, *Chem3*, a global performance-related pay system was devised through strong input from the UK and US HR subsidiaries; both already operated such systems which were drawn on in the design of the new corporate scheme. In another chemicals firm, *Chem2*, the HQ adopted a directors' bonus scheme for the global company and for the domestic German operation. This followed the introduction in the UK three years earlier of such a system (already operating in the US subsidiary) in which bonuses were linked to budget targets and other objectives. In a Third company, *Chem5*, the UK introduced a new system for objective-setting based on a combination of competencies and work targets; the Spanish subsidiary meanwhile introduced a similar principle. This approach was subsequently developed by European personnel managers for adoption throughout Europe.

The characteristics of national business systems shape RD through their influence on the *diffusability* – what Taylor et al. (1996) refer to as the 'context generalisability' – of practices, and the *receptiveness* of the domestic plants to particular practices. Some practices are easier to transfer across national business systems than others. A key feature influencing diffusability across business systems is the degree to which knowledge is 'codified' or 'tacit', a distinction going back to Polanyi (1962). Lam (1997) argues that – the characteristics of the UK business system make firms less adept at absorbing new practices from Japan than vice versa. The Japanese 'organisational' model, based on on-the-job experience, flexible utilisation of skills, and the organic development of collective knowledge in groups and teams, makes knowledge embedded in this system far less easy to transfer than the codified, standardised, 'professionalised' forms of knowledge typical of the UK model. The Japanese style of knowledge is also likely to suffer from what Szulanski (1996, p. 31) refers to as 'causal ambiguity', in which 'the precise reasons for success or failure in replicating a capability in a new setting cannot be determined', again reducing the chances of successful transfer.

The extent to which domestic plants are able to adopt and operationalise information diffused from foreign subsidiaries depends on their receptiveness, or what Szulanski (1996) calls their 'absorptive capacity' (also Andersson et al. 2001, Tasi 2001). This refers to the ability of organisational actors in the home country to institutionalise new knowledge – the greater this ability, the more receptive is the business system to RD. Like diffusability, receptiveness is strongly influenced by the characteristics of business systems, both individually and relative to each other. One of the British MNCs, *Engineering Products*, demonstrates the way that MNCs may try to improve its absorptive capacity. Through collaboration with one of its key customers, a Japanese car producer, the firm had set up a programme of 'organisational learning' that resulted in the introduction of new mechanisms capable of identifying and transferring innovations across its sites. In this way, the company was able to increase its absorptive capacity, and thereby engage in RD more easily than would otherwise have been the case.

The study of German MNCs found that the transfer of Anglo-Saxon HR practices to the domestic plants of German MNCs was subject to the institutional constraints imposed by the German model. For example, the introduction of Anglo-Saxon-style performance-related pay systems was constrained by the fact that they had to be negotiated with the company works council, a finding confirmed by Kurdelbusch's comprehensive study (2002). However, (as Lam's arguments imply) deregulated, liberalised host systems do not necessarily have greater absorptive capacity, since they may lack the broader 'institutional complementarities' (Hall/Soskice 2001) necessary to underpin particular practices.

In sum, we have seen that RD is not a phenomenon common to all MNCs, but rather the evidence indicates that it is promoted and retarded by the presence or absence of characteristics of subsidiaries, organisations and national business systems. These three sets of characteristics are strongly inter-related. For example, foreign subsidiaries stand a greater chance of acquiring 'vanguard' status or being given 'mandates' by the HQ in 'Open Hybrid' or 'transnational' firms since such companies actively seek to learn from the variety of national systems in which they operate. Moreover, the chances of a particular subsidiary acquiring a mandate from the HQ is shaped by its embeddedness in its national business system and the characteristics and performance of this system. We proceed by distinguishing between different forms of RD.

The Impact of RD

In this section we use the distinction made in the methodology between different forms of RD according to its impact on the companies in which it occurs: RD can be *evolutionary* in that it is directed towards an optimal mix of practices within an existing *modus operandi*, or it can be transformative in that it has the effect of moving the firm towards a new *modus operandi*. We argue that whether RD is evolutionary or transformative is shaped in part by the position of the country of origin in the international economy. As many authors suggest (e.g. Porter 1990), MNCs from strong domestic economies are likely to draw on the strength of the home country by adopting practices in their foreign subsidiaries which are characteristic of this economy. The logic of this argument is that MNCs from 'dominant' countries are those most likely to use RD as a way of consolidating their existing strengths and, hence, RD is likely to be evolutionary.

In contrast, MNCs from non-dominant countries have a stronger incentive to engage in transformative RD by using foreign subsidiaries as a way of bringing about fundamental change. In other words, they may see RD as a way of 'catching up' with MNCs from dominant countries by using those foreign operations in economically successful business systems as a way of gaining first-hand knowledge of practices they perceive as contributing to this success. Of course, attempts to do so may be frustrated where the factors promoting RD identified in the previous section are not present. The evolutionary-transformative dimension is also influenced by the stage of internationalization of the multinational. In their early stages of development MNCs are likely to use RD as a way of learning about internationalisation and so engage in transformative RD; long-established MNCs, in contrast, are more likely to use RD as a way of building on existing practices.

Our findings produced several instances of transformative RD. In some cases this involved diffusion at the level of international HR strategy, including issues such as control and co-ordination of HRM across sites, with the impact of RD in this area shifting the MNC towards a new *modus operandi*. This form of RD is most common in MNCs whose home-country ways of controlling and co-coordinating plants are seen as inappropriate for international operations and, relatedly, in firms relatively new to the international scene. The evidence from the German MNC study indicates that increasing internationalisation among German firms in recent years has been accompanied by a move away from traditional German hierarchical decision-making structures, which are seen as inappropriate for rapidly evolving international markets, towards more devolved business units characteristic of large British and American MNCs. In one of the electronics firms in our study, for example, devolved responsibility for 'bottom line' results had been introduced at international business divisional level following its introduction in the UK subsidiary. Many German MNCs have introduced other Anglo-Saxon practices at the strategic level, such as the use of performance-related pay for senior managers. The impact of this 'Anglo-Saxonisation' has been to transform the approach to international HRM of many German firms.

There is some evidence that a similar shift to being oriented towards 'Anglo-Saxon' norms has occurred in MNCs originating elsewhere in continental Europe. Hayden and Edwards (2001) show how a Swedish multinational used its British subsidiaries, and their links to UK business schools, to establish policies designed to identify a cadre of 'high potentials' as a key part of the firm's approach to succession planning. This is a common characteristic of the approach to IHRM of British and American MNCs. Mtar (2001) provides evidence of French firms using their British subsidiaries to learn about new ways of restructuring. She shows that companies such as Vivendi and Saint Gobain have taken practices from the UK operations and adopted them in France in an attempt to move away from rigid, centralised and bureaucratic modes of control in domestic plants.

The impact of transformative RD can also be felt at plant level, typically in those MNCs for which the home country does not provide a model of organising production to compete with those of 'dominant' countries. The British MNC *Engineering Products* provided an example of this form of RD. This multinational had developed a process of disseminating 'best practice' based on the principles of 'lean production' characteristic of Japanese MNCs. Indeed, links with a Japanese MNC in the UK had provided the impetus for this move. Within the new *modus operandi*, plants were encouraged to develop new practices along these lines and share them with other plants. Thus the Spanish plant pioneered the creation of production cells within which teams of workers were required to perform a range of tasks and share responsibility for the quality and pace of production. Moreover, the French plant had reorganised its factory into a series of small units which had responsibility for 'internal customers' within the plant. Both practices were seen by HQ as fitting the new organising template and so were diffused to all the other plants in the division, including those in the UK. In this way, one aspect of HR practice at plant level was transformed.

Our findings also produced instances of evolutionary RD, in which the impact of diffusion was to consolidate rather than transform an existing *modus operandi*. Evolutionary RD can operate at the level of international HR structures and mechanisms, building on and developing those already in place rather than introducing an entirely new set. We hypothesise that this form of RD is likely to be found in MNCs which have operated internationally for some time and, consequently, have considerable experience of international HRM. Forsgren et al. (1992) argue that many Swedish MNCs are characterised by 'internationalisation of the second degree' in which strategic functions, such as R&D, are located outside the home country. In such firms the role of the HQ is concerned with establishing mechanisms which facilitate the transfer of expertise across the organisation. ABB, the Swiss-Swedish group, is often cited as an example of such a company (e.g. Bélanger et al. 1999).

The impact of evolutionary RD is also felt in the implementation of policies at plant level. RD of this type is characteristic of MNCs from countries which have HR practices perceived as successful, with RD contributing new practices within this *modus operandi*. There is evidence of this form of RD in some Japanese MNCs (Bird et al. 1998, Cutcher-Gershenfeld et al. 1998, p. 44). For instance, Sewell and Wilkinson's (1993, p. 144) study of a Japanese MNC detailed the way in which HQ identified improvements in work organisation in its foreign subsidiaries and diffused them to all factories through a standard manual.

The impact of RD, transformative or evolutionary, is in part a function of the way in which the recipient unit processes the diffused practice. A given practice may not operate in the same fashion in the recipient as in the donor unit but, rather, may undergo *transmutation* as actors in the recipient seek to adapt it to pre-existing patterns of behaviour and power relations (a process that

Boyer et al. 1998 refer to as 'hybridisation'). The evidence from the study of German MNCs demonstrates that many have borrowed the concept of 'corporate culture' from an Anglo-Saxon context where it is formalised in the shape of mission statements, corporate 'vision' and so on. This was particularly in response to investor pressures as companies floated on foreign stock markets. In the German context, the form and the language of the mission statement was retained, but it had to accommodate to an older, more organic and inclusive concept of culture within German companies – the *Betriebsgemeinschaft*, or the 'works community' – which accorded legitimacy to the collective interests and aspirations of the workforce and emphasised trust and cooperation (Ferner/Varul 1999). Unlike in US or UK companies, explicit 'mission statements' and corporate 'values' rarely became part of the general discourse of management in German companies, and they were rarely 'cascaded' down into lower level plans and policies.

A second example is that of work organisation. The well-known adoption by US (and other) motor manufacturers of Japanese forms of production organisation encapsulated in the term 'lean production', while not strictly an example of RD, reflects a pattern of transformative diffusion from Japanese competitors. US MNCs have incorporated such innovations within a distinctive pattern of employee relations, based on a strong orientation to the external labour market and a distinctive hierarchy within work organisation, so that 'lean production' acquires a particular coloration within the American business context (e.g. Maccoby 1997).

The way in which apparently transformative innovations are incorporated into existing institutional frameworks, and their meaning is thereby 'transmuted', is clearly evident from Ortiz's (1998) analysis of the adoption of teamworking by car companies in Britain and Spain. Ortiz argues that unions will resist those aspects of an innovative diffusion that challenge their core organisational interests. Thus in Britain the unions successfully resisted the election of team leaders since this would have represented a challenge to the shop stewards' traditional workplace role. This analysis has the merit of drawing attention to the importance of the relations of power and influence between the multiple actors involved in both recipient and donor, an issue taken up further below.

The case study of Engineering Products provides another example of the power dimension of RD. One of the practices diffused was a form of cellular assembly which significantly reduced the number of operators required. In the company's British plants unions were well organised and represented a high proportion of workers, forcing the company to negotiate the introduction of the practice. Management secured union agreement after giving assurances on redeployment and the avoidance of compulsory redundancies. When the same practice was diffused to the American plants, which were all union-free, the surplus labour was disposed of through redundancies.

In general, the idea that reverse-diffused practices are subject to transmutation calls into question the conventional information-processing approaches to diffusability: the original function of the practice in the donor unit may be irrelevant to the purposes assigned to it in the recipient unit; this may be true even of highly 'codified' practices. The new function may not necessarily be that originally intended but instead may emerge out of the interaction between the diffused practice and the interests of actors in the MNC. The converse of Ortiz's argument is that apparently minor tactical or operational diffusions within a given mode of operation may end up having a transformative impact at a strategic level, for example through their cumulative effect on existing power relations between actors.

Thus, in short, the impact of RD appears to be complex and ambiguous. The features of the domestic business system influence the extent to which RD is transformative or evolutionary, but they do not determine this; the nature of the impact is also strongly shaped by internal power relations. This means that some apparently transformative practices may be adapted by actors in the recipient business culture, resulting in the impact becoming less marked. Equally, however, actors in the recipient units may reinterpret a diffused practice in such a way that increases its impact. The importance of power relations between different levels of actors in MNCs demands a closer inspection of the process of RD.

The Mechanisms and Processes of Reverse Diffusion

As noted earlier, the *process* whereby practices are diffused has been generally overlooked in the literature, with some exceptions, notably Szulanski (1996) who stresses the 'stickiness' of the transfer process, and Birkinshaw and Fry (1998) who explore the gradual, informal coalition-building through which the subsidiary acquires a 'mandate' within the wider MNC. This section considers three issues to do with the process of RD: the coordination and control of the RD process; the mechanisms whereby practices are transferred from subsidiaries to other parts of the corporation; and the organisational politics that is an integral part of the diffusion process.

Coordination and Control of RD

From our empirical data, a key variable appears to be the extent to which RD is coordinated and controlled by headquarters. Does it result from a deliberate effort by the centre to achieve synergies between operations in different countries (Edwards 1998, p. 698), or is it a more organic, grassroots process? There appears to be a spectrum of possible situations. At one extreme, the RD process is strongly under the control of the centre, which establishes mechanisms for defining, identifying and transferring what is considered to be 'best practice'. At the other extreme, diffusion occurs on the margins of – or even despite – central policy through the one-to-one contacts of actors at the working level, leading to a fragmented and uncoordinated diffusion. Adopting the description used by one of our respondents in a British unit of a German multinational, we label this phenomenon 'bush-fire' diffusion, conveying the way it spreads in an uncontrolled, patchy and unpredictable way. An example was provided by a UK HR manager in a German chemical company (*Chem1*) who described the piecemeal adoption of elements of a competency framework by managers at corporate headquarters. Between these two extremes, the centre may play a variety of co-ordinating roles, creating a framework that brings together actors from different national subsidiaries and allows them varying degrees of influence over what is diffused and how.

It seems plausible to hypothesise that the role played by the centre in RD will vary systematically according to factors such as the basic orientation of the MNC. The stronger the desire of the centre to impose a uniform headquarters approach to policy, the less likely it is to allow subsidiaries anything more than an instrumental role in the diffusion process. It is likely to reserve to itself decisions on the criteria of what constitutes a diffusable practice, how the practice is to be identified, and how it is to be disseminated. Some central coordination seems likely where RD is highly routinised within a given, stable modus operandi, in other words where it is evolutionary rather than transformative. Conversely, lack of central control and coordination over the process of RD may be found where corporate headquarters is so ethnocentric that it has yet to acknowledge the possibility of exploitable knowledge in the 'periphery'. RD can still occur in such MNCs through 'bush-fire' diffusion. RD in polycentric MNCs is also likely to be in this ad hoc manner. Paradoxically, therefore, the process of RD (where it occurs) is likely to be very similar in both highly ethnocentric and highly polycentric MNCs. Finally, in strongly networked companies, subsidiary actors are highly involved in policy generation and diffusion, albeit under the clear coordination of headquarters managers, as was the case in the Swedish multinational studied by Hayden and Edwards (2001).

The Mechanisms of Reverse Diffusion

Our research points to a variety of transmission mechanisms whereby HR/IR practices are reverse-diffused in MNCs. Some are systematic and routinised with a degree of continuity over time, others more ad hoc and opportunistic. Some are highly formalised systems, others much more informal. A basic division is between 'procedure-based' mechanisms of transmission, and 'person-based' mechanisms. The former are often linked to formalised management control systems. 'Best practice' may be established on the basis of internal benchmarking among plants in different countries, with 'league tables' and managerial target-setting (e.g. Bélanger et al. 1999, Birkinshaw et al. 1998). In essence, RD may then be generated by internal competition between plants and operating units in different countries. Thus in *Engineering Products* the willingness of the plants, including those in the UK, to engage in diffusion – both by adopting practices originating elsewhere and by identifying practices that other plants could adopt – was a key factor shaping the way that the HQ allocated resources. In other words, increased investment or production quotas may provide an incentive for subsidiaries to absorb 'best practices' from other plants wherever located (cf. Coller 1996).

Person-based mechanisms of RD are linked to the movement of personnel across borders. These may be formalised – as with the use of international HR committees in many MNCs – or relatively informal, such as the use of expatriation, short business trips, informal contacts, international workshops and so on. O'Dell and Grayson (1998) refer to the 'pollination' approach of senior managers' visits to subsidiaries around the world. (Using a related metaphor, Harzing (1996) talks of expatriates as corporate 'bumble bees'.) Such visits may be institutionalised. In a large electrical engineering company in the German study (*Elec6*), for example, a special team comprising permanent HQ staff and seconded managers from operations around the world conducted systematic management audits of policies and processes in different subsidiaries, making recommendations on the basis of best practice elsewhere and monitoring subsequent implementation. Similarly, in *Swedco*, people from the UK were brought in on discussions of policy development in relation to training programmes and management development.

We would argue that person-based systems are particularly important for tacit knowledge transfer, and also in the implementation phase of diffusion of complex practices, through direct personal transfers of expertise from experienced sites. Data from the UK study illustrates this. *Engineering Products* made extensive use of internal consultants and the transfer of technical experts to get new practices implemented. In *ChemCo*, a manufacturer of paint and plastic goods, the head of training in the UK was an American brought over with the brief of introducing techniques developed in the US operations.

The German study strongly suggests that international HR managers' meetings are a major conduit for reverse diffusion, typically in internationally-integrated chemicals or pharmaceuticals MNCs. Subcommittees or working groups of managers from key subsidiaries were established under the coordination of the central HR function to draw up regional or world-wide group policy on such HR issues as performance management, management development, graduate recruitment and pensions. Managers from subsidiaries which were the repositories of relevant knowledge were often given leadership roles; for example, in one chemicals-pharmaceutical company (*Chem3*), a new global performance-related pay system was designed in an international project group on which there was German representation but which was initially led by the UK HR director. These international forums were an increasingly important mechanism for transferring strategic knowledge about international HR: such knowledge was not readily available in a German context in which HRM innovation was constrained by the strong statutory rights of works councils.

The Organisational Politics of Reverse Diffusion

Diffusion has largely been conceptualised in the literature in terms of knowledge flows. An overriding managerial rationality is often taken for granted, diffusion being seen as almost a 'neutral', technical matter of, for example, setting up appropriate conduits. By contrast, our research indicates that knowledge flows are paralleled by corresponding power and resource flows: the transfer of knowledge involved in RD is a *political* as much as a technical problem, in that it involves expending resources to overcome resistance, and it makes manifest the interplay of different sectional interests and the deployment of appropriate 'vocabularies of motive' (Mills 1963) – that is, systems of argument legitimising selected courses of action – within the wider corporation.

Discussions of diffusion have acknowledged the resource cost implications. Szulanski (1996), for example, argues that the cost of diffusion increases the more tacit the knowledge, because there is greater 'stickiness' associated with the transfer, and the process is relatively intensive in expertise. Conversely, the widespread use of standard operating procedures can ensure relatively low-cost transfers, since the knowledge is highly codified.

What the literature says much less about is the need to deploy resources to overcome resistance to transfer rather than technical problems of diffusability. Szulanski's comment (1996, p. 31) on the power dimension of diffusion – which can apply equally to RD – is suggestive but tantalisingly brief:

> A knowledge source may be reluctant to share crucial knowledge for fear of losing ownership, a position of privilege, superiority; it may resent not being adequately rewarded for sharing hard-won success; or it may be unwilling to devote time and resources to support the matter.

It points to some key elements in the power dynamics of the transfer. Most importantly, it cannot be assumed that the potential source is a willing participant in RD. One motive for resistance is the resource cost of transfer, especially the investment of staff time in codifying tacit aspects of the practice to be diffused, hosting multiple visits from central personnel, helping implement the practice in the recipient unit, and so on. A second aspect, no more than hinted at by Szulanski, is the increasing context of inter-site competition in internationally-integrated MNCs, in which, as discussed earlier, the allocation of investment and production quotas to plants is linked to performance on benchmarking measures. A successful subsidiary may be unwilling to jeopardise its position by diffusing to competing units the very practices that have given it a competitive edge. Thus Tregaskis (forthcoming) found that the British subsidiary of a Swedish multinational was reluctant to share innovations with other plants because they were seen as a source of local competitive advantage. It may be hypothesised therefore that a source subsidiary will engage in a variety of behaviours designed to increase the causal ambiguity and tacitness of practices, at least to observers from other parts of the corporation. A final factor in resistance is that the infrastructure of knowledge transfer is likely to be introduced in parallel with a change in status of the subsidiary from relative autonomy to closer integration into international structures. The centre's search for reverse-diffusable practices may be seen as a symptom of the subsidiary's increasing subservience to central control and may thus provoke resistance. However, our own studies – like that of Szulanski – have thrown up little evidence on subsidiary resistance to RD, and further research is needed.

In contrast, our research does hint at *central* resistance to RD, an issue barely touched on by Szulanski. We identified a number of sources of corporate resistance to RD. Most important was that RD practices would undermine the existing organisational status or rewards of particular corporate interest groups. In the German study, British subsidiaries often pointed to central resistance to 'Anglo-Saxon' HR and other business practices. To overcome such resistance, some UK subsidiary managers argued that it was necessary to understand and play by the 'rules of game' in operation at HQ, speaking the appropriate 'language' and taking the trouble to build the necessary networks to increase the receptivity of the centre to subsidiary ideas. Although we have little direct evidence, UK respondents believed that central resistance resulted from the challenge posed by RD to the *modus operandi* of a strongly entrenched administrative stratum of managers below director level at HQ. The importation of 'Anglo-Saxon' practices could be regarded as threatening established ways of doing things, themselves reflecting the strong German institutional framework, to which the individual power, influence and career structures of these middle managers were intimately linked. It may be hypothesised that there will be particular opposition to 'bushfire' diffusion, since it could be seen as undermining existing authority relations by promoting ad hoc change outside the control of central management.

Different forms of RD are likely to provoke resistance in different corporate interest groups and strata at the centre. In *Engineering Products*, a form of cellular assembly was reverse-diffused from Spain to the UK plants. This had implications for employee practice and for skill divisions and status distinctions, provoking opposition particularly from skilled UK shopfloor employees whose previous monopoly of certain skills was diluted by the change. Such resistance had impeded but not prevented the introduction of the new practice. In other instances, one would expect RD practices to provoke resistance from trade unions or other representative employee bodies. As mentioned above, Ortiz's (1998) findings on union responses to teamworking suggest that resistance is more likely when RD challenges actors' core interests. This is one reason why, as argued above, RD practices may undergo transmutation following their transfer to the centre.

However, the politics of RD is not merely about resistance. Both parties to diffusion may see their interests as being furthered by RD, and will thus be willing to bear the immediate resource costs of transferring the practice and overcoming resistance. In the source subsidiary, the costs may be judged worthwhile if RD is perceived as an opportunity to strengthen the position of the unit within the overall corporation, raise its 'profile' and status, enable it to gain 'intra-organisational legitimacy', and thus help it bank a set of important (and not necessarily tangible) resources for future use (e.g. Birkinshaw et al. 1998, Tregaskis forthcoming). The RD of cellular manufacturing from the Spanish subsidiary of *Engineering Products* could be seen as increasing the power of Spanish management in relation to other managerial groups in the company, potentially allowing the subsidiary to ignore corporate guidelines in certain areas without risk of sanction. Identifying practices for reverse diffusion can also advance the position of individual managers. For example, the plant manager of the French subsidiary which had provided a new form of work organization to the rest of the group was accorded the position of 'internal consultant', roaming across the group advising on the implementation of the practice. Similarly, in *ChemCo*, another of the British MNCs, experience of practices viewed favourably by HQ was a key factor in the promotion of an American to the position of corporate head of training.

In this way, 'vanguard' subsidiaries may manipulate their status as exemplars to strengthen their strategic position within the corporation and to increase their future claim on resources. This could well be a phase in the process described by Birkinshaw and Fry (1998) whereby subsidiaries win global mandates from headquarters through building credibility, networking with the centre and constructing international alliances with other groups in the MNC. RD can be seen as contributing to all these aspects of the process.

The centre too may have an interest in encouraging the flow of RD as a relatively unproblematic way of increasing productivity and efficiency in the corporation. Beyond that, RD may be seen by senior tiers of central managers as providing it with leverage in the face of resistance to change on the part of particular groups in the centre. De facto alliances may therefore emerge between subsidiary actors keen to raise their standing and central actors anxious to exploit vanguard practices in foreign subsidiaries to lever change at the centre. Complex games may also be played by sectional groups at the centre who see RD as an opportunity to enhance their group or individual status and power. Thus where British or US models of performance-related remuneration are adopted as global policy – as happened in several German MNCs – a new central corporate responsibility is thereby created. This may 'unfreeze' existing functional responsibilities, opening the way for sectional interests to stake claims to control of the new system. The introduction of performance-related remuneration, and other forms of 'variable' pay, may also benefit many at HQ materially as well. In *Swedco*, for instance, many senior managers had seen their pay packages rise significantly as a result of the introduction of bonuses and debenture schemes.

In short, therefore, RD seems to require both an 'infrastructure' of mechanisms of diffusion, and the wielding of power resources at both ends of the transfer in order to overcome the 'stickiness' caused by the inherent resource costs and by the resistance of differentially affected corporate interest groups. Reverse diffusion is not unique in being highly political; forward diffusion also involves the mobilisation of power resources and the overcoming of resistance. What is significant about it, however, is that an apparently one-off instance of RD can lead to a lasting shift in power relations between various organisational actors. In particular, senior managers in a donor unit may use the identification of a practice that has benefits elsewhere in order to increase their chances of promotion to corporate positions, while the unit as a whole may be in a stronger position to receive investment and orders from the centre, thereby helping to secure its future.

Conclusions

This paper has addressed the potentially important concept of reverse diffusion in the field of HRM, building on the patchy evidence in the literature by drawing on empirical evidence from German and British MNCs. This fresh evidence, drawn from a number of case studies, has not been used to establish empirical generalisations but has revealed much about a number of aspects of RD. Three particular arguments have been made about RD. First, RD is not found in all MNCs but is promoted by the presence of certain structural aspects of subsidiaries, organisations and national business systems. Second, a distinction was drawn between the evolutionary and transformative impact of RD. Third, RD depends on the exercise of power by organisational actors.

At the outset we noted that RD has potentially important implications for both the MNCs themselves and the domestic national business system. On the first of these, a key consequence of RD is its ability to erode the 'country-of-origin effect'. Thus our evidence demonstrates that many German firms are adopting practices characteristic of British and American MNCs, thereby potentially watering down their 'Germanic' traits. A further consequence relates to the impact of RD on power relations within the multinational. We have argued that RD may be contested; both in subsidiaries and headquarters, some groups see RD as threatening their interests, while others see it as an opportunity to advance either their own individual position or that of their unit.

In relation to the impact of RD on the home country, the paper has demonstrated the significance of the changes to HR policy and practice which RD can bring. It might be argued that since the content of RD is influenced by the nature of 'dominance effects' this will contribute to the convergence of different national patterns of HRM. However, our analysis indicates that this may not be the case. Practices which are reverse-diffused may undergo transmutation as organisational actors across countries interpret and implement them in different ways. Thus RD can exert a significant impact on the home country without necessarily contributing to convergence.

One interesting question concerns whether the arguments are specific to HR or have more general applicability. It might be argued that HR practices are more dependent on, and embedded in, particular legal, institutional and cultural contexts than practices in the areas of, say, technology, finance or marketing: HR is often regarded as an area in which MNCs adopt a more decentralized, polycentric approach than other areas. A number of implications for RD flow from this. The scope for RD would appear to be more constrained in HR than in other functions, and where RD of HR practices does occur the process may be more strongly contested since actors can draw on the system of employment in their own country to argue that the practice makes little sense there. However, many of the arguments have more general applicability. For instance, the factors promoting RD apply across all areas, while power relations between organizational actors will be central to the process of RD irrespective of the practice under consideration. Moreover, while HR practices are embedded in distinct national systems, so too are practices in other areas: technological innovations must be implemented in particular socio-cultural settings (Hall/Soskice 2001), financial practices must comply with national regulations, and a MNC's approach to marketing must to some extent be responsive to national variations in consumer tastes. This would suggest that the arguments in the paper to some extent have implications beyond HRM.

A related question is how far the processes described are specific to German and British MNCs? While a systematic comparison by nationality was not a primary aim of the paper, two points stand out. First, the constraints posed by the home-country system of employment are likely to be greater in 'co-ordinated market economies' (ibid.), such as Germany, in which regulations and institutions strongly underpin economic activity, compared with 'liberal market economies', such as the UK, in which hierarchies and competitive relations between firms are more influential. Thus the German study suggested that diffused practices often underwent significant transmutation, whereas the adaptations to the UK context in British MNCs were more modest. Second, the data suggest that the *substance* of RD will vary according to the country of origin of the multinational. RD in the British MNCs was in areas in which the domestic system did not provide a strong basis on which firms could compete in international markets, namely training and work organisation. In contrast, RD in German MNCs was primarily in the areas of decision-making structures, performance management, and the development of managerial and professional staff, all areas where the German system would not be easily exported to other countries. Thus the evidence from both studies suggests that the nature of reverse-diffused practices will reflect perceptions of the extent to which the country-of-origin business system provides an attractive and feasible basis on which to build an internationally integrated set of operations.

Finally, the paper has provided a set of arguments about RD, but the supporting evidence from the case studies is indicative rather than comprehensive, and needs more systematic confirmation from further research. One issue to be addressed is how MNCs access new policies and practices for subsequent RD. One possibility is that companies may use joint ventures or strategic alliances as a way of learning about alternative *modus operandi* (Parkhe 1991). Acquisitions could serve a similar purpose, and the gathering of expertise from recently acquired subsidiaries may be an important driver of the acquisition in the first place. How quickly, and through what mechanisms, does the parent seek to absorb and utilize the expertise? Under what conditions do actors in the acquired units seek to block or promote the diffusion process? Thus an area that could usefully be researched concerns the role of joint ventures, strategic alliances and acquisitions in enhancing a MNC's potential for RD. A second issue relates to the politics of reverse diffusion. Although we were able to demonstrate that there is potential resistance to diffusion, significant gaps remain in our understanding of the factors affecting the willingness of subsidiaries to diffuse practices to the rest of the group, and of home-country actors to adopt reverse-diffused practices from foreign subsidiaries. And what tactics does the centre use in order to overcome any resistance at either level? Third, the empirical work used in this paper could usefully be extended to MNCs of other nationalities, notably to American MNCs which still account for by far the largest proportion of FDI. A number of intriguing questions arise when considering RD in US MNCs. How, for instance, does the traditional centralized 'command and control' approach of many American MNCs affect their ability to absorb knowledge from other countries? Does the deregulated, weakly institutionalized labour market give management a relatively free hand in implementing practices from abroad, or might the relative absence of broadly-based skills amongst most American workers impede it? Do the regional structures increasingly in evidence in US MNCs, at European and 'Asia-Pacific' levels for example, reduce scope for RD to the US, or do they raise the profile of foreign subsidiaries and provide a focal point through which practices can be reverse-diffused? Fourth, while investigative case study-based research has been invaluable in many respects, this approach is not well suited to assessing the extent of RD across MNCs. In this context, surveys have the potential to make a significant contribution by, for example, charting the incidence of the corporate characteristics that we argued in section 4 promote RD; by gathering information on the prevalence of the mechanisms identified in section 6 as being capable of reverse diffusing practices; and by capturing the perception of a key actor in a multinational concerning the form and nature of RD in their firm. We hope that the arguments advanced in this paper provide the basis on which these issues can be addressed.

Acknowledgements

1 We are very grateful for comments on earlier drafts of this paper from anonymous MIR referees and from participants at the conference on Multinationals and Industrial Relations at Wayne State University, Detroit, USA, 1st–3rd April 2000.
2 The empirical research on German MNCs was funded with financial support from the Anglo-German Foundation for the Study of Industrial Societies, and from the UK Economic & Social Research Council.

Appendix 1. Topics and Issues Covered in the Interviews in both Projects

The interviews were all semi-structured and so did not follow rigid formats. Within each project the precise nature of the questions varied somewhat according to the respondent's position and responsibility, the organisational context, and the extent of our prior knowledge of the company concerned. There was also some variation between the two projects; for example, the interviews in the study of German MNCs focused partly on the 'Germanness' of the company. Despite these variations, the interviews covered many common areas and these are outlined below.

Context: The Facilitating Characteristics of RD

- Products/customers (including extent of diversification)
- Geographical breakdown on the company and its main activities
- Structure – divisionalised or regionalised
- Extent of integration of international operations
- Method of Growth – acquisitions or greenfield investments
- Age of international operations

Context: Reporting Relations

- Role of company board/senior managerial team
- Budgets (including nature of targets and possible sanctions)
- Approval process for investment
- Control over managerial appointments and remuneration at plant level

The Process of RD: International Co-ordination

- Mechanisms to facilitate the transfer of 'best practice' e.g. task forces, committees, working parties
- Role of Corporate personnel/HR function e.g. the nature and extent of formal policies
- Comparisons of performance across sites and the use to which these are put
- The role and purpose of the transfer of staff across sites

The Substance and Impact of RD: Substantive areas of employment practice in domestic plants

- Pay and appraisal
- Work organisation
- Training and development
- Communication, participation and involvement

Appendix 2. German Case Study Companies by Sector and Employment

Pseudonym	Sector	Subsidiary employment	Size of Parent
Autodist1	Motor vehicle comps dist'n	2000	Very large
Autodist2	Motor vehicles dist'n	100	Very large
Autopart1	Motor vehicle comps	300	Small
Autopart2	Motor vehicle comps	1000	Very large
Autopart3	Motor vehicle comps	300	Small
Autopart4	Motor vehicle comps	600	Small
Autopart5	Motor vehicle comps	500	Medium
Autopart6	Motor vehicle comps	200	Very large
Machinery2	Industrial machinery	300	
Autopart7	Motor vehicle comps	300	Very large
Autopart8	Motor vehicle comps	400	Small
Business Serv's	Business Services	500	Medium
Chem1	Chemicals and Pharma	1000	Very large
Chem2	Chemicals and Pharma	3000	Very large
Chem3	Pharma	700	Large
Chem4	Pharma	400	Medium
Chem5	Chemicals	700	Very large
Chem6	Chemicals	300	Very large
Chem7	Chemicals	400	Medium
Distrib1	Retail distribution	5000	Very large

Appendix 2. German Case Study Companies by Sector and Employment (continued)

Pseudonym	Sector	Subsidiary employment	Size of Parent
Distrib2	Trading	350	Very large
Distrib3	Timber	500	Very large
Elec1	Electrical engineering	200	Small
Elec2	Electrical engineering	200	
Elec3	Electrical engineering	700	Very large
Elec4	Communication services	800	Very large
Elec5	Electrical engineering	200	
Elec6	Electrical engineering	10000+	
Elec7	Electrical engineering	300	
ResearchCo	Research and development	400	
Food1	Food products	700	Small
Food2	Food products	300	Small
Instruments	Scientific Instruments	200	Medium
Leisure1	Leisure products	400	Very large
Leisure2	Leisure products	10000+	Large
Machinery1	Industrial machinery	600	Large
Material	Paper products	400	Small
Metal	Metal products	600	Large
ManuCo	Plastic products	700	Medium
Transport	Transport services	600	Small

Notes: "Autopart" includes manufacturers which could be classified under other categories – e.g. plastics, metal, and electrical products.
"Distrib" includes wholesale and retail distribution (other than motor vehicle distributors), and trading. "Elec" includes electrical and electronic products.
Elec1 and Elec2 are subsidiaries of the same parent; the same is true of ResearchCo, Elec4, Elec5, and Elec6; and of Autopart6 and Machinery2.
In addition to the firms listed, we conducted three interviews in the HQ of two firms where we were unable to gain access to UK subsidiaries.
Figures for Distrib2 include only the UK-based employees; a further 1600 were based overseas at the time of the research.
To avoid identification, figures for subsidiaries are rounded to the nearest '00 or '000.
For the parent companies, the following size categories are used:
small = 1–5,000; medium = 5–20,000; large = 20,000–50,000; very large = over 50,000
For further details see Ferner and Varul, 1999.

References

Andersson, U./Forsgren, M/Holm, U., Subsidiary Embeddedness and Competence Development in MNCs – A Multi-level Analysis, *Organization Studies*, 22, 6, 2001, pp. 1013–1034.
Archibugi, D./Michie, J. (eds.), *Technology, Globalisation and Economic Performance*, Cambridge: CUP 1997.
Bartlett, C./Ghoshal, S., *Managing Across Borders*, 2nd edition, London: Hutchinson 1998.
Bélanger, J./Berggren, C./Björkman, T./Köhler, C., *Being Local Worldwide: ABB and the Challenge of Global Management*, Ithaca: ILR Press 1999.

Bird, A./Taylor, S./Beechler, S., A Typology of International Human Resource Management in Japanese Multinational Corporations, *Human Resource Management*, 37, 2, 1998, p. 159-172.

Birkinshaw, J., How Multinational Subsidiary Mandates are Gained and Lost, *Journal of International Business Studies*, Third quarter 1996, pp. 467-495.

Birkinshaw, J./Fry, N., Subsidiary Initiatives to Develop New Markets, *Sloan Management Review*, 39, 3, Spring 1998, pp. 51-62.

Birkinshaw, J./Hood, N./Jonsson, S., Building Firm-Specific Advantages in Multinational Corporations: The Role of Subsidiary Initiative, *Strategic Management Journal*, 19, 1998, pp. 221-241.

Boyer, R./Charron, E./Jürgens, U./Tolliday, S., *Between Imitation and Innovation. The Transfer and Hybridization of Productive Models in the International Automobile Industry*, Oxford: OUP 1998.

Child, J./McGrath, R. G., Organizations Unfettered: Organizational Form in an Information-intensive Economy, *Academy of Management Journal*, 44, 6, 2001, pp. 1135-1148.

Coller, X., Managing Flexibility in the Food Industry: A Cross-National Comparative Case Study in European Multinational Companies, *European Journal of Industrial Relations*, 2, 2, 1996, p. 153-172.

Cutcher-Gershenfeld, J. et al., *Knowledge-Driven Work: Unexpected Lessons from Japanese and United States Work Practices*, Oxford: Oxford University Press 1998.

Edwards, T., Multinationals, Employment Practices and the Process of Diffusion, *International Journal of Human Resource Management*, 9, 4, 1998, p. 696-709.

Edwards, T., Multinationals, International Integration and Employment Practice in Domestic Plants, *Industrial Relations Journal*, 31, 2, 2000, pp. 115-129.

Ferner, A., Country of Origin Effects and HRM in Multinational Companies, *Human Resource Management Journal*, 7, 1, 1997, pp. 19-37.

Ferner, A./Varul, M., *The German Way? German Multinationals and the Management of Human Resources in their UK Subsidiaries*, London: Anglo-German Foundation for the Study of Industrial Society 1999.

Ferner, A./Varul, M., "Vanguard" Subsidiaries and the Diffusion of New Practices: A Case Study of German Multinationals, *British Journal of Industrial Relations*, June, 38, 1, 2000, pp. 115-140.

Forsgren, M./Holm, U./Johanson, J., Internationalisation of the Second Degree: The Emergence of European-Based Centres in Swedish Firms, in Young, S., Hamill, J. (eds.), *Europe and the Multinationals*, Aldershot: Edward Elgar 1992, pp. 235-253.

Ghoshal, S./Nohria, N., Horses for Courses: Organizational Forms for Multinational Corporations, *Sloan Management Review*, 34, 2, Winter 1993, pp. 23-36.

Gupta, A./Govindarajan, V., Knowledge Flows and the Structure of Control within Multinational Corporations, *Academy of Management Review*, 16, 4, 1991, pp. 768-792.

Gupta, A./Govindarajan, V., Knowledge Flows within Multinational Corporations, *Strategic Management Journal*, 21, 2000, pp. 473-496.

Hall, P./Soskice, D., An introduction to varieties of capitalism, in Hall, P./Soskice, D. (eds.), *Varieties of Capitalism. The Institutional Foundations of Comparative Advantage*, Oxford: OUP, 2001, pp. 1-68.

Hamill, J., Labour Relations Decision Making in Multinational Corporations, *Industrial Relations Journal*, 15, 2, 1984, pp. 30-34.

Harzing, A., Environment, Strategy, Structure, Control Mechanisms and Human Resource Management in Multinational Companies, Research Report, University of Limburg 1996.

Hayden, A./Edwards, T., The Erosion of the Country of Origin Effect: A Case Study of a Swedish Multinational Company, *Relations Industrielles/Industrial Relations*, 56, 1, 2001, pp. 116-140.

Hedlund, G., The Hypermodern MNC, *Human Resource Management*, 25, 1, 1986, pp. 9-36.

Kopp, R., International Human Resource Policies and Practices in Japanese, European, and United States Multinationals, *Human Resource Management*, 33, 4, 1994, pp. 581-599.

Kurdelbusch, A., Multinationals and the Rise of Variable Pay in Germany, *European Journal of Industrial Relations*, 8, 3, November 2002.

Lam, A., Embedded Firms, Embedded Knowledge, *Organization Studies*, 18, 6, 1997, pp. 973-996.

Maccoby, Just Another Car Factory? Lean Production and its Discontents, *Harvard Business Review*, November-December, 75, 6, 1997, pp. 161-168.

Mills, C. W., *The New Men of Power. America's Labor Leaders*, New York: Harcourt Brace 1963.

Mtar, M., *French Multinationals' International Strategy*, PhD thesis, University of Warwick, Coventry 2001.

O'Dell, C./Grayson, C., If Only We Knew What We Know: Identification and Transfer of Internal Best Practices, *California Management Review*, 40, 3, 1998, pp. 154–174.

Oliver, N./Wilkinson, B., *The Japanization of British Industry*, Oxford: Blackwell 1992.

Ortiz, L., Unions' Response to Teamwork: Differences at National and Workplace Level, *Industrial Relations Journal*, 29, 1, March 1998, pp. 42–57.

Parkhe, A., Interfirm Diversity, Organisational Learning and Longevity in Global Strategic Alliances, *Journal of International Business Studies*, 22, 4, 1991.

Perlmutter, H., The Tortuous Evolution of the Multinational Firm, *Columbia Journal of World Business*, January–February 1969, pp. 9–18.

Polanyi, M., *Personal Knowledge*, New York: Harper 1962.

Porter, M., *The Competitive Advantage of Nations*, London/Basingstoke: Macmillan 1990.

Rugman, A./Verbeke, A., Subsidiary-specific Advantages in Multinational Enterprises, *Strategic Management Journal*, 22, 2001, p. 237–250.

Sewell, G./Wilkinson, B., Human Resource Management in "Surveillance" Companies, in Clark, J. (ed.) *Human Resource Management and Technical Change*, London: Sage 1993, pp. 137–154.

Smith, C./Meiksins, P., System, Society and Dominance Effects in Cross-National Organisational Analysis, *Work, Employment and Society*, 9, 2, 1995, pp. 241–267.

Szulanski, G., Exploring Internal Stickiness: Impediments to the Transfer of Best Practice within the Firm, *Strategic Management Journal*, 17, Winter Special Issue 1996, pp. 27–43.

Tasi, W., Knowledge Transfer in Intraorganizational Networks: Effects of Network Position and Absorptive Capacity on Business Unit Innovation and Performance, *Academy of Management Journal*, 44, 5, 2001, pp. 996–1004.

Taylor, S./Beechler, S./Napier, N., Toward an Integrative Model of Strategic International Human Resource Management, *Academy of Management Review*, 21, 4, 1996 pp. 959–985.

Tregaskis, O., Learning Networks, Pwer and Legitimacy in Multinational Subsidiaries, *International Journal of Human Resource Management* 14, 3, 2003, pp. 431–447.

United Nations, *World Investment Report*, New York: United Nations 2001.

Zanfei, A., Transnational Firms and the Changing Organisation of Innovative activities, *Cambridge Journal of Economics*, 24, 2000, pp. 515–542.

mir *Edition*

Andreas Wald

Network Structures and Network Effects in Organizations

A Network Analysis in Multinational Corporations

2003, XVIII, 238 pages, pb., € 49,90 (approx. US $ 49,90)
ISBN 3-409-12395-4

Network structures have been praised as the organizational form of today's multinational corporation. Building on conceptual work on network organizations, a quantitative network analysis of formal and informal organizational structures is performed in this study. It is tested whether network structures can be identified empirically. Moreover, the effects of organizational structures on strategic decision making in two multinational corporations are analyzed. A theoretical framework is provided by an exchange model and by social capital theory.

The book is addressed to scholars of international management and organizational studies.

Betriebswirtschaftlicher Verlag Dr. Th. Gabler GmbH, Abraham-Lincoln-Str. 46, 65189 Wiesbaden

Brent B. Allred/K. Scott Swan

Global Versus Multidomestic: Culture's Consequences on Innovation[1]

Abstract

- This study examines the relationship of national culture to firm innovation, moderated by the type of industry in which the firm competes.
- Hypotheses are developed and tested using data from 536 companies across ten countries competing in four global and four multidomestic industries.

Key Results

- The findings generally support the hypotheses. Individualism, low power distance, and low uncertainty avoidance are more positively related to innovation within multidomestic industries, while Confucian dynamism is more positively related to innovation within global industries. There is no significant moderation effect of industry type on the relationship between masculinity/femininity and innovation.

Authors

Brent B. Allred, Assistant Professor of Business Administration, School of Business, The College of William & Mary, Williamsburg, Virginia, USA.

K. Scott Swan, Associate Professor of Business Administration, School of Business, The College of William & Mary, Williamsburg, Virginia, USA.

Introduction

A growing literature stream addresses a wide range of issues associated with the internationalization of R&D (Cantwell/Mundambi 2000, Chiesa 1995, Kotabe/Swan 1994, Kuemmerle 1997, Peng/Wang 2000, Ronstadt 1978, Teigland/Fey/Birkinshaw 2000). Recent empirical and conceptual research examines cultural characteristics, based primarily on Hofstede's (1980) dimensions, and how they relate to indices of innovation: specifically, societal inventiveness (Shane 1992), R&D productivity (Kedia/Keller/Julian 1992), the ability to source or adopt innovations (Herbig 1994, Herbig/Miller 1992), national rates of innovation (Shane 1993), organizational entrepreneurship (Morris/Davis/Allen 1994), initiation and implementation of new product development (Nakata/Sivakumar 1996), and locational cultural profiles supporting R&D strategy classifications (Jones/Davis 2000).

We pursue the impact of industry type and test its influences on the relationship between national culture and innovation (Jones/Davis 2000). The type of industry may range from purely domestic to entirely global (Bartlett/Ghoshal 1989, Prahalad/Doz 1987, Yip 2003). At one end, firms within *global* industries are integrated and interdependent (Hout/Porter/Rudden 1982). At the other end, firms within *multidomestic* industries are relatively autonomous across countries and focus on the needs of the local market (Porter 1986).

Research employing the global integration – local responsiveness framework has generally been limited to multinational companies (MNCs) based in a single country such as the US (Johnson 1995, Mauri/Phatak 2001, Roth/Morrison 1990), or to various MNCs doing business in a single country such as Canada (Birkinshaw 1997) or Taiwan (Hannon/Huang/Jaw 1995). This study takes a multi-country focus and empirically tests the relationship between national culture and firm innovation, moderated by whether the firm competes in a global or multidomestic industry. We utilize data from 536 companies across ten countries competing in four global and four multidomestic industries as identified by Ghoshal and Nohria (1993).

Conceptual Framework

The internationalization of research and development capabilities is increasingly vital to the success of multinationals (Jones/Davis 2000). Past researchers have identified motivations, orientations, and expectations that affect the decision of where to locate R&D (Cantwell 1992, Casson/Singh 1993, De Meyer/Mizushima

1989, Julian/Keller 1991). Given a global business environment, there is a growing interest in exploring the relationship between national culture and R&D. The following synthesis of the literature identifies the cultural profiles and industry contexts that support innovation activities. We use the enduring organizational theory that a firm's structure and management process must "fit" its environment (Yip 2003). Additionally, a resource-based view is invoked.

Culture and Innovation

Innovation is the basis by which an entrepreneur either creates new wealth-producing resources or endows existing resources with enhanced potential for creating wealth (Drucker 1985). These resources and capabilities can lead to distinctive competencies and are expected to result in competitive advantages (Barney 1991, Peteraf 1993, Prahalad/Hamel 1990, Wernerfelt 1984). Both local and global factors influence innovation (Lindqvist/Solvell/Zander 2000). For example, increasingly sophisticated consumers, heightened domestic and foreign competition, and access to more advanced resources all create pressures on firms to innovate. At the national level, innovation "is one of the most crucial dimensions of economic success" (Hall/Soskice 2001, p. 44).

Culture refers to learned behavioral standards, socially transmitted through personal values, norms, activities, attitudes, cognitive processes, interpretation of symbols, feelings, ideas, reactions, and morals (Hofstede 1980, Morris/Davis/Allen 1994). Culture exists at multiple, but interrelated levels. The cultural propensities of a society influence the strategic thinking and actions of its members. Culture at an organizational level is in general congruence with the broader societal culture (Hofstede 1991). In line with this literature stream, we use Hofstede's national culture dimensions (Hofstede 1980, Hofstede/Bond 1988). We next review past research on the direct influence of culture on innovation, add the stage of the product development process, and then consider the industry type context.

Direct Effects

Jones and Davis (2000) provide a review of the conceptual and empirical research linking national culture to firm innovation and associated measures (e.g., R&D productivity, innovative capacity, technological development, inventiveness, and innovativeness). In their summary, they find that cultures characterized by low power distance, low uncertainty avoidance, high individualism, and masculinity are generally associated with positive innovative attributes. Cultures with a longer-term orientation or high Confucian dynamism are also positively associated with innovation.

Direct Effects Within Stages

Nakata and Sivakumar (1996) separate the innovation process into two stages of new product development: *initiation* and *implementation*. In the *initiation* stage, research and development investments focus on idea generation, screening, and concept testing. Expenditures in the *implementation* stage are not associated with traditional R&D since they fund test marketing, product launch, and manufacturing efficiencies. In the *implementation* stage, the relationships between culture and innovation are different than in the *initiation* stage due to a firm's changing needs and objectives.

Jones and Davis' (2000) summary of direct culture – innovation relationships generally mirrors Nakata and Sivakumar's (1996) *initiation* stage of new product development, except for the influence of masculinity on innovation. While Jones and Davis' (2000) summary suggests that this relationship is positive, Nakata and Sivakumar (1996) propose that the influence of masculinity on innovation is positive in the *implementation* stage only. During the *initiation* stage, they suggest this relationship is negative, since cooperation, rather than competition, is needed for the development of new ideas and products. In the *initiation* stage, cultures characterized by low power distance, low uncertainty avoidance, high individualism, femininity, and high Confucian dynamism are associated with positive innovative attributes. This study focuses the initiation stage.

Effects Within the Initiation Stage Moderated by Industry Type

Jones and Davis (2000) incorporate the stages idea and offer broad propositions as to the relationship between national culture and innovation across industry types. We develop these ideas further by including the moderating role of global – multidomestic industry type and then empirically test them.

MNCs cannot simply adopt generic strategies, but must appropriately respond to competing pressures for global integration and local responsiveness. Firms adopt strategies in the context of competition in their industry (Roth/Morrison 1990). It is through the efficient positioning and coordinating of assets, subsidiaries, technology, and knowledge that a globally-oriented firm achieves a competitive advantage over rivals. Interestingly, national-level influences have been downplayed as less relevant in the current global business environment (Ohmae 1995), yet, "in spite of the shrinking world, location still matters", (Krugman 1994, p. 464, Porter 1990). The environment provides both resources and exerts pressure on firms to adopt appropriate innovation strategies.

Globally-oriented firms must integrate their activities on a worldwide basis to capitalize on synergistic linkages among operations in different countries, either within or between businesses (Hout/Porter/Rudden 1982, Morrison/Roth

Figure 1. Industry Type Interaction Model

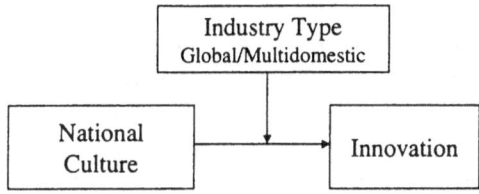

1992). Firms in multidomestic industries allow their foreign subsidiaries to be relatively autonomous in order to better respond to local markets. In multidomestic industries, R&D expenditures are aligned with specific markets (Ring/Lenway/Govekar 1990). Thus, R&D expenditures are in response to the industry type.

In the following section we develop a model and hypotheses outlining the moderating role of global – multidomestic industry types on the culture – innovation relationship (see Figure 1). In particular, we focus on R&D expenditures that are closely aligned with the initiation stage of product development. We extend the logic proposed by Nakata and Sivakumar (1996) concerning the initiation stage in our moderation model. We then compare our direct relationship results with their initiation stage direct propositions.

Model Development and Hypotheses

Cultural differences have been associated with patterns of innovation across countries (Shane 1992, 1993, 1995). The same values that operate at the national level operate on the firm level. Accordingly, companies that operate in more innovation-supporting cultures tend to be more innovative (Shane 1992).

Our general proposition is that Hofstede's national culture dimensions have a greater relationship to innovation in multidomestic than in global industries. R&D personnel in multidomestic industries perceive strong forces for local responsiveness, while R&D personnel in global industries detect strong forces for global integration (Ghoshal/Nohria 1993). Global integration is biased toward ignoring cultural differences and developing products that will entice consumers by decreasing price, increasing quality, and enhancing preference through global availability, serviceability, and recognition (Yip 2003). In contrast, local responsiveness requires a greater understanding of the culture to adapt products. This approach, although generally more costly, suggests a "let a thousand flowers bloom" orientation that can lead to greater innovation.

Power Distance

Hofstede's (1980) first cultural dimension assesses the degree to which individuals or institutions in a society accept inequalities of power. Low power distance cultures will be less tolerant of inequality and attempt to negate the advantage of other societies. Accordingly, low power distance cultures are more inventive (Shane 1992) and actively pursue strategies that enhance competitiveness and speed development.

In multidomestic industries, local science and technology infrastructure is important, as local R&D efforts rely less on centralized R&D advances. A self-sustaining path moves a firm from relying on R&D efforts that were the result of home market R&D (Dunning 1994) to decentralized R&D (Casson/Singh 1993, Chiesa 1995). High power distance could make this transition slower and more difficult and could be seen as autocratic and intolerable. A decentralized setting would equalize capabilities across the firm and increase motivation (Nakata/Sivakumar 1996).

"Organistic" firms characterized by low dependence on hierarchy provide higher yields per R&D output than "mechanistic" (centralized and formal) organizations (Azumi/Hull 1990). Centralized structures are more commonly found in global settings and are efficient for managing current business activities. They are not as conducive to providing change dynamics in NPD as decentralized structures, generally found with multidomestic settings (Johne/Snelson 1988). Decentralized structures also enable direct access to people and resources, resulting in quicker decision-making and decreased internal competition (Griffin 1992, Murphy 1992). Decentralization's superiority in innovation may lie in the reduction of information overload at higher organizational levels (Henke/Krachenberg/Lyons 1993), an atmosphere of free exchange with minimal risks, and a more direct, immediate attack on problems (Olson/Walker/Ruekert 1995). Therefore,

Hypothesis 1. High power distance will be more negatively related to firm innovation in multidomestic industries than in global industries.

Uncertainty Avoidance

A dynamic marketplace brings uncertainty as firms simultaneously deal with rapid changes in national and global environments as well as technology. Cultures that are high on uncertainty avoidance will attempt to buffer themselves from global uncertainty through activities such as protectionism, trade barriers, or nationalism. These activities stifle competition and innovation and hinder a country's development (Porter 1990). Cultures that are more tolerant of uncertainty recognize that change is inevitable and can be advantageous if they will develop a degree of flexibility. Shane (1995) finds that uncertainty-accepting societies are more innovative. This flexibility allows them to develop robust innovations that can be offered outside the home country (Casson/Singh 1993, Chiesa 1995). Thus, the degree of uncertainty avoidance that exists in a culture influences the roles and attitudes of managers regarding innovation.

Uncertainty avoidance can be related to innovation through planning and risk aversion (Nakata/Sivakumar 1996). The inherent messiness about the innovation process does not readily lend itself to control and formalization (Gresov 1984, Quinn 1979). Informal, non-standardized procedures during the initiation phase are more conducive to creative problem-solving and feedback (Johne 1984). Additionally, risk-taking promotes innovation (O'Reilly 1989). Global industries are more likely to have formal controls while multidomestic industries generally have greater informality, non-standardization, and environmental complexity (Ghoshal/Nohria 1993). Thus, firms in multidomestic industries are more likely to be negatively affected by high uncertainty avoidance in the pursuit of innovation.[2] Therefore,

Hypothesis 2. High uncertainty avoidance will be more negatively related to firm innovation in multidomestic industries than in global industries.

Individualism

Individualistic cultures foster entrepreneurial, innovative behavior and seek greater personal autonomy. Successful risk-takers accrue rewards. Individualism, entrepreneurism, and risk-taking create a cultural cluster that is mutually reinforcing (Herbig/Miller 1992). Hofstede (1980) has found that wealth is positively associated with individualism. Individualistic societies develop more competitive economies (Shane 1992, 1993).

Innovators are associated with product success (Maidique 1980). They are described as nonconformist and self-confident, with strong perseverance, who drive the innovation process by generating possibilities and overcoming obstacles (Nakata/Sivakumar 1996). They typically operate autonomously (Goldhar/Bragaw/Schwartz 1976). While individualism generally fosters innovation, a collectivist approach is better when communication, cooperation, and harmony are required between marketing and R&D, where there is a willingness to work toward a common vision or purpose (Gupta/Wilemon 1988, Johne 1984, Souder 1988).

Multidomestic industries are better suited for individualistic cultures, while global industries are better matched with collectivist cultures. In a multidomestic industry the approach is to maximize the number and range of options. This individualistic behavior is accomplished through a loose structure in the initiation stage (Johne 1984). If the dynamics require cohesion and single-minded purpose – a strength in global industries – then a collectivist approach is preferred. Therefore,

Hypothesis 3. Individualism will be more positively related to firm innovation in multidomestic industries than in global industries.

Masculinity-Femininity

Generally, masculine cultures are expected to be more assertive, competitive, achievement-oriented, and exhibit a higher need for recognition versus feminine nurturance (Hofstede 1980). Pennings (1993) asserts that executives in more masculine cultures favor a large portion of variable compensation, since rewards are desired for individual risk-taking and accomplishments. "Masculinity" at the individual and societal levels is expected to lead to more innovative behavior.

However, masculinity is also associated with purposefulness and formalization (Nakata/Sivakumar 1996). During the initiation stage of NPD, highly structured organizations and procedures may stifle innovativeness. The more feminine characteristics of trust, communication, and low conflict have been associated with successful NPD (Thwaites 1992). Organic internal environments enable NPD participants to cope with the uncertainty of their work (Burns/Stalker 1961).

While global industries are more likely to be characterized by directedness and formalization, multidomestic settings are more closely aligned with a focus on people and a supportive atmosphere in uncertain environs. Multidomestic industries tend to be informal, non-standardized, and environmentally complex (Ghoshal/Nohria 1993). Thus, national cultures (e.g., masculine) that do not fit with the industry environment (e.g., multidomestic) are likely to be less innovative. Therefore,

Hypothesis 4. Masculinity will be more negatively related to firm innovation in multidomestic industries than in global industries.

Confucian Dynamism

Confucian dynamism indicates a future-oriented mentality. High Confucian dynamism cultures can also be characterized by persistence, hard work, thrift, shame, and regard for friendships. This is in contrast to cultures that maintain a static mentality focused on past and present, reciprocation, and tradition (Hofstede/Bond 1988). Innovation requires that investments be made in uncertain technologies with uncertain payoffs and time frames (Steensma et al. 2000). These investments involve a great deal of risk and are undertaken with a hope of long-term viability. Long-term oriented cultures are more likely to see the benefits of innovation strategies. For more short-term oriented cultures, the focus is more on the past and present and investing in things that generate immediate gains. Franke, Hofstede, and Bond (1991) have found that cultures high on Confucian dynamism have higher economic growth.

High Confucian dynamism is thought to promote NPD in both the initiation and implementation stages by emphasizing action and future possibilities (Nakata/Sivakumar 1996). While culture has been proposed to be generally more meaningful within multidomestic settings, globally-orientated industries are usually associated with a more long-term focus since they proactively move and respond to overall consumer shifts toward new innovations (Yip 2003). Multidomestic industries are more likely to be tradition bound and protectionist for short-term gain. There seems to be compelling motivation for this cultural dimension to be more positively related to innovation in global industries. Therefore,

Hypothesis 5. High Confucian dynamism will be more positively related to firm innovation in global industries than in multidomestic industries.

Methodology

Sources of Data

This study draws from a Datastream database of approximately 14,500 companies in 47 countries. It includes national-level data from the International Monetary Fund, worldwide government sources, and other providers of national and macro economic data. Additional national-context data is drawn from the World Development Indicators (World Bank 1997), The World Factbook (CIA 1997), and the World Reference Atlas (Dorling Kindersley 1996).

Sample

The Datastream database uses an industry classification scheme based on the Standard Industrial Classification (SIC) codes used in the US. Initially, 1,609 companies from 47 countries are identified in eight industries, based on the 4 digit SIC code. We then limit the sample to the ten highest represented countries in the sample and all firms with a compete set of data. Recent concerns have been raised that most studies using Hofstede's measures rely on not enough countries (i.e., only two) or on countries that do not provide an adequate variance

Table 1. Sample Data (536 Companies)

Country		Industry	
Australia	12	Beverage	25
Canada	13	Food	73
France	11	Household Appliances	16
Germany	12	Rubber	26
India	44	Construction Machinery	47
Japan	116	Industrial Chemicals	90
South Korea	25	Nonferrous Metals	42
Taiwan	22	Scientific Instruments	237
United Kingdom	72		
United States	209		

in the culture variables to generate meaningful results (Sivakumar/Nakata 2001). This selection criterion allows for adequate variance, representation, and completeness of study variables. The final sample includes seven industrialized countries and three developing/newly-industrialized countries. This offers broad geographic coverage: two countries from North America, three from Europe, three from Asia, Australia, and India. Due to missing values for key variables and other abnormalities in the firm level data, a final sample of 536 firms results (see Table 1).

Measures

The firm, industry, and country-level data are drawn from archival sources for the 1995 period. These variables are continuous measures.

Innovation

R&D Intensity, the measure of innovation, is used extensively as a proxy for innovation (Baysinger/Hoskisson 1989, Hambrick/MacMillan 1985, Hitt/Hoskisson/Kim 1997). R&D intensity is calculated by dividing R&D expenditures by sales (Hoskisson et al. 1993). The general proposition is that the higher the R&D intensity, the greater the firm's strategic focus on innovation. R&D intensity is positively related to other important measures of innovation output, such as new product introductions: correlation = 0.510, $p < 0.001$ (Hitt et al. 1996) and patents: correlation = 0.221, $p < 0.01$ (Hitt et al. 1991).

National Culture

The independent variables are taken from Hofstede (1980) and Hofstede and Bond (1988). A proxy value for Confucian dynamism for France, which was not provided in early work, is calculated by regressing the other culture dimensions onto Confucian dynamism.

International Industry Setting

Like Ghoshal and Nohria (1993), we use Kobrin's (1991) index of integration. Industries are categorized as having either strong or weak forces for global integration based on the degree of local regulation and local customer preferences. A resulting two by two matrix identifies four industry settings: global, transnational, international, and multinational. This study focuses on two opposing industry settings: global and multinational (i.e., multidomestic). Global industries, classified as "0", are those that have strong forces for global responsiveness and weak forces for local responsiveness. Multidomestic industries, classified as "1", are characterized as having weak forces for global integration and strong forces for local responsiveness (Ghoshal/Nohria 1993). Since industry setting is not defined by industry structure, the influences of industry structure can be tested without tautological concerns.

Following Ghoshal and Norhia (1993), construction and mining machinery, industrial chemicals, nonferrous metals, and scientific instruments are categorized as global industries. Beverages, food, household appliances, and rubber are categorized as multidomestic industries. We have excluded engines, which Ghoshal and Norhia (1993) classify as a global industry, and tobacco, which is classified as a multidomestic industry, because of the limited number of firms available for these industries and their lack of representation across countries. We have included manufacturing industries because of the nature of innovation through R&D investments and their greater consistency in reporting procedures for R&D expenses over services or non-profit industries.

Control Variables

We control for industry and country effects. We use *munificence, dynamism,* and *complexity* to capture the key elements that comprise industry structure (Dess/Beard 1984, Keats/Hitt 1988), since industry structure has been associated with R&D investment (Kuemmerle 1999). Specifically, the moderating variables are trying to capture a dimension of industry structure and so other related measures may confound the genuine relationships between the IVs and DV as moderated by global multidomestic industry type. Industry measures are calculated using data from all 47 countries and 1,609 companies in the eight industries following the method employed by Boyd (1990). *Munificence*, the measure of the abundance of resources in the industry environment, is calculated by taking the industry's total sales for the five years from 1991–1995 and regressing the year onto

Table 2. Correlations and Descriptive Statistics

Variable	Mean	S.D.	1	2	3	4	5	6	7	8	9	10	11	12
1. R&D Intensity	3.56	4.39	1.000											
2. Industry Munificence	7.01	9.39	−0.083	1.000										
3. Industry Dynamism	4.34	3.21	−0.053	0.828***	1.000									
4. Industry Complexity	0.05	0.03	−0.306***	0.379***	0.356***	1.000								
5. Home Country GDP	4,250	2,931	0.358***	−0.066	−0.079	−0.245***	1.000							
6. Home Co. GDP Growth	2.55	1.65	−0.124**	0.082	0.124**	0.114**	−0.355***	1.000						
7. Home Co. Urban Pop. %	74.65	15.19	0.178***	−0.081	−0.106*	−0.227***	0.207***	−0.446***	1.000					
8. Power Distance	47.42	12.35	−0.343***	0.050	0.060	0.261***	−0.401***	0.419***	−0.782***	1.000				
9. Uncertainty Avoidance	58.15	21.55	−0.210***	−0.048	−0.074	0.064	0.016	−0.134**	0.139**	0.422***	1.000			
10. Individualism	69.78	25.28	0.383***	−0.020	−0.028	−0.226***	0.467***	−0.406***	0.313***	−0.769***	−0.728***	1.000		
11. Masculinity	66.85	16.26	−0.066	−0.121**	−0.143**	−0.053	0.328***	−0.730***	0.218***	−0.010	0.555***	−0.146**	1.000	
12. Confucian Dynamism	46.89	23.92	−0.349***	−0.020	−0.018	0.185***	−0.242***	0.178***	−0.265***	0.731***	0.838***	−0.219***	0.427***	1.000
13. Industry Type	0.26	0.44	−0.346***	0.305***	0.051	−0.034	−0.246***	0.142**	−0.035	0.172***	0.122**	−0.051	0.175***	

N = 536; *** $p < 0.001$; ** $p < 0.01$; * $p < 0.05$

the total sales for that year. The resulting regression slope coefficient is then divided by the mean value of the five years of sales to calculate the munificence of the industry for 1995 (Dess/Beard 1984).

Dynamism, the measure of volatility or instability in the industry environment, is calculated by taking the standard error of the regression slope coefficient from the same regression used for calculating munificence. This is then divided by the mean value of the five years of sales to compute the industry dynamism for 1995 (Boyd 1990).

Complexity, the measure of heterogeneity or concentration of resources in the industry environment (Aldrich 1979), is measured by creating a concentration ratio following the Herfindahl-Hirschman index of industry complexity (Herfindahl 1950, Hirschman 1945). The top 4, 8, 20, or 50 firms in an industry are suggested for use in this index. All four indices levels are highly correlated (Schmalensee 1977), and have a Cronbach's alpha of 0.998 for the data in this study. We use the concentration index of the top 20 firms in each of the industries.

As with industry structure, national-context control measures are included to tap into different aspects of the national environment that can influence firm innovation (Kuemmerle 1999). Our measures include *Gross Domestic Product* (i.e., munificence or resource availability), *GDP Growth* (i.e., dynamism), and *Urban Population Percentage* (i.e., complexity or concentration). *Gross Domestic Product (GDP)* is stated in US $ terms (in Billions). *GDP Growth* is the growth and stability of the economy over the period from 1990–1995. *Urban Population Percentage* is included as proxy for sophistication and homogenization of consumers, as well as the ease of product diffusion through the distribution and concentration of the population. A relatively high urban population could improve cost/benefit analysis for innovation investments and desire for its outputs. The controls for industry and country effects improve the robustness of the findings and have not been previously utilized in this research stream. See Table 2 for descriptive statistics and correlations among the study variables.

Analysis

We employ hierarchical regression and an interaction methodology[3] to test the hypotheses in this study (Aiken/West 1991, Baron/Kenny 1986, James/Brett 1984). Once the significance of an interaction is determined, it can be interpreted by plotting the moderation effect (Aiken/West 1991). The plotting procedure[4] follows Cohen and Cohen (1983), and the plots are presented in Figures 2–5.

The variables involved in the interaction (i.e., the independent variable and moderator variable) are centered prior to creating the interaction term (Aiken/West 1991). The centered variables and interaction term are then entered into

Table 3. Regression Analysis for the Moderation Model

Variables	R&D Intensity						
	Direct Effects Model	Base Model	Power Distance	Uncertainty Avoidance	Individualism	Masculinity	Confucian Dynamism
Constant	3.5640***	6.1440	6.0670	6.5020	7.0530+	5.9500	5.8540
Industry Munificence		0.1120**	0.1080**	0.1170**	0.1120**	0.1130**	0.1160***
Industry Dynamism		−0.1750+	−0.1710+	−0.1790+	−0.1710+	−0.1760+	−0.1770+
Industry Complexity		−38.3170***	−35.9610***	−37.7750***	−35.6310***	−38.3070***	−35.9080***
Home Country GDP		0.0003*	0.0003*	0.0003*	0.0002+	0.0003*	0.0002+
Home Country GDP Growth		−0.3550	−0.3270	−0.3660	−0.4120	−0.3400	−0.3340
Home Country Urban Population %		−0.0143	−0.0149	−0.0186	−0.0245	−0.0122	−0.0117
Power Distance	−0.0532*	−0.0564	−0.0645	−0.0628	−0.0703	−0.0531	−0.0512
Uncertainty Avoidance	0.0378*	0.0056	0.0062	0.0038	0.0093	0.0056	0.0064
Individualism	0.1510***	0.0204	0.0301	0.0248	0.0404	0.0201	0.0338
Masculinity	−0.0738***	−0.0822*	−0.0791+	−0.0808+	−0.0839*	−0.0813*	−0.0773+
Confucian Dynamism	0.0992*	0.0293	0.0381	0.0353	0.0468	0.0279	0.0361
Industry Type		−3.5180***	−3.6210***	−3.6310***	−3.7440***	−3.5320***	−3.7320***
Industry Type X Power Distance			0.0662*				
Industry Type X Uncertainty Avoidance				0.0308+			
Industry Type X Individualism					−0.0459**		
Industry Type X Masculinity						0.0070	
Industry Type X Confucian Dynamism							0.0441**
R^2	0.176	0.332	0.339	0.336	0.345	0.332	0.342
Adj. R^2	0.168	0.317	0.322	0.320	0.328	0.315	0.326
F	22.573***	21.651***	20.570***	20.350***	21.112***	19.960***	20.887***
Change in R^2 from base model			0.007	0.004	0.013	0.000	0.010
F			5.414*	3.497+	10.114**	0.108	8.166**

$N = 536$; + $p < 0.10$; * $p < 0.05$; ** $p < 0.01$; *** $p < 0.001$
Following Aiken and West (1991), the independent and moderator variables were centered prior to calculating the interaction terms and being entered into the regression.

Figure 2. Industry Type Interaction Model

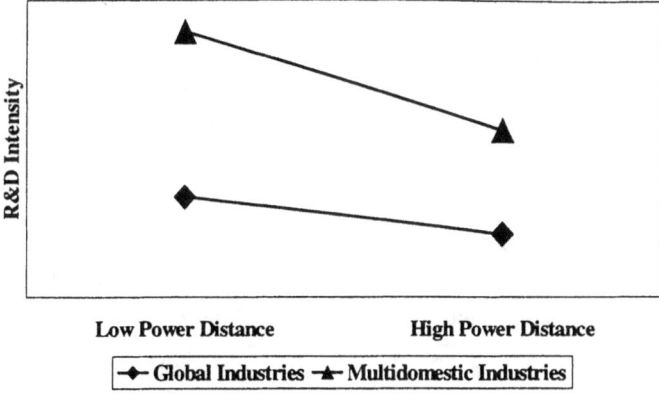

Figure 3. Industry Setting X Uncertainty Avoidance Interaction

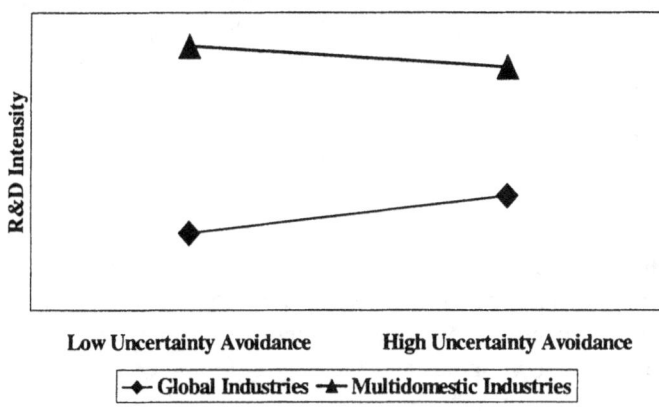

Figure 4. Industry Setting X Individualism Interaction

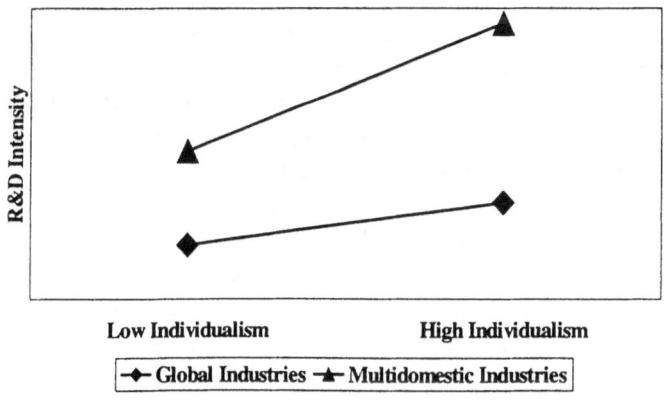

Figure 5. Industry Setting X Confucian Dynamism Interaction

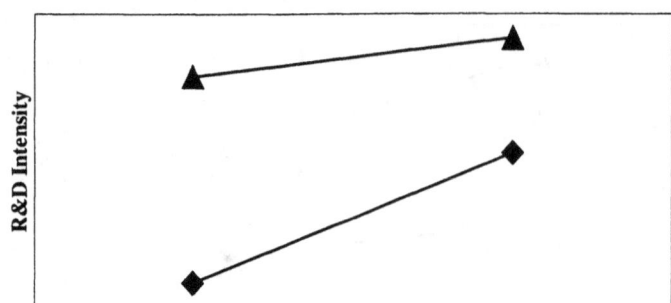

the regression. By centering the variables, any multicollinearity that exists between the variables in the interaction and the interaction term itself is reduced and robustness is improved without degrading the quality of the data.

Results

The results of the analyses generally support the hypotheses that industry setting moderates the relationship between national culture and firm innovation. The base model includes the control variables for industry effects and country effects, as well as the five culture variables and industry type moderator. The base model is highly significant ($R^2 = 0.332$; $p < 0.001$).

It is not clear appriori which industry type would be more R&D intensive. While the initial level of R&D intensity within each industry type may be of interest, it could be an artifact of the industries identified as global versus multidomestic. The interaction between industry type and cultural dimensions along with their relationship to innovation offer important insights.

Hypothesis 1 predicts that high power distance will be more negatively related to firm innovation in multidomestic industries than in global industries. The interaction term is significant and the relationship is as hypothesized, supporting *Hypothesis 1*. The R^2 for the power distance model is 0.339 ($p < 0.001$). The change in R^2 from the base model is 0.007 ($p < 0.05$). Table 3 offers a summary of the regression results for the hypotheses tests.

Hypothesis 2 states that high uncertainty avoidance will be more negatively related to firm innovation in multidomestic industries than in global industries. The interaction term is marginally significant and the relationship is as hypothesized, providing limited support for *Hypothesis 2*. The R^2 for the uncertainty avoidance model is 0.336 (p < 0.001). The change in R^2 from the base model is 0.004 (p < 0.10).

Hypothesis 3 posits that individualism will be more positively related to firm innovation in multidomestic industries than in global industries. The interaction term is significant and the relationship is as hypothesized, providing support for *Hypothesis 3*. The R^2 for the individualism model is 0.345 (p < 0.001). The change in R^2 from the base model is 0.013 (p < 0.01).

Hypothesis 4 proposes that masculinity will be more negatively related to firm innovation in multidomestic industries than in global industries. The interaction term is not significant, which fails to support *Hypothesis 4*. The R^2 for the masculinity model is 0.332 (p < 0.001). There was no change in R^2 from the base model.

Hypothesis 5 predicts that high Confucian dynamism will be more positively related to firm innovation in global industries than in multidomestic industries. The interaction term is significant and the relationship is as hypothesized, which supports *Hypothesis 5*. The R^2 for the power distance model is 0.342 (p < 0.001). The change in R^2 from the base model is 0.010 (p < 0.01).

Discussion and Implications

This study set out to empirically test the influence of national culture on firm innovation across industry type. We extend the conceptual work of Jones and Davis (2000) and Nakata and Sivakumar (1996) by considering this influence within the context of the industry type, i.e., global versus multidomestic. Generally, the relationship between national culture and innovation is more pronounced for firms competing in multidomestic industries, where the needs of local markets have the greatest strategic imperative. Confucian dynamism has a different influence profile. It is more associated with a global and long-term orientation. While our hypotheses were supported for four national culture dimensions, the result concerning masculinity is intriguing and deserves further exploration.

Power distance is more negatively associated with firm innovation in multidomestic industries than in global industries. This suggests not only that power distance has a greater influence on firm innovation in multidomestic industries, but also that cultures more tolerant of inequality in the distribution of power may be less innovative. In low power distance cultures, less rigid hierarchies and a tendency to break down power barriers encourage and reward innovation. Similarly, innovation is greatest in multidomestic industries for cultures low in uncertainty avoidance. When uncertainty is present and mechanisms to buffer or limit competition are not employed, firms tend to be more innovative and use uncertainty to their advantage. Firms competing in global industries transcend national boundaries, seek balance, and can better hedge uncertainty and risk, as a result of organizational and competitive dynamics. This suggests that firms in global industries have a different innovation dynamic and national-level factors have a less pronounced effect on strategic behavior and outcomes.

Individualism, moderated by industry context, is also a key predictor of firm innovation. Highly individualistic cultures foster risk-taking and reward entrepreneurial behavior. While our findings are consistent with Shane (1992, 1993), we further contribute by offering evidence that this relationship is much more pronounced in multidomestic industries than global industries. In industries where competition is on a country-by-country basis, innovation and strategic behavior must be focused on the needs of the local market. Although the national culture of the home country for firms competing in global industries may influence innovation, in multidomestic industries national culture will influence not only firm behavior, but also competition, regulation, and consumer behavior in those markets.

The masculinity hypothesis is not supported, since no interaction effect is found. Interestingly, masculinity is the only cultural dimension that has a significant direct effect in any of the models after the control variables are included. Masculinity has a negative direct effect on firm innovation, consistent with the findings of Nakata and Sivakumar (1996). In contrast, there is a significant industry-type interaction for Confucian dynamism. There is a positive relationship between Confucian dynamism and firm innovation, consistent with Herbig and Miller (1992), Nakata and Sivakumar (1996), and Jones and Davis (2000). Unlike the others, this relationship is more pronounced in global industries than in multidomestic industries. Whereas global industries transcend national boundaries and innovation is more long-term oriented, domestic factors such as regulation, consumer demands, and especially investor expectations may drive firms in multidomestic industries to focus relatively more on short-term activities and returns.[5]

Firms in multidomestic industries have more of an imperative to customize and innovate for each market, which is likely to require greater investment but achieve fewer economies of scale. We do not test investment effectiveness, only measure innovation by R&D intensity. Future research is needed to determine whether the increased spending in multidomestic industries may be more or less efficient than in global industries.

We did not intend that this study would cast doubts on Hofstede's national cultural framework. On the contrary, we hypothesize and find significant moderating effects of Hofstede's cultural dimensions on innovation. However, the moderation models reveal that four of the five dimensions of culture have no direct effects, contrary to the consensus of past research in this area. One explanation is that we have included control variables for industry and national environment that have not been included in previous studies. This suggests that there are concerns about how far the prevailing national culture approach, based on Hofstede's research, for comparative business studies contributes to our understanding of and ability to explain national differences in innovation activities.[6] Other approaches, e.g., national-institutionalist[7] (Hall/Soskice 2001), Culture Distance (Shenkar 2001), or the Schwartz values framework (1992, 1994, 1996),[8] might account for what has previously been attributed to a pure national culturalist approach – although this is speculative from our results. We also acknowledge that some of our national-level control variables are crude.

This study's limitations are consistent with international research involving numerous countries and industries. First, the availability and comparability of data for countries, companies, and industries is a concern through potential shortcoming in worldwide data availability, comparability, reliability, and robustness. We significantly reduced these limitations in the data collection stage by using a high quality database. Second, data is available for only publicly traded companies. While these companies typically represent the major firms in a given country or industry, private or national companies are not represented. Third, company-level data is more heavily represented in certain countries and industries. These concerns are common for research using archival databases and country as well as industry effects were controlled for in the analyses. As such, the findings in this study may not be generalizable to all firms, industries, and countries. Future research could replicate this study in alternative countries and non-manufacturing industries. Additionally, we do not develop the host environment issues. Assessing the host environments for firms doing business in multiple environments would be difficult to measure and analyze; however, this would be an excellent follow-up study.

Fourth, there are challenges with developing a meaningful measure of innovative output (Pakes 1985). Several researchers have used patents, but not all R&D activity leads to patents and not all innovations are patented. Additionally, patent grants and use are not consistent across countries (Kotabe 1992). One reason is that the appropriability regime may make it more prudent to use company secrets than reveal the innovations in patent disclosures. Comparative rates of new product introductions are also used, but comparing relative innovativeness is difficult.

We recognize that R&D intensity is not a perfect measure of innovation; one reason is that it is likely to be lower in large firms. To the extent that a firm skillfully leverages it resources by successfully marketing new products and services, low R&D intensity ratios may be a positive indicator of innovation within reasonable limits of sales and time (Baysinger/Hoskisson 1989). In addition, firms involved in products and services that require low levels of R&D investment to maintain competitiveness should not be perceived as having low innovation levels. This is generally an industry rather than a firm-level issue. Thus, it should not be a major concern, since industry-level controls have been included. Among firms drawn from the database, these differences should be non-systematically distributed or can be adjusted by controlling for intervening influences in the regression equations. Despite careful model-building, caution must be used in interpreting the results of R&D intensity. It is meant to reflect only what it measures – the intensity of investment in the inputs supporting the innovation process.

Finally, this study has focused on the *initiation* stage of new product development (Nakata/Sivakumar 1996). We test this assumptive hypothesis by comparing the direct relationships between culture and innovation (Table 3) with the Nakata and Sivakumar (1996) propositions for the initiation stage and discover general congruence (except uncertainty avoidance). A research extension would be to consider whether industry type moderates the effect of national culture on innovation in the *implementation* stage. Nakata and Sivakumar (1996) suggest that the direct effect of national culture on innovation may be different during the implementation stage than the initiation stage. Additionally, exploring different levels of innovation (e.g., dynamically discontinuous, discontinuous, and incremental) may yield valuable insights into this innovation research stream.

Endnotes

1 We would like to thank James Olver, two anonymous reviewers, as well as this special issue's editors, David Brock and Julian Birkinshaw, for their valuable comments.
2 Firms in multidomestic industries have more adapted innovation versus firms in global industries with more standardized innovation. Adapted innovation requires a greater number of solutions and is likely to be more costly. While firms in both multidomestic and global industries innovate, we are exploring relative differences within a national culture context.
3 According to Aiken and West (1991), two steps are required to perform the moderation test. First, the dependent variable (DV) is regressed onto the independent variable (IV) and moderator variable. Second, the DV is regressed onto the interaction term (the product of the IV and moderator variable), along with the IV and moderator variables. If moderation exists, the interaction term will be significant. There should also be a significant change in R^2 from the first model to the second.
4 Once the significance of the interaction is determined, it must be interpreted by plotting the moderation effect (Aiken/West 1991). The interaction variables are calculated at both high and low levels. Using Cohen and Cohen (1983), high is considered one standard deviation above the mean and low is considered one standard deviation below the mean. The interaction is plotted by calculating the DV (innovation) in the regression equation by including the Hofstede IVs in the model at their mean value and the interaction variables at first a high level and then a low level. For example, one variable is used for the interactions in this study: global – multidomestic. From this, four points can be calculated and plotted to create two lines: one line between high

IV and Low IV for global and one line between high IV and Low IV for multidomestic. The moderation effect can then be viewed and interpreted. For both global and multidomestic industries, the moderated relationship between the culture IVs and the innovation DV is shown.
5 While Ghoshal and Nohria (1993), Yip (2003), and Porter (1986) frameworks develop the ideas that global and multidomestic are environmental uncontrollables, alternative views suggest that they can also be corporate strategic choices, philosophies, and approaches (Bartlett/Ghoshal 1989 and Prahalad/Doz 1987).
6 We thank an anonymous reviewer for helpful suggestions in this section.
7 Hall and Soskice's (2001) "Varieties of Capitalism" provides a broad institutionalist perspective for the study of comparative business. The national-institutionalist approach moves beyond traditional cultural and economic comparative advantage explanations of firm behavior and performance. Instead, the concept of *comparative institutional advantage* is introduced. With this concept, advantage is not *absolute* and determined solely by the availability and growth in capital or labor. Static ideas of culture or values are replaced with a more evolutionary perspective of national business systems. Values and national institutions are interrelated and result in dynamic patterns of firm innovation, capabilities that are essential for long-term success and survival. National economies consist of networks of inter-corporate linkages that foster the innovation process. This perspective goes beyond what the culture values approach generally ignores and may be better able to explain differences in national patterns of product and process innovation.
8 Schwartz (1992, 1994, 1996) provides a universal theory of the content and structure of personal values through the tension between personal drives and cultural requirements. Management, marketing, and consumer behavior studies are often concerned with individual behaviors or aggregated individual behaviors rather than with characterizing cultures or societies as wholes. These areas benefit from an understanding of national character along dimensions that relate directly to individuals and groups (Gregory/Munch 1996).

References

Aiken, L. S./West, S. G., *Multiple Regression: Testing and Interpreting Interaction*, Newbury Park, CA: Sage Publications 1991.
Aldrich, H. E., *Organizations and Environment*, Englewood Cliffs, NJ: Prentice-Hall 1979.
Azumi, K./Hull, F., Inventive Payoff from R&D in Japanese Industry: Convergence with the West?, *IEEE Transactions on Engineering Management*, 37, 1990, pp. 3–9.
Barney, J. B., Firm Resources and Sustained Competitive Advantage, *Journal of Management*, 17, 1991, pp. 99–120.
Baron, R. M./Kenny, D. A., The Moderator-Mediator Variable Distinction in Social Psychological Research: Conceptual, Strategic, and Statistical Considerations, *Journal of Personality and Social Psychology*, 51, 1986, pp. 1173–1182.
Bartlett, C. A./Ghoshal, S., *Managing Across Borders: The Transnational Solution*, Boston, MA: Harvard Business School Press 1989.
Baysinger, B. D./Hoskisson, R. E., Diversification Strategy and R&D Intensity in Larger Multiproduct Firms, *Academy of Management Journal*, 32, 1989, pp. 310–332.
Birkinshaw, J, Entrepreneurship in Multinational Corporations: The Characteristics of Subsidiary Initiatives, *Strategic Management Journal*, 18, 1997, pp. 207–229.
Boyd, B., Corporate Linkages and Organizational Environment: A Test of the Resource Dependence Model, *Strategic Management Journal*, 11, 1990, pp. 419–430.
Burns, R./Stalker, G. M., *The Management of Innovation*, London: Tavistock Publications 1961.
Cantwell, J., The Internationalization of Technology Activity and its Implications for Competitiveness, in Granstrand, O./Hakanson, L./Sjolander, S. (eds.), *Technology Management and International Business*, Chichester: John Wiley and Sons 1992, pp. 75–95.
Cantwell, J./Mudambi, R., The Location of MNE R&D Activity: The Role of Investment Incentives, *Management International Review*, 40, 2000, pp. 127–148.

Casson, M./Singh, S., Corporate Research and Development Strategies: The Influence of Firm, Industry, and Country Factors on the Decentralization of R&D, *R&D Management*, 23, 1993, pp. 91–107.

Central Intelligence Agency, *The World Factbook*, Washington, D.C.: Central Intelligence Agency 1997.

Chiesa, V., Globalizing R&D Around Centres of Excellence, *Long Range Planning*, 28, 1995, pp. 19–28.

Cohen, J./Cohen, P., *Applied Multiple Regression/Correlation Analyses for the Behavioral Sciences* (2nd edition), Hillsdale, NJ: Lawrence Erlbaum 1983.

De Meyer, A./Mizushima, A., Global R&D Management, *R&D Management*, 19, 1989, pp. 135–146.

Dess, G. G./Beard, D. W., Dimensions of Organizational Task Environments, *Administrative Science Quarterly*, 29, 1984, pp. 52–73.

Dorling Kindersley, *World Reference Atlas*, London: Dorling Kindersley 1996.

Drucker, Peter F., *Innovation and the Entrepreneur*, New York: Harper & Row 1985.

Dunning, J. H., Multinational Enterprises and the Globalization of Innovatory Capacity, *Research Policy*, 23, 1994, pp. 67–88.

Franke, R. H./Hofstede, G./Bond, M., Cultural Roots of Economic Performance: A Research Note, *Strategic Management Journal*, 12, 1991, pp. 165–173.

Ghoshal, S./Nohria, N., Horses for Courses: Organizational Forms for Multinational Corporations, *Sloan Management Review*, 34, 1993, pp. 23–35.

Goldhar, J. D./Bragaw, L. K./Schwartz, J. J., Information Flows, Management Styles, and Technological Innovation, *IEEE Transactions on Engineering Management*, EM-23, 1976, pp. 51–62.

Gregory, G. D./Munch, J. M., Reconceptualizing Individualism-Collectivism in Consumer Behavior, in Corfman, K./Lynch, J. (eds.) *Advances in Consumer Research*, Provo, UT: Association for Consumer Research, 23, 1996, pp. 104–110.

Gresov, C., Designing Organizations to Innovate and Implement: Using Two Dilemmas to Create a Solution, *Columbia Journal of World Business*, 19, 1984, pp. 63–67.

Griffin, A., Evaluating QFD's Use in US Firms as a Process for Developing Products, *Journal of Product Innovation Management*, 9, 1992, pp. 171–187.

Gupta, A. K./Wilemon, D., The Credibility-Cooperation Connection at the R&D-Marketing Interface, *Journal of Product Innovation Management*, 5, 1988, pp. 20–31.

Hall, P. A./Soskice, D., An Introduction to Varieties of Capitalism, in Hall, P. A./Soskice, D. (eds.), *Varieties of Capitalism : The Institutional Foundations of Comparative Advantage*, Oxford, England: Oxford University Press 2001, pp. 1–68.

Hambrick, D. C./MacMillan, I. C., Efficiency of Product R&D in Business Units: The Role of Strategic Context, *Academy of Management Journal*, 28, 1985, pp. 527–547.

Hannon, J. M./Huang, I./Jaw, B., International Human Resource Strategy and its Determinants: The Case of Subsidiaries in Taiwan, *Journal of International Business Studies*, 26, 1995, pp. 531–554.

Henke, J. W./Krachenberg, A. R./Lyons, R. F., Perspective: Cross-Functional Teams: Good Concept, Poor Implementation!, *Journal of Product Innovation Management*, 10, 1993, pp. 216–229.

Herbig, P., *The Innovation Matrix: Culture and Structure, Prerequisites to Innovation*, Connecticut: Quorum Books 1994.

Herbig, P./Miller, J. C., Culture and Technology: Does the Traffic Move in Both Directions?, *Journal of Global Marketing*, 6, 1992, pp. 97–104.

Herfindahl, O. C., *Concentration in the Steel Industry*, Ph.D. dissertation, New York: Columbia University 1950.

Hirschman, A. O., *National Power and the Structure of Foreign Trade*, Berkley, CA: University of California Press 1945.

Hitt, M. A./Hoskisson, R. E./Ireland, R. D./Harrison, J. S., Effects of Acquisitions on R&D Inputs and Outputs, *Academy of Management Journal*, 34, 1991, pp. 693–706.

Hitt, M. A./Hoskisson, R. E./Johnson, R. E./Moesel, D. D., The Market for Corporate Control and Firm Innovation, *Academy of Management Journal*, 39, 1996, pp. 1084–1119.

Hitt, M. A./Hoskisson, R. E./Kim, H., International Diversification: Effects on Innovation and Firm Performance in Product Diversified Firms, *Academy of Management Journal*, 40, 1997, pp. 767–798.

Hofstede, G., *Culture's Consequences: International Differences in Work-Related Values*, Beverly Hills, CA: Sage Publications 1980.

Hofstede, G./Bond, M. H., The Confucius Connection: From Cultural Roots to Economic Growth, *Organizational Dynamics*, 16, 1988, pp. 4–21.

Hofstede, G., *Cultures and Organizations: Software of the Mind*, Berkshire, England: McGraw-Hill Book Company 1991.

Hoskisson, R. E./Hitt, M. A./Johnson, R. A./Moesel, D. D., Construct Validity of an Objective (Entropy) Categorical Measure of Diversification Strategy, *Strategic Management Journal*, 14, 1993, pp. 215–235.

Hout, T./Porter, M. E./Rudden, E., How Global Companies Win Out, *Harvard Business Review*, 60, 1982, pp. 98–108.

James, L. R./Brett, J. M., Mediators, Moderators, and Tests for Mediation, *Journal of Applied Psychology*, 69, 1984, pp. 307–321.

Johne, F. A., How Experienced Product Innovators Organize, *Journal of Product Innovation Management*, 4, 1984, pp. 210–223.

Johne, F. A./Snelson, P., Success Factors in Product Innovation: A Selective Review of the Literature, *Journal of Product Innovation Management*, 5, 1988, pp. 114–128.

Johnson, J. H., An Empirical Analysis of the Integration-Responsiveness Framework: U.S. Construction Equipment Industry Firms in Global Competition, *Journal of International Business Studies*, 26, 1995, pp. 621–635.

Jones, G. K./Davis, H. J., National Culture and Innovation: Implications for Locating Global R&D Operations, *Management International Review*, 40, 2000, pp. 11–39.

Julian, S. D./Keller, R. T., Multinational R&D Siting: Corporate Strategies for Success, *Columbia Journal of World Business*, 26, 1991, pp. 46–57.

Keats, B. W./Hitt, M. A., A Causal Model of Linkages Among Environmental Dimensions, Macro Organizational Characteristics, and Performance, *Academy of Management Journal*, 31, 1988, pp. 570–598.

Kedia, B. L./Keller, R. T./Julian, S. T., Dimensions of National Culture and the Productivity of R&D Units, *Journal of High Technology Management*, 3, 1992, pp. 1–18.

Kobrin, S. J., An Empirical Analysis of the Determinants of Global Integration, *Strategic Management Journal*, 12, 1991, pp. 17–31.

Kotabe, M., A Comparative Study of U.S. and Japanese Patent Systems, *Journal of International Business Studies*, 23, 1992, pp. 147–168.

Kotabe, M./Swan, K. S., Offshore Sourcing: Reaction, Maturation, and Consolidation of U.S. Multinationals, *Journal of International Business Studies*, 25, 1994, pp. 115–140.

Krugman, P., Location and Competition: Notes on Economic Geography, in Rumelt, R. P./Schendel, D. E./Teece, D. J. (eds.), *Fundamental Issues in Strategy*, Boston, MA: Harvard Business School Press 1994, pp. 463–493.

Kuemmerle, W., The Drivers of Foreign Direct Investment into Research and Development: An Empirical Investigation, *Journal of International Business Studies*, 30, 1999, pp. 1–24.

Kuemmerle, W., Building Effective R&D Capabilities Abroad, *Harvard Business Review*, 75, 1997, pp. 61–70.

Lindqvist, M./Solvell, O./Zander, I., Technological Advantage in the International Firm – Local and Global Perspectives on the Innovation Process, *Management International Review*, 40, 2000, pp. 95–126.

Maidique, M. A., Entrepreneurs, Champions and Technological Innovation, *Sloan Management Review*, 21, 1980, pp. 59–76.

Mauri, A. J./Phatak, A. V., Global Integration as Inter-Area Product Flows: The Internalization of Ownership and Location Factors Influencing Product Flows Across MNC Units, *Management International Review*, 41, 2001, pp. 233–249.

McSweeney, B., Hofstede's Model of National Cultural Differences and their Consequences: A Triumph of Faith A Failure of Analysis, *Human Relations*, 55, 2002, pp. 89–118.

Morris, M. H./Davis, D. L./Allen, J. W., Fostering Corporate Entrepreneurship: Cross-Cultural Comparison of the Importance of Individualism and Collectivism, *Journal of International Business Studies*, 25, 1994, pp. 65–89.

Morrison, A. J./Roth, K., A Taxonomy of Business-Level Strategies in Global Industries, *Strategic Management Journal*, 13, 1992, pp. 399–418.

Murphy, K., Venture Teams Help Companies Create New Products, *Personnel Journal*, 71, 1992, pp. 60–67.

Nakata, C./Sivakumar, K., National Culture and New Product Development: An Integrative Review, *Journal of Marketing*, 60, 1996, pp. 61–72.

Olsen, E./Walker, C./Ruekert, R. W., Organizing for Effective New Product Development: The Moderating Role of Product Innovativeness, *Journal of Marketing*, 59, 1995, pp. 48–62.

Ohmae, K., *The End of the Nation State: The Rise of Regional Economies*, New York: Free Press 1995.

O'Reilly, C., Corporations, Culture, and Commitment: Motivation and Social Control in Organizations, *California Management Review*, 31, 1989, pp. 9–25.

Pakes, A., On Patents, R&D, and the Stock Market Rate of Return, *Journal of Political Economy*, 93, 1985, pp. 390–409.

Pennings, J. M., Executive Reward Systems: A Cross-National Comparison, *Journal of Management Studies*, 30, 1993, pp. 261–280.

Peng, M. W./Wang, D. Y., Innovation Capability and Foreign Direct Investment: Toward a Learning Option Perspective, *Management International Review*, 40, 2000, pp. 79–93.

Peteraf, M. A., The Cornerstones of Competitive Advantage: A Resource-Based View, *Strategic Management Journal*, 14, 1993, pp. 179–191.

Porter, M. E., Competition in Global Industries: A Conceptual Framework, in Porter, M. E. (ed.), *Competition in Global Industries*, Cambridge, MA: Harvard University Press 1986, pp. 15–60.

Porter, M. E., *The Competitive Advantage of Nations*, New York: Free Press 1990.

Prahalad, C. K./Doz, Y., *The Multinational Mission: Balancing Local Demands and Global Vision*, New York: Free Press 1987.

Prahalad, C. K./Hamel, G., The Core Competence of the Corporation, *Harvard Business Review*, 68, 1990, pp. 79–91.

Quinn, J. B., Technological Innovation, Entrepreneurship, and Strategy, *Sloan Management Review*, 20, 1979, pp. 19–30.

Ring, P. S./Lenway, S. A./Govekar, M., Management of the Political Imperative in International Business, *Strategic Management Journal*, 11, 1990, pp. 141–151.

Ronstadt, R. C., International R&D: The Establishment and Evolution of Research and Development Abroad by Seven US Multinationals, *Journal of International Business Studies*, 9, 1978, pp. 7–24.

Roth, K./Morrison, A. J., An Empirical Analysis of the Integration-Responsiveness Framework in Global Industries, *Journal of International Business Studies*, 21, 1990, pp. 541–564.

Schmalensee, R., Using the H-index of Concentration with Published Data, *Review of Economics and Statistics*, 59, 1977, pp. 186–213.

Schwartz, S. H., Universals in the Context and Structure of Values: Theoretical Advances and Empirical Tests in 20 Countries, in Zanna, M. (ed.), *Advances in Experimental Social Psychology*, Orlando, FL: Academic Press, 25, 1992, pp. 1–65.

Schwartz, S. H., Are There Universal Aspects in the Structure and Contents of Human Values?, *Journal of Social Issues*, 50, 1994, pp. 19–45.

Schwartz, S. H., Value Priorities and Behavior: Applying a Theory of Integrated Value Systems, in Seligman, C./Olson, J. M./Zanna, M. P. (eds.), *The Psychology of Values: The Ontario Symposium*, Mahwah, NJ: Lawrence Erlbaum Associates, 8, 1996, pp. 1–24.

Shane, S., Why Do Some Societies Invent More than Others?, *Journal of Business Venturing*, 7, 1992, pp. 9–46.

Shane, S., Cultural Influences on National Rates of Innovation, *Journal of Business Venturing*, 8, 1993, pp. 59–74.

Shane, S., Uncertainty Avoidance and the Preference for Innovation Championing Roles, *Journal of International Business Studies*, 26, 1995, pp. 47–68.

Shenkar, O., More Rigorous Conceptualization and Measurement of Cultural Differences, *Journal of International Business Studies*, 32, 2001, pp. 519–535.

Sivakumar, K./Nakata, C., The Stampede Toward Hofstede's Framework: Avoiding the Sample Design Pit in Cross-Cultural Research, *Journal of International Business Studies*, 32, 2001, pp. 555–574.

Souder, W. E., Managing Relations Between R&D and Marketing in New Product Development Products, *Journal of Product Innovation Management*, 5, 1988, pp. 6–19.

Steensma, H. K./Marion, L./Weaver, K. M./Dickson, P. H., The Influence of National Culture on the Formation of Technology Alliances by Entrepreneurial Firms, *Academy of Management Journal*, 43, 2000, pp. 951–975.

Teigland, R./Fey, C. F./Birkinshaw, J., Knowledge Dissemination in Global R&D Operations: An Empirical Study of Multinationals in the High Technology Electronics Industry, *Management International Review*, 40, 2000, pp. 49–77.

Thwaites, D., Organizational Influences on the New Product Development Process in Financial Services, *Journal of Product Innovation Management*, 9, 1992, pp. 303–313.

Wernerfelt, B., A Resource-Based View of the Firm, *Strategic Management Journal*, 5, 1984, pp. 171–180.

World Bank, *World Development Indicators*, Washington, D.C.: World Bank 1997.

Yip, G. S., *Total Global Strategy II*, Englewood Cliffs, NJ: Prentice-Hall 2003.

Neuerscheinungen

Doris Lindner
Einflussfaktoren des erfolgreichen Auslandseinsatzes
Konzeptionelle Grundlagen – Bestimmungsgrößen – Ansatzpunkte zur Verbesserung
2002
XX, 341 S. mit 38 Abb., 21 Tab.,
(mir-Edition),
Br. € 59,–
ISBN 3-409-11952-3

Tobias Specker
Postmerger-Management in den ost- und mitteleuropäischen Transformationsstaaten
2002
XX, 431 S. mit 60 Abb., 28 Tab.,
(mir-Edition),
Br. € 64,–
ISBN 3-409-12010-6

Jörg Frehse
Internationale Dienstleistungskompetenzen
Erfolgsstrategien für die europäische Hotellerie
2002
XXVI, 353 S. mit 48 Abb.,
(mir-Edition),
Br. € 59,–
ISBN 3-409-12349-0

Anja Schulte
Das Phänomen der Rückverlagerung
Internationale Standortentscheidungen kleiner und mittlerer Unternehmen
2002
XXII, 315 S. mit 17 Abb., 2 Tab.,
(mir-Edition),
Br. € 59,–
ISBN 3-409-12375-X

Andreas Wald
Netzwerkstrukturen und -effekte in Organisationen
Eine Netzwerkanalyse in internationalen Unternehmen
2003
XVIII, 238 S. mit 19 Abb., 61 Tab.,
(mir-Edition),
Br. € 49,90
ISBN 3-409-12395-4

Nicola Berg
Public Affairs Management
Ergebnisse einer empirischen Untersuchung in Multinationalen Unternehmungen
2003
XXXIV, 471 S. mit 20 Abb., 67 Tab.
(mir-Edition),
Br. € 64,–
ISBN 3-409-12387-3

Betriebswirtschaftlicher Verlag Dr. Th. Gabler GmbH, Abraham-Lincoln-Str. 46, 65189 Wiesbaden

Stephen B. Tallman/J. Michael Geringer/David M. Olsen

Contextual Moderating Effects and the Relationship of Firm-Specific Resources, Strategy, Structure and Performance among Japanese Multinational Enterprises[1]

Abstract

- This paper develops and tests a path analytic model of resource value-strategy-structure-performance relationships for multinational enterprises (MNEs) in which resource and strategic variables are interdependent.
- The model is tested using multi-year data from a sample of large Japanese industrial MNEs in order to examine the effects of *keiretsu* membership on hypothesized relationships.

Key Results

- Results suggest that resource value, strategy, and structure have significant interdependencies and simultaneously impact performance.
- *Keiretsu* membership has significant moderating effects under some circumstances.

Authors

Stephen B. Tallman, Professor of Management, Management Department, David Eccles School of Business, University of Utah, Salt Lake City, UT, USA.
J. Michael Geringer, Professor of Strategy and International Management, College of Business, California Polytechnic University, San Luis Obispo, CA, USA.
David M. Olsen, Adjunct Assistant Professor, Management Department, David Eccles School of Business, University of Utah, Salt Lake City, UT, USA.

Stephen B. Tallman/J. Michael Geringer/David M. Olsen

Introduction

The literature of the multinational enterprise (MNE) treats geographic expansion of the market scope and operational reach of a firm across national boundaries as strategies that should improve performance by opening new markets in which the firm can employ its idiosyncratic resources and capabilities. Models of the MNE assert that such firms must have certain firm-specific (Rugman 1979) or ownership-tied (Dunning 1981) assets that provide superior competitive advantage in international markets, otherwise they could not overcome the natural disadvantages of operating in foreign markets. The theory of the MNE has taken an ever more explicitly Resource-Based View (RBV) approach (Tallman/Li 1996, Hitt/Hoskisson/Kim 1997) in which access to increased customer bases, economies of scope, market power, risk reduction, and internal financial markets lead consistently to improved performance by increasing opportunities to exploit strategic resources. At the same time, investigations of foreign direct investment from an internalization or transaction cost economics perspective have addressed the impact of non-marketable assets on alternative governance structures for international transactions (Buckley/Casson 1976, Rugman 1979, Teece 1986, Casson 1987). Most empirical studies provide partial support for the RBV-based conceptual arguments studies (Grant 1987, Grant/Jammine/Thomas 1988, Geringer/Beamish/daCosta 1989, Tallman/Li 1996, Hitt/Hoskisson/Kim 1997, Delios/Beamish 1999a), but seldom confirm the RBV perspective completely (Geringer/Tallman/Olsen 2000). Yet other work suggests that international expansion *per se* offers no advantage, but rather reflects the superior resources that also underlie superior performance (Dess/Gupta/Hennart/Hill 1995, Morck/Yeung 1991).

Part of the problem of mixed outcomes for studies of MNEs is that empirical studies continue to address only portions of the full resource-strategy-structure-performance relationship at the core of the RBV. From a configurational perspective (Miller 1986), studies that only examine the influence of firm characteristics on diversification or that only examine the effect of diversification on performance are incomplete – these relationships are interdependent and simultaneous. This study examines the simultaneous effects of superior firm specific resources (FSRs) on multinationality and the effects of both on performance. Taking an explicit RBV approach considers the effect of superior resources on international diversification strategies and governance structures, explicitly differentiates international diversification strategy and governance structure while examining their relationship, and examines the impact of all these inputs on performance. We believe that measures of multinationality, expressed as geographical scope and governance structure, are different but interdependent constructs that must be separated. Geringer et al. (1989), Hitt et al. (1997), Tallman and Li (1996), Delios and Beamish (1999a), and others use various measures of international sales, number of foreign investments, and size of foreign subsidiaries. This confuses results, in part by failing to discriminate between considerations for the relative focus on international markets (sales measures) and considerations for the relative use of hierarchical governance structures in foreign markets (investment site counts, size of overseas operations). We measure both the strategic scope of international sales and the relative use of hierarchical versus market governance. Finally, our configurational approach suggests that only the proper combination of FSRs, geographical diversification strategies, international governance structure, and contextual conditions (rather than unique resources alone) can lead firms to superior performance – again, these are not independent relationships. We use path analytic estimation techniques (Stimpert/ Duhaime 1997) in order to test empirically the simultaneous relationships predicted by our model.

Further, models of international diversification strategies have generally ignored or inferred exogenous factors that might moderate the effect of resources and strategy on performance, although Delios and Beamish (1999a) and Geringer et al. (2000) suggest that the Japanese situation has produced somewhat different outcomes than have Anglo-American samples studied previously. This paper uses measures of a unique national institution in Japanese industry, the *keiretsu*, as a moderating variable on the simultaneous relationships described in the basic model. We expect that different organizational contexts will result in different values for the strategy-structure-performance relationships of the individual firms that we are studying. The idea that exogenous conditions do not just impact the performance outcomes of strategic inputs but also will change the strategies of individual firms is not surprising in itself, but has not been measured directly in prior studies of international strategy.

A Model of Resources, International Scope, and Firm Performance

This paper develops and tests a model in which FSR value, international diversification strategy, and internalization of international operations are interdependent and also explain performance differences among firms in a group of the largest Japanese industrial MNEs over the period from 1985 until 1998. The model presented in this section seeks to demonstrate the interdependencies among our explanatory variables through the use of endogenous explanatory variables. The simultaneous estimation of multiple structural equations in a path-analytic framework permits us to estimate the effects of various inputs on performance and also to understand the interdependencies of those causal variables

Figure 1. The Predicted Structural Model

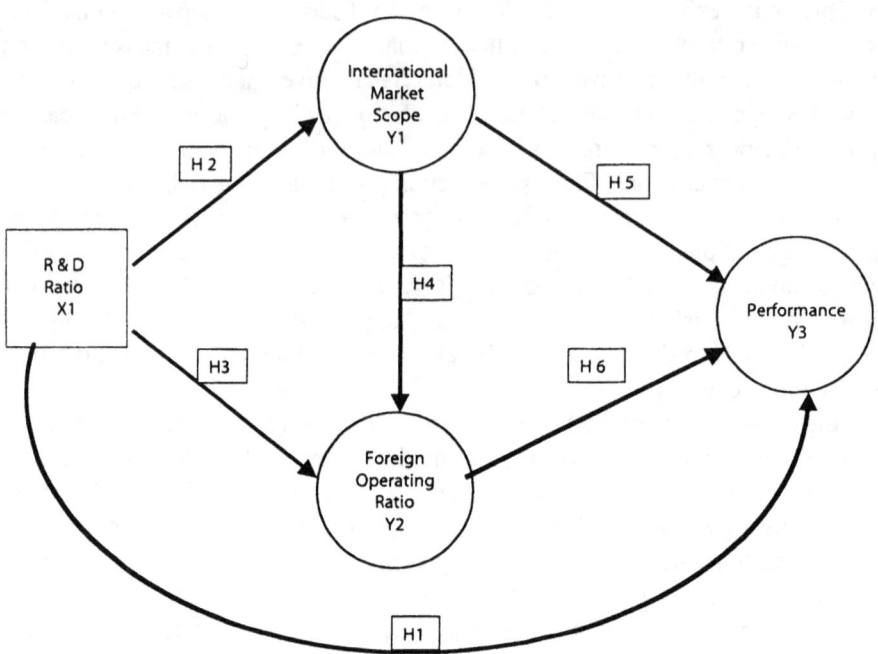

(Stimpert/Duhaime 1997, Delios/Beamish 1999a). The impact of contextual differences is examined further by comparing results for the same system of equations estimated under alternative conditions. The general model is illustrated in Figure 1 and the hypothesized relationships are described in the next sections. We begin by presenting a set of theory-driven hypotheses, then introduce our moderating variable and predict its effects on the original hypotheses.

Hypotheses

Resources and Performance

In his Eclectic Model of the MNE, Dunning (1981) developed the Ownership Factor construct to describe the unique internal capabilities of MNEs. As discussed by Hitt et al. (1997), though, international economics-based models of the MNE focus on the economic consequences of FSR possession, not on their strategic implications. Hitt et al. follow Fladmoe-Lindquist and Tallman (1994) in using the RBV to provide conceptual guidance in characterizing these sources of strategic advantage. The resource-based view of the firm proposes that above-normal performance is based on possession of valuable FSRs, not merely on industry conditions. In its most basic form, the RBV suggests a direct association of the value of unique, non-contestable resources and capabilities with sustainable competitive advantage and therefore with superior performance (Barney 1991, Rumelt 1991). In this vein, Morck and Yeung (1991) suggest that only superior resources provide value to MNEs, with internationalization having at best an indeterminate effect on performance.

Hypothesis 1. The greater the value of an MNE's firm-specific resources, the better its performance.

Resources and Multinational Strategy

This simple but all-encompassing view of FSRs has led to charges that the RBV is a simple tautology: "Possession of rent-yielding resources generates superior performance, so superior performance is evidence of the possession of such resources." From a configuration perspective, though, if a firm does not have the strategic management competencies to create a bundle of firm-specific and complementary resources and then to use this capability in the marketplace to exploit its strategic resources, it should not be able to gain advantage from its FSRs. In other words, strategy counts.

For the MNE, access to larger international markets provides increased opportunities to gain rents from its FSRs, and should provide benefits. Empirically, Delios and Beamish (1999a) show, contrary to Morck and Yeung (1991), that the performance effects of FSRs and multinationality are simultaneous, and that international diversification has positive performance effects even when resource inputs are taken into account. International business theory suggests that there are natural disadvantages to the MNE of being foreign. A logical consequence of this condition, according to international business theory, is that only firms with strong FSRs will be successful in international markets (Caves 1971, Kogut 1991). This should be the case whether firms use exports, licensing, or direct investment to access these markets – firms with strong FSRs should sell more in international markets. Ito and Pucik (1993) show that higher investment in R&D results in greater exports for Japanese firms, while Delios and Beamish (1999a) show that greater R&D investment is tied to more, and more widespread, foreign investment. While previous studies have mixed firm and industry-level technology intensity, we believe that the effect is best depicted as a firm-level phenomenon.

Hypothesis 2. The greater the value of its FSRs, the greater the International Market Scope of an MNE.

International business theory suggests that the use of internally governed international operations should be positively related to possession of "know-how" (Rugman 1979) or invisible (Itami 1987) resources (our FSRs), since the firm wishes to protect and fully exploit these critical strategic assets (Hennart 1982, Grant 1987, Delios/Beamish 1999a). Internalization models based on transaction cost economics and RBV models of the MNE establish that multinational operations in the presence of valuable, rent-yielding, tacit, organizational FSRs that cannot be transmitted readily through markets will encourage the use of internal means rather than market means of control (Teece 1986, Tallman 1992). First, these characteristics are subject to opportunism if exposed; second, they are difficult or impossible to adequately represent in marketable form; and third, their application with suitable complementary resources must be managed close to the market in order to fully develop their rent-yielding potential. Studies in international business suggest that firms in industries characterized by high knowledge investment are more likely to use foreign direct investment in international markets as compared to market means to control international sales (Caves 1971, Buckley/Casson 1976, Rugman 1979). Using counts of foreign investments, Delios and Beamish (1999a) show this to be true for individual firms. We apply this same logic by comparing sales by foreign operating units to export sales (Foreign Operating Ratio) for individual MNEs.

Hypothesis 3. The greater the value of its FSRs, the greater the Foreign Operating Ratio of an MNE.

Strategy and Structure

Our configuration approach suggests that the scope of international market diversification and the degree of internalization of overseas sales are related to each another (Miller 1986). Strategic management models suggest that the potential quasi-rents to ownership of the resources are best extracted by a strategy that identifies, protects, and exploits strategic resources, combined with an efficient organizational structure (Rumelt 1984). As in Chandler's (1962) strategy-structure-performance model of business strategy, the firm's international market scope strategy also affects the choice of governance structure, or overall level of internalization. We expect that the greater the MNE's geographical spread, the more likely that it will produce internationally (to tap local complementary resources and avoid economic and political barriers to trade) and also that it will keep overseas operations under its control (to bring its tacit managerial capabilities to bear and to avoid opportunistic transaction partners). Use of exports is subject to exchange risks, transport costs, trade barriers, and the vagaries of increasing numbers of distributors as MNEs grow. Establishment of international operations to produce for international sales acts to reduce possible negative transactional effects that could reduce performance as international market scope increases, as well as providing a direct means to move tacit strategic resources into international markets. While this direct relationship has not been applied in previous studies of internationalization and performance, it is in close keeping with studies of internationalization, showing that increasing international presence is related to increasing internalization of foreign operations (Johanson/ Vahlne 1977).

Hypothesis 4. The greater a MNE's International Market Scope, the higher will be its Foreign Operating Ratio.

Strategy and Performance

The above hypotheses predict that possession of unique and valuable strategic resources will encourage diversification into international markets and lead to greater use of internalized operations as firms attempt to leverage their proven rent-yielding FSRs, and that greater international market scope will be associated with more internal foreign production. The RBV further suggests that strategies that properly apply the firm's FSRs will generate competitive advantage (Dierickx/Cool 1989, Miller 1986). While simple possession of unique FSRs may improve performance somewhat, to a large extent the benefits of superior resources will be seen only through successful strategic choices in application of these resources (Miller 1986, Rumelt 1974, Chandler 1962). Strategic decisions about the international scope of a firm's sales should directly affect performance in a resource-based model of the MNE by leveraging FSRs in the international marketplace, independent of the value of those FSRs (Fladmoe-Lindquist/Tallman 1994, Hitt et al. 1997, Delios/Beamish 1999a). Delios and Beamish (1999a) show that a greater number of international subsidiaries in more countries leads to superior economic performance even when resource value is estimated simultaneously. Therefore, so long as the ownership factors can be applied profitably, greater international market scope should generate higher performance levels (Grant 1987, Kim/Hwang/Burgers 1993), even when accounting for separate FSR effects. Some studies suggest a curvilinear effect of international strategy on performance, with the bureaucratic costs of excessive diversification eventually leading to lower accounting performance, other studies do not produce such results and suggest that learning effects permit MNEs to overcome short-term difficulties in new markets (Tallman/Li 1996). Lu and Beamish (2001) suggest an S-curve, with early inexperience overcome as internationalism increases, but with eventually high costs to excessive international spread. Most predictions of declining performance at high levels of international diversity focus not on international sales, but on numbers of foreign subsidiaries, which increase the bureaucratic costs of internalized transactions as they increase. We expect that our IMS measure, including both market and hierarchically controlled international sales, will be less subject to bureaucratic cost effects than measures addressing only the size or number of overseas subsidiaries, further supporting a linear formulation. In addition, the use of the FOR variable to specifically address the relative use of hierarchy and market transactions provides a direct measure of the effects of governance efficiencies typically assigned to variables representing market scope.

Hypothesis 5. The greater a MNE's International Market Scope, the better its performance.

The transactional literature of the MNE (Buckley 1988, Dunning 1993) suggests that *where* international operations are located and *how* they are controlled are as important to MNE performance as the decision *whether* to pursue such activities. Exports (market governance) are efficient for cross-border movement of simple products, but complex technology-based products are more efficiently handled by internal means of control, intra-firm transfer, and local production (Dunning 1993, Teece 1986). Firm-level resource-based models predict that the exploitation of FSRs for rents is better accomplished through the greater degree of control associated with direct investment in subsidiaries (Fladmoe-Lindquist/ Tallman 1994). Use of international operations permits superior combination of FSRs and local complementary resources, thus increasing competitive advantage and minimizing the risks of using markets to transmit high rent-yielding tacit resources and capabilities. We conclude from the RBV literature that the performance effects of superior FSRs will be enhanced by a reduced use of market governance of sales from the home country (exports) and an increased use of internally controlled international operations to produce for international markets (foreign direct investment). On the other hand, the transaction cost literature suggests a natural limit to the internalization of transactions after which the bureaucratic costs of a larger organization exceed the benefits of reducing market risks (Williamson 1975). This theoretical argument supports the empirical finding that very large numbers of foreign subsidiaries or operating locations will lead to declining performance (Hitt/Hoskisson/Kim 1997). This suggests that the direction of effect of increased FOR depends on the range of multinationality in the sample. It is also the case that over time MNEs should develop capabilities for managing their subsidiaries more efficiently, so that over time higher ranges of FOR would not reduce performance. A realistic perspective is that over time MNEs will either develop efficient governance and raise their performance levels or they will shift to alternative governance structures (or lower IMS) in order to become competitive again. Given our multi-year sample, we make a positive prediction for the effect of increased FOR on performance, while mindful that the alternative arguments have considerable validity.

Hypothesis 6. The greater its Foreign Operating Ratio, the better the performance of an MNE.

The Effects of Context as a Moderating Variable

The final concern in our model is exploration of the impact of environmental or contextual factors on the relationships within the resource-strategy-structure configuration and between it and firm performance (Miller 1986, Geringer/Tallman/ Olsen 2000). Strategy theory requires that the firm's operations and outputs be suited to its environment in order to maximize performance, suggesting that the success of a strategy will be contingent on contextual factors (Dierickx/Cool 1989, Wernerfelt 1984). The performance effects of a particular strategy and structure in individual foreign markets will be influenced by home and host country characteristics and the global strategy (Tallman 1992). Individual host market effects are not observable in this study. We do test whether home country-tied factors in the organizational environment will influence the relationships among the parts of our basic model and their impact on performance at the individual firm level.

Home country conditions will influence strategic choices, independent of resource value. Legal, regulatory, and customary restrictions on organizational choices should impact the form of resource-strategy-structure (Kogut 1991). Thus, strategy may vary with identifiable locational factors, whatever the absolute logic of resource endowments would suggest. It is possible that the unique aspects of the Japanese business environment might lead to different strategies, objectives, and outcomes than those found for a similar group of firms in the Euro-American context. A notable aspect of large Japanese industrial MNEs is that many of them are members of *keiretsu*, families of firms with interlocking ownership and unique inter-firm relationships. In choosing a sample of Japanese MNEs, we should anticipate that membership in a *keiretsu* group will affect the set of strategic relationships that we are modeling. Internal sales, the existence of group trading companies, and possible negative competitive effects are discussed by Hundley and Jacobson (1998) as being related to lower export sales on the part of members of horizontal or financial *keiretsu* (*kigyoshudan*) – horizontal corporate groups (Johnston/McAlevey 1998).[2] Their analysis suggests that horizontal *keiretsu* membership does not affect the use of foreign direct investment, but Delios and Beamish (1999b) show a negative effect of *sogo shosha* partnerships on ownership levels in individual transactions. As *sogo shosha* are affiliated with many *keiretsu*, this suggests that *keiretsu* affiliation may reduce the Foreign Operating Ratio. We suggest that *keiretsu* membership will limit the scope of international market access, whether by export or by direct investment, for a given strategic resource value, as market power in the domestic market reduces the need to look abroad. Thus, *keiretsu* membership might be expected to have a negative effect on the relationship between FSR value and both international market scope and foreign operating ratio. *Keiretsu* groups are typically highly diversified, suggesting a decreased direct impact of FSR value on performance (Tallman/Li 1996). On the other hand, we could expect that the availability of group related complementary assets such as *sogo shosha* and intimate ties to large international banks will enhance the effects of increased international sales and operations on performance. Simultaneous effects on multiple relationships among endogenous variables are not easily analyzed, but we make the following predictions:

Hypothesis 7: Membership in a horizontal keiretsu should:
    a. Reduce the effect of FSR value on performance
    b. Result in a negative relationship between FSR Value and International Market Scope
    c. Result in a negative relationship between FSR Value and Foreign Operating Ratio
    d. Have no impact on the IMS – FOR relationship
    e. Positively affect the impact of the international measures on performance.

The Variables

Table 1. The Variables

Variable	Measurement
Independent Variable	
X1: R&D Ratio (RDR)	R&D Expenditures/Sales (Centered by industry group)$_t$
Mediating Variables	
Y1: International Market Scope (IMS)	(Foreign Sales + Export Sales)/Total Sales
Y2: Foreign Operating Ratio (FOR)	Foreign Sales/Export Sales
Dependent Variable	
Y4: Accounting Performance	(ROS) Return on Sales (Z Scores by Industry Group)
	(ROA) Return on Assets (Z scores by Industry Group)

Performance

We estimate our model using two different measures of accounting performance as outcome variables. These are after-tax Return on Sales (ROS) and Return on Total Assets (ROA), both adjusted for industry group means. These measures have been used in previous studies of diversification, permitting us direct comparisons to previous work (Grant 1987, Geringer et al. 1989, 2000, Tallman/Li 1996). Although accounting-based measures of a firm's profitability have received criticism from some authors (e.g., Aaker/Jacobson 1987), their use has been justified extensively in the diversification literature. Return on Sales and Return on Assets reflect somewhat different time horizons for performance meas-

Table 2. Industry Groups

Group #	Group Name	N Firms	Constituent Industries
1	Consumer Products	12	Apparel Beverages Food Publishing and Printing Soaps and Cosmetics Toys
2	Transport	21	Industrial and Farm Equipment Motor Vehicles and Parts Transport Equipment
3	High Tech and Electronics	26	Computers and Office Equipment Electronics Scientific Equipment
4	Metals and Industrial Materials	16	Building Materials Metal Products Metals
5	Chemicals and Related	16	Chemicals Pharmaceuticals Rubber and Plastics
6	Primary Industries	7	Forest Products Mining and Crude Oil Petroleum Refining
7	Textiles	9	Textiles

urement, and both are used extensively (Grant 1987), so we use both measures in our analysis. Industry effects are widely considered to influence accounting performance and must be controlled in tests of individual firm performance. We do so by limiting the sample to MNEs that were principally in manufacturing (US SIC codes 20 to 39) and further by using firm Z-scores calculated by industry group in place of raw data for each observation (see Table 2).

International Market Scope

Measures of multinational diversity strategies should reflect the relative importance of foreign and domestic activities to the firm (Grant 1987). Based on prior studies and theory on the role of markets versus hierarchies, our preferred measure of geographic diversification strategy combines one used in several prior studies (i.e., foreign subsidiary sales), with a measure particularly suited to the Japanese context (i.e., export sales). Consistent with prior studies, these two measures of international activity are added and the sum divided by total sales (Grant et al. 1988, Geringer et al. 1989, Stopford 1983). Similar measures were highly correlated with measures of scope in Hitt et al. (1997) and Tallman and Li (1996). We expect that such strategy variables will require time to affect performance, so this variable and the following measure of transaction structure are both lagged one year behind performance. We use ((Sales by Foreign Operations + Export Sales)/Total Sales)$_{t-1}$ to operationalize this variable.

Foreign Operating Ratio

We used the ratio of sales by foreign operations to export sales to represent the degree to which international value-adding activities were located abroad in internally controlled operations. This ratio indicates structural multinationalism, or the overall degree of internalization of international operations, representing the relative use of internal versus market governance of operations generating international sales, per the internalization school of the MNE (Buckley 1988). Again, we use a one-year lag to assess the performance effects of this variable (Sales by Foreign Operations/Export Sales)$_{t-1}$.

Firm-Specific Resource Value

In resource-based models of the firm, the basis for superior performance is possession of unique and valuable FSRs (Barney 1991). Core competency models (Prahalad/Hamel 1990) suggest that the most successful corporations can apply core competencies across product lines and (presumably) geographical markets. In the sense that diversification decisions are typically corporate, examining the overall effect of rent-yielding FSRs on corporate strategy seems appropriate and conservative. Such resources are impossible to measure directly, so various indicators of the extent and value of proprietary assets have been used in past studies. One variable that has been used often to represent the value of technical resources is research and development (R&D) expenditures divided by total sales (R&D Ratio) (Hitt et al. 1997, Stimpert/Duhaime 1997, Delios/Beamish 1999a). Firms that make larger investments in research are presumed to have higher innovative resource value (rent earning capacity), and firms with superior innovative capabilities are assumed to be more international (Hitt et al. 1997) and to show superior performance (Delios/Beamish 1999a). Thus R&D/Sales is often taken as a proxy for superior technical innovative skills. Conceptually, R&D expenditures as a proxy for superior FSRs must be considered in relation to competitive standards, and as these expenditures vary considerably across industries, this variable is adjusted for industry by replacing raw scores with industry-based Z-scores for each observation. Also, as we expect the impact of increased FSRs (as represented by R&D expenditures) on strategy to develop over time as strategic decisions are made and implemented, the R&D Ratio is lagged one year behind the strategy variables: $(R\&D/Sales)_{t-2}$. Our use of lagged effects is also intended to reduce confusion of the direction of the relationships between resources, strategy, and performance.

Moderating Variable

We expect that membership in one of the six major financial or horizontal *keiretsu* groups, similar to the formulation in Hundley and Jacobson (1998), will moderate the effects described in the model (Keiretsu Membership) as described in *Hypothesis 7*. The literature has focused on these groups, which have been generally stable for over 30 years and have strong institutional ties (Flath 1993, Yoshinari 1992, Lawrence 1991). Data on group membership come from *Kigyo Keiretsu Soran*, an annual publication of Toyo Keiai, Tokyo, and were confirmed through *Dodwell's Industrial Groupings in Japan*, published by Dodwell Consulting Group, and the *Japan Company Handbook*. Keiretsu membership in this study refers only to firms with the closest level of affiliation, those companies that are part of the "president's council" or equivalent. Hundley and Jacobson (1998) provide a good discussion of the effects and meaning of such affiliation. As we expect possible effects on all the modeled relationships among the variables, the model is calculated on split samples which are determined using LISREL multiple group analytic techniques.

Sample and Results

The sample

Using criteria for MNEs consistent with those adopted by Stopford (1983), the 108 largest Japanese industrial MNEs were identified for 1981. These MNEs were chosen, and ranked, according to their consolidated worldwide sales as identified from Nikkei's "NEEDS" database. The sample was checked against a similar listing drawn from the *Kaigai Shinshutu Kigyo Soran*, using identical criteria. The latter set included essentially the same companies, with some minor variations in rankings, as those obtained from the "NEEDS" database. The consistency of companies included in the separate lists exceeded 95 percent, confirming the reliability of the sample as representing the 108 largest Japanese industrial MNEs. The majority of our data were extracted from the Daiwa Securities Co., Ltd. *Analyst's Guide*, an annual produced by Daiwa Institute of Research, Ltd., Tokyo, Japan, and covered the years 1985–1998.[3] Additional data were collected from the *Japan Company Handbook*, annual reports of the identified companies, the Worldscope database on Nexis/Lexis, and *Hoover's Global 500*.

Estimation of the Path Analytic Model

As our model proposes several simultaneous equations and treats the strategy variables as endogenous explanatory variables, it is appropriate to use structural equation modeling in estimating the model (Goldberger 1973, Stimpert/Duhaime 1997). The data on the 108 firms over 14 years were pooled and parameters estimated for the path analytic model in Figure 1 using LISREL 8 (Joreskog/Sorbom 1993).[4] Our use of lags in estimating the effect of technical FSRs on strategy and structure and the effect of strategy and structure on performance allow us to make stronger statements about causal relationships than is the case in single period data. Earlier work suggested minor autocorrelation effects for a subset of our year-to-year observations of individual firms. However, we did not average observations for each firm in order to retain as much variance as possible in our lagged effects. As noted above, z-score values for R&D Ratio for one year were assumed to impact values of International Market Scope and Foreign Operating Ratio for the subsequent year, and all of these variables were assumed to have a further year's delay in affecting accounting returns. The correlation table for the full sample is shown in Appendix 1. In Table 3, the first column in each section shows the coefficients for ROS and ROA for the full sample. We see that in each case, the effect of R&D Ratio on performance two years later is significant. This supports *Hypothesis 1* and the assertions of the resource-based and transaction cost theories of competitive advantage that stronger capabilities predict superior performance. We see further that the coefficient of the path from R&D Ratio to International Market Scope is negative and significant, contrary to *Hypothesis 2*. This finding suggests that more investment in research and development results in lower relative levels of international sales for Japanese MNEs. We see a similar significant negative effect of R&D Ratio on Foreign Operating Ratio, suggesting that firms with more R&D/Sales are more likely to enter foreign markets through exports than through foreign operations. These findings are contrary to the expectations of most theories of organizational economics. We also see that greater International Market Scope predicts a lower Foreign Operating Ratio, contrary to *Hypothesis 3* and suggesting that Japanese industrial firms with greater international sales use a higher, not lower, percentage of exports to support international sales. Finally, greater International Market Scope generates lower accounting performance on both measures, contrary to *Hypothesis 5*, and Foreign Operating Ratio has no significant effect on either measure of performance, so that *Hypothesis 6* is not supported. That so many findings are significantly contrary to hypotheses that we see as fairly standard and typically supported (Stimpert/Duhaime 1997, Delios/Beamish 1999a) is unexpected. As a step toward understanding these results, we turn to our analysis of the data separated by keiretsu membership.

Table 3. Results of the Structural Equation Model – Standardized Estimates (t-values)

Structural Model	Predicted Sign	Dependent Variable					
		ROS			ROA		
		Full Sample	Keiretsu Member	Keiretsu Non-member	Full Sample	Keiretsu Member	Keiretsu Non-member
H7: Predicts significant differences in parameters between groups consisting of keiretsu members (n = 53) and non-members (n = 55)			Chi-square test shows a significant difference between the groups for ROS as d.v.: Chi-square = 28.44, P < 0.00			Chi-square test shows no significant difference between the groups for ROA as d.v.: Chi-square = 4.49, P < 0.21	
H1: R&D Ratio → Performance (γ_{1-3})	+	0.23 (8.15*)	0.10 (2.48*)	0.28 (6.99*)	0.19 (6.90*)	–	–
H2: R&D Ratio → International Market Scope (γ_{1-1})	+	-0.06 (2.14*)	0.18 (4.57*)	-0.20 (4.94*)	-0.05 (2.14*)	–	–
H3: R&D Ratio → Foreign Operating Ratio (γ_{1-2})	+	-0.09 (3.12*)	-0.17 (4.31*)	-0.01 (0.25)	-0.09 (3.12*)	–	–
H4: International Market Scope → Foreign Operating Ratio (β_{1-2})	+	-0.24 (8.40*)	-0.19 (4.82*)	-0.27 (6.80*)	-0.24 (8.40*)	–	–
H5: International Market Scope → Performance (β_{1-3})	+	-0.07 (2.48*)	0.10 (2.37*)	-0.14 (3.51*)	-0.07 (2.40*)	–	–
H6: Foreign Operating Ratio → Performance (β_{2-3})	+	0.01 (0.40)	0.04 (1.02)	-0.03 (0.84)	0.02 (0.86)	–	–

* $P < 0.05$

Our split sample analysis tests the effects of core membership in a horizontal or financial keiretsu on the model. This technique treats the grouping variable as a qualitative moderating variable for the entire model (Jaccard/Wan 1996). Identification of groups was accomplished by means of LISREL multiple groups analysis (Joreskog/Sorbom 1989).[5] This technique allows for a test of the equality of covariance matrices across groups. Groups may be different regions, populations, recipients of different treatments, and so on. The only requirement for group identification is that they are mutually exclusive and clearly defined. For the present test, groups are defined by membership (N = 53) or non-membership (N = 55) in a keiretsu. Using the recommended Chi-Square test, we found significantly different path coefficients for the ROS measure of performance (Chi-square = 28.44, p = 0.000), but not for ROA. For ROS only, we see that FSR Value has a positive effect on performance in both samples, but that the coefficient for *keiretsu* members is considerably smaller than for non-members, supporting *Hypothesis 7a*. *Hypothesis 7b* is not supported, indeed the results are the opposite of those expected, in that FSR Value is related to increased IMS for *keiretsu*-related firms, and decreased IMS for independent MNEs. *Hypothesis 7c* is supported as only the *keiretsu* firms show significant negative effects of FSR Value on FOR. We see a significant negative effect of International Market Scope on Foreign Operating Ratio for both groups, as was found for the entire sample, so *Hypothesis 7d* is supported. IMS has a positive effect on ROS for keiretsu members, and a negative effect for non-members, but the results for FOR are not significant, even though properly signed, so *Hypothesis 7e* has only partial support. We see that the patterns of the effect of R&D Ratio on international activity and of international activity on returns on sales indeed are different across the two groups. The importance of institutionalized business networks to the outcomes of resource-strategy-structure-performance relationships is apparent.

Discussion

Our results prove interesting on both theoretical and practical levels. Our primary innovation from a theoretical perspective is modeling and testing a complete resources-strategy-structure-performance system, rather than analyzing only a part or parts of the RBV framework. As a part of this effort, we incorporated measures of both international strategic scope (IMS) and the relative use of hierarchical versus market governance (FOR) in international markets simultaneously. We found that FSR value had an independent and simultaneous effect on performance together with our measure of international scope (IMS). This tends to support Delios and Beamish (1999a) as opposed to Morck and Yeung (1991) and suggests that multinationality has an independent, if possibly negative impact on performance from FSR value. We also found significant effects of FSR value on both international scope and on governance structure, and found a significant relationship between these two measures. While we did not always see the signs that we expected, we did find significant relationships along all pathways in the structural equation model. Modeling all the parts of the RBV theoretical configuration is shown to be useful.

What we found in analyzing these relationships was often out of line with our expectations, and provides considerations of both conceptual and pragmatic value. Particularly intriguing, for a set of multinational firms from what is commonly seen as a trading nation, is that higher levels of research intensity generally result in lower International Sales to Total Sales ratios. However, this strategic response appears rational since higher relative international sales typically result in lower profit performance. In the one instance of a positive relationship between R&D Ratio and International Market Scope, for *keiretsu* member firms, we also see a positive performance relationship. It seems that, contrary to some "popular wisdom", Japanese firms are not indifferent to accounting profitability, but rely on domestic markets for much of that profitability. This is of particular note at a time when Japan is again trying to export its way out of economic stagnation.

Of equal interest, considering the importance to standard international business theory of the role of hierarchical governance, is the observation that firms with greater international market focus and higher research intensity consistently make greater use of exports rather than an emphasis on international operations.[6] Yet, Foreign Operating Ratio has a consistently neutral or weakly positive but non-significant effect on profitability. Standard models from the theories that we have applied would suggest that more research intensive and more international firms should seek the greater control over value that is offered by internalized foreign operations over export markets, yet this is not the case. These outcomes suggest that these Japanese firms still locate the majority of their value-adding activities in the home country, so that exports are more valuable than are sales from foreign subsidiaries. Considering that these exports include sales of intermediate goods to foreign subsidiaries, these intermediate goods appear to be high-value items. The overall pattern shows that Japanese industry is still largely export-dependent, despite more than a decade of increased foreign direct investment. It may also be that the transaction cost economics notion of increasing bureaucratic costs for overly diversified companies is relevant – Japanese manufacturing MNEs may feel that exports are a more efficient way of dealing with more internationalized markets. It may also be that concerns for home-country employment still motivate Japanese multinational firms, even as this becomes an expensive and limiting goal.

Our other innovation, modeling a distinguishing feature of the national environment as a moderating variable, also had an effect on our results. Looking at our sub-group analyses, we see that the outcomes for keiretsu-related firms and non-keiretsu firms are not identical. The former, as noted, are more likely to tie research intensity directly to increased international sales. This may reflect the international trading traditions of the financial keiretsu, which traditionally have been built around a trading company and a bank. Competency and experience with international markets seem to have made profitability possible even in the face of a generally strong yen over the period studied. The size and activity of the Japanese economy, even in the 1990s, may have kept newer firms without *keiretsu* ties from exploiting their skills in international markets where a generally strong yen limited sales or required minimal profit margins – either of which would generate the negative results observed for *Hypothesis 5* in the overall sample. In general, a historically strong home currency reduces the level and/or profitability of exports, and we see that more the international these firms are, the more their international sales rely on exports. The positive effect of International Market Scope on ROS for keiretsu members may well reflect greater experience, efficiency, and a greater use of affiliated competencies through *sogo shosha* and export banks.

Overall, we see a pattern of higher R&D to Sales ratios resulting in less international scope for non-keiretsu firms and more international revenues for keiretsu members. We also see more internationally focused sales resulting in less commitment to international production compared to exporting, suggesting that international investment is a response to weakness at home rather than strength for these Japanese firms (Mascarenhas 1986). Further, the impact of overall international sales on profits has a much more positive effect on *keiretsu* than non-*keiretsu* firms, a possible indicator of more efficient organizational capabilities in international markets.

Conclusions

We have shown that predicting outcomes for separated parts of a conceptually integrated system of relationships between resources, strategy, structure, and performance is likely to lead to inaccurate results and inferences. A complex configurational system such as the RBV requires complex modeling for conceptual accuracy. We also find that developing strategy theory in isolation from environmental factors is a fundamentally flawed process – context matters to what firms choose to do and to the effect of these choices on competitive advantage. For instance, the overall sign on the coefficients for the indirect path from IMS to performance through FOR is negative for keiretsu firms but positive for non-keiretsu firms, the opposite of the direct paths. The full sample alone obscures this, and relying on IMS alone to measure multinationality could well have obscured these significant but opposite effects with a non-significant overall finding. More complete specification of the model and disaggregation of the sample have advantages in sorting out complex relationships.

Our study does have limitations in data – all firms are large manufacturing concerns, and are Japanese, so that specific relationships cannot be extended to either smaller firms, service firms, or to non-Japanese companies. The last point, of course, reflects one of our key assertions: that studies of diversification in American firms too often generalize beyond the scope of their data. Our use of secondary data makes the use of multiple measured variables difficult in most cases, so rather than mix multiple measures with single measures, we have simply used our best representative measure for each construct. The use of multiple measured variables would provide better reliability, but secondary data do not provide the high levels of correlation between measured variables needed for such analysis. We did not use measures of product diversification, often seen to moderate the effects of international diversification (Hitt et al. 1997). Bringing product diversification into this model is an apparent next step, as is the application of more exogenous moderating variables, such as industry types or macroeconomic variables. Identification of multiple measures to allow for the development of latent variables in our structural equations would permit better exploitation of the capabilities of LISREL and would reduce concerns about single measures of complex constructs.

We produced several findings with potential practical value. Our most consistent finding is representative of these outcomes. It is that, for large Japanese MNEs, the *more* they rely on international sales, the *less* they rely on sales by foreign operations. This is seemingly contrary to Western practice as described in the literature. It is also somewhat anomalous in the light of our performance findings. While greater international scope is associated significantly with lower performance (excepting *keiretsu* members), a higher foreign operating ratio is at best neutral in relation to profitability (positive, but not significant in most cases). Innovation-oriented Japanese MNEs appear to have a strong attachment to home production and export in the light of strict economic rationality. This pattern, though, does reflect common ideas about Japanese industry and its traditional commitment to home employment, suggesting that path determinacy in strategic decision making is very relevant in Japan today. It may also reflect a specific example of the larger question of how best to apply home-country derived capabilities with high cultural content. In such cases, exploitation through home-based production and export may be essential to firm-level advantage. These conclusions must be considered to offer useful insights on the strategies of Japanese manufacturing MNEs for practicing managers. We trust that they also will offer food for thought about strategic theory and processes for both managers and scholars, and provide a foundation for further research on the resource-strategy-structure-performance relationship across a range of temporal and institutional contexts.

Endnotes

1 The authors acknowledge the assistance of Daiwa Securities and the comments and assistance of Colette Frayne, Karin Fladmoe-Lindquist, and Shige Makino.
2 While our sample for industrial group members are all in horizontal *keiretsu* or *kigyoshudan*, we will use the more familiar term *keiretsu* in the rest of the paper to designate these groups.
3 Although the sample was chosen based on data from 1981, reliable data for the variables used in this paper were only available from 1985 onward.
4 While LISREL can be used to estimate latent variables from multiple measurement variables, it is also possible to use it single indicator variables, as we do here (Stimpert/Duhaime 1997, Jaccard/Wan 1996). Use of secondary data rather than survey data designed for factor analysis, as is the case here, limits the potential for identifying multiple measured variables.
5 LISREL multiple groups analysis proceeds in three steps. First, a LISREL solution is obtained across groups that are hypothesized to be different. No constraints are imposed in the first step, and a chi-square statistic is obtained for the unconstrained solution. Second, a LISREL multiple group solution is obtained for the same groups as in step 1, except that parameters across groups are constrained to be equal. A chi-square statistic is also obtained for this second step. Third, the chi-square value obtained for the constrained solution is subtracted from the chi-square value obtained for the unconstrained solution. This difference is also distributed as a chi-square statistic with degrees of freedom equal to the difference between the degrees of freedom of the constrained and unconstrained solutions. Consequently, the difference in chi-squares can be used to test for equality of covariance matrices of the two solutions.
6 This may be due to the existence of FSRs associated with complex organizational routines, highly tacit knowledge bases, high context cultural circumstances, or related factors that are (or are perceived to be) difficult to transfer successfully into other national contexts.

Appendix 1. Correlation (Spearman's Rho) Table for the Full Sample

Key for Correlation Table Variables

R&DR	R&D Ratio
IMS	International Market Scope
FOR	Foreign Operating Ratio
ROS	Return on Sales (Performance)
ROA	Return on Assets (Performance)

	Mean	Median	Std. Dev.	R&DR	IMS	FOR	ROS	ROA
R&DR	0.032	0.028	0.025	1.000				
IMS	0.329	0.274	0.220	0.285**	1.000			
FOR	2.492	0.571	6.076	−0.351**	−0.132**	1.000		
ROS	0.020	0.018	0.026	0.267**	0.062*	−0.033	1.000	
ROA	0.019	0.017	0.023	0.244**	0.021	−0.027	0.921**	1.000

*$p < 0.05$; **$p < 0.01$

References

Aaker, D./Jacobson, R., The Role of Risk in Explaining Differences in Profitability, *Academy of Management Journal*, 30, 1987, pp. 277–296.

Barney, J. B., Firm Resources and Sustained Competitive Advantage, *Journal of Management*, 17, 1991, pp. 99–120.

Buckley, P. J., The Limits of Explanation: Testing the Internalization Theory of the Multinational Enterprise, *Journal of International Business Studies*, 19, 1988, pp. 181–194.

Buckley, P. J./Casson, M., *The Future of the Multinational Enterprise*, London: Holmes & Meier 1976.

Casson, M., *The Firm and the Market*, Oxford: Basil Blackwell 1987.

Caves, R. E., International Corporations: The Industrial Economics of Foreign Investment, *Economica*, 38, 1971, pp. 1–27.

Chandler, A. D., *Strategy and Structure*, Cambridge, MA: MIT Press 1962.

Delios, A./Beamish, P. W., Geographic Scope, Product Diversification and the Corporate Performance of Japanese Firms, *Strategic Management Journal*, 20, 1999a, pp. 711–728.

Delios, A./Beamish, P. W., Ownership strategy of Japanese firms: Transactional, Institutional and Experience Influences, *Strategic Management Journal*, 20, 1999b, pp. 915–934.

Dess, G. G./Gupta, A./Hennart, J.-F./Hill, C. W. L., Conducting and Integrating Strategy Research at the International, Corporate, and Business Levels: Issues and Directions, *Journal of Management*, 28, 1995, pp. 357–393.

Dierickx, I./Cool, K., Asset Stock Accumulation and Competitive Advantage, *Management Science*, 12, 1989, pp. 1504–1511.

Dunning, J. H., *International Production and the Multinational Enterprise*, London: George Allen and Unwin 1981.

Dunning, J. H., *The Globalisation of Strategy*, London: Routledge 1993.

Fladmoe-Lindquist, K./Tallman, S. B., Resource-based Strategy and Competitive Advantage among Multinationals, in, Shrivastava, P./Huff, A./Dutton, J. (eds.), *Advances in Strategic Management*, 10, Greenwich, CT: JAI Press 1994, pp. 45–72.

Flath, D., Shareholding in the Keiretsu, Japan's Biggest Groups, *Review of Economics and Statistics*, 75, 1993, pp. 249–257.

Geringer, J. M./Beamish, P. W./daCosta, R. C., Diversification Strategy and Internationalization: Implications for MNE Performance, *Strategic Management Journal*, 10, 1989, pp. 109–119.

Geringer, J. M./Tallman, S./Olsen, D. M., Product and International Diversification among Japanese Multinational Firms, *Strategic Management Journal*, 21, 2000, pp. 51–80.

Goldberger, A. S., Structural Equation Models: An Overview, in Goldberger, A. S./Duncan, O. D. (eds.), *Structural Equations in the Social Sciences*, New York: Seminar Press 1973.

Grant, R. M., Multinationality and Performance among British Manufacturing Companies, *Journal of International Business Studies*, Fall 1987, pp. 79–89.

Grant, R. M./Jammine, A. P./Thomas, H., Diversity, Diversification, and Profitability among British Manufacturing Companies, 1972–1984, *Academy of Management Journal*, 31, 1988, pp. 771–801.

Hennart, J.-F., *A Theory of the Multinational Enterprise*, Ann Arbor: University of Michigan Press 1982.

Hitt, M. A./Hoskisson, R. E./Kim, H., International Diversification: Effects on Innovation and Firm Performance in Product-Diversified Firms, *Academy of Management Journal*, 31, 1997, pp. 771–801.

Hundley, G./Jacobson, C. K., The Effects of the Keiretsu on the Export Performance of Japanese Companies: Help or Hindrance, *Strategic Management Journal*, 19, 1998, pp. 927–938.

Itami, H., *Mobilizing Invisible Assets*, Cambridge, MA: Harvard University Press 1987.

Ito, K./Pucik, V., R&D Spending, Domestic Competition, and Export Performande of Japnaese Manufacturing Firms, *Strategic Management* Journal, 14, 1993, pp. 61–75.

Jaccard, J./Wan, K. C., *LISREL Approaches to Interaction Effects in Multiple Regression*, Thousand Oaks, CA: Sage Publications, Inc 1996.

Johanson, J. K./Vahlne, J. E., The Internationalization Process of the Firm: A Model of Knowledge Development and Inceasing Foreign Market Commitments, *Journal of International Business Studies*, 8, 1977, pp. 23–32.

Johnston, S./McAlevey, L., Stable Shareholdings and Japan's Bubble Economy: An Historical Overview, *Strategic Management Journal*, 19, 1998, pp. 1101–1107.

Joreskog, K. G./Sorbom, D., *LISREL 8: Structural Equation Modeling with the SIMPLIS Command Language*, Hillsdale, HJ: Lawrence Erlbaum Associates Publishers 1993.

Joreskog, K. G./Sorbom, D., *LISREL 7 A Guide to the Program and Applications*, Chicago: SPSS, Inc 1989.

Kim, W. C./Hwang, P./Burgers, W. P., Multinationals' Diversification and the Risk-Return Trade-Off, *Strategic Management Journal*, 14, 1993, pp. 275–286.

Kogut, B., Country Capabilities and the Permeability of Borders. *Strategic Management Journal*, 12, 1991, pp. 33–47.

Lawrence, R. Z., Efficient or Exclusionist? The Import Behavior of Japanese Corporate Groups, *Brookings Papers on Economic Activity, Vol. 1*, Washington, DC: Brookings Institution 1991, pp. 311–341.

Lu, J. W./Beamish, P. W., The Internationalization and Performance of SMEs, *Strategic Management Journal*, 22, June–July 2001, pp. 565–586.

Mascarenhas, B., International Strategies of Non-Dominant Firms, *Journal of International Business Studies*, 17, 1986, pp. 1–26.

Miller, D., Configurations of Strategy and Structure: Towards a Synthesis, *Strategic Management Journal*, 7, 1986, pp. 233–249.

Morck, R./Yeung, B., Why Investors Value Multinationality, *Journal of Business*, 64, 1991, pp. 165–187.

Prahalad, C. K./Hamel, G., The Core Competence of the Corporation, *Harvard Business Review*, May–June 1990, pp. 79–91.

Rugman, A. M., *International Diversification and the Multinational Enterprise*, Lexington, MA: Lexington Books 1979.

Rumelt, R. P., *Strategy, Structure, and Economic Performance*, Cambridge, MA: Harvard University Press 1974.

Rumelt, R. P., Towards a Strategic Theory of the Firm, in: Lamb, R. B. (ed.), *Competitive Strategic Management*, Englewood Cliffs, NJ: Prentice-Hall 1984.

Rumelt, R. P., How Much Does Industry Matter, *Strategic Management Journal*, 12, 1991, pp. 167–186.

Stimpert, J. L./Duhaime, I. M., Seeing the Big Picture: The Influence of Industry, Diversification, and Business Strategy on Performance, *Academy of Management Journal*, 40, 1997, pp. 560–583.

Stopford, J. M., *The World Directory of Multinational Enterprises, 1982–1983*. London: Macmillan 1983.

Tallman, S. B., A Strategic Management Perspective on Host Country Structure of Multinational Enterprises, *Journal of Management*, 18, 1992, pp. 455–472.

Tallman, S. B./Li, J. T., The Effects of International Diversity and Product Diversity on the Performance of Multinational Firms, *Academy of Management Journal*, 39, 1996, 179–196.

Teece, D. J., Transactions Cost Economics and the Multinational Enterprise, *Journal of Economic Behavior and Organization*, 7, 1986, pp. 21–45.

Wernerfelt, B., A Resource-based View of the Firm, *Strategic Management Journal*, 5, 1984, pp. 171–180.

Williamson, O.E., *Markets and Hierarchies*, New York: Free Press 1975.

Yoshinari, M., The Big 6 Horizontal Keiretsu, *Japan Quarterly*, 34, 1992, pp. 186–199.

Mark V. Cannice/Roger (Rongxin) Chen/John D. Daniels

Managing International Technology Transfer Risk: Alternatives and Complements to Ownership Structure[1]

Abstract

- This exploratory study builds propositions for protecting technology when exploiting it through foreign production. It uses transaction cost as a preliminary basis to explore alternative methods to predict and assess firms' methods of managing international technology transfer risks. It adds theoretical explanations based on the experiences of nine US high-tech companies' entries and operations in Asia.

- We propose that companies rely not only on ownership structure (e.g. entry mode selection) to protect against technology misappropriation, but also on making transferred technologies more tacit and headquarters-dependent. Finally, viewing technology transfer from the transferee's perspective, we develop a theoretical framework on managing international technology transfer risks.

Key Results

- Firms rely on their transferred technologies' tacitness to increase the difficulty of misappropriation.

- Firms make their internationally transferred technologies' dependent on headquarters-controlled technology to decrease the value of those technologies to potential misappropriators, thus decreasing the motivation to misappropriate.

- Firms use more technology protection levers for core technologies than for peripheral technologies.

Authors

Mark V. Cannice, Associate Professor of Finance and Entrepreneurship, School of Business and Management, University of San Francisco, San Francisco, CA, USA.
Roger (Rongxin) Chen, Associate Professor of Management, School of Business and Management, University of San Francisco, San Francisco, CA, USA.
John D. Daniels, Professor of Management, Department of Management, School of Business, University of Miami, Coral Gables, FL, USA.

Introduction

Organizational theorists have long debated the relationship between strategies and structures (Chandler 1962, Porter 1980, Hall/Saias 1980, Miller 1986). Nevertheless, they agree that companies must develop strategies to utilize their competencies and devise appropriate means to implement these strategies effectively. Concomitantly, they agree that companies face new implementation considerations internationally because different foreign environments can either amplify or constrain their alternatives. A primary means of implementation is structure, which theorists have studied from both a global operating standpoint and from a foreign operating standpoint – both at the country and regional level. Structure, itself, may refer either to lines of communications (reporting structure) or entry mode (ownership structure) (Davis/Desai/Francis 2000). Early studies concluded that many companies are using mechanisms to enhance their reporting structures (Bartlett 1983, Pitts/Daniels 1984). Thus, this study, by exploring companies' use of mechanisms to replace or complement ownership structure, is a natural extension of work done on reporting structures. Specifically, this study examines the experience of a small group of companies competing primarily on technology[2] intensity, while they seek simultaneously to exploit and protect their technologies in foreign markets.

"Knowledge is arguably the most important resource a firm possesses" (Liebeskind 1996, p. 93), but, as a public good, it is also the most tenuous (Arrow 1962, Narula 2001). Therefore, "the management of knowledge is increasingly considered as a main source of competitive advantage for corporations" (Schulz/Jobe 2001, p. 140). Further, the exploitation of knowledge in foreign markets lies at the heart of the study of the multinational company (MNC) (Hymer 1960, Buckley/Casson 1976, Rugman 1981). Because of the liability of foreignness, MNCs need a compensating advantage in foreign markets. In technology-intensive MNCs, the transfer of knowledge and the commercialization of superior technology are usually the primary compensating advantages (Isobe/Makino/Montgomery 2000).

Yet, theorists inadequately understand the link between the innovative process and firms' strategy and structure (Dosi et al. 1988, Teece 1996). We can improve our understanding of the link through analyzing international technology transfer. Researchers have examined international technology transfer directly and indirectly from different theoretical perspectives. In organizational research literature, scholars have analyzed the organizational process of duplicating and transferring technologies. They have looked at the tacit or implicit nature of technologies, the impact of these technologies on organizational learning, and the knowledge dissemination process (Kogut/Zander 1992, Kim/Hwang 1992, Zander/Kogut 1995, Mowery/Oxley/Silverman 1996, Schulz/Jobe 2001). Other scholars have examined alliance firms' intent or 'race to learn' from each other (Hamel 1991, Khanna/Gulati/Nohria 1998). Madhok (1997) has advocated the organizational capability perspective of value creation over cost minimization in determining firm boundaries during international expansion.

However, most studies on international technology transfer risk rely on transaction cost theory to analyze international technology transfers; i.e. they examine companies' use of ownership as the primary method to diminish the possibility of technology loss (Contractor 1990, Kim/Hwang 1992). This perspective is consistent with earlier studies, which argue that, due to the public goods nature of technologies, internalizing technologies within organizational boundaries (internalization) is the way to protect technologies (Buckley/Casson 1976, Rugman 1981, Osborn/Baughn 1990). Nevertheless, high technology sectors tend to have a higher share of contractual agreements (or a lower rate of internalization) than medium or low technology sectors (Hagedoorn/Narula 1996). Thus, companies logically protect technology by other means (Daniels/Magill 1991, Liebeskind 1996). These alternative means (levers) give managers more protective options when they exploit knowledge to gain technology-based competitive advantages abroad.

Our study's primary purpose is to extend existing theoretical perspective on international technology protection by examining the ownership lever alongside non-ownership levers to protect against technology misappropriation in foreign markets. Specifically, we examine high technology companies' use of internalization when transferring technology abroad, their use of non-ownership levers, and their differentiation among levers based on the importance to them of the technology they transfer to foreign markets. Following the discussion of our methodology, we'll discuss the theories that caused us to expect companies to (a) use ownership as a protective device and (b) be more concerned about the transfer of core than peripheral technology. We'll then present our findings and our arguments. We'll posit premises based on our findings and theoretical explanations, explain how our premises differ from transactions cost theory, and conclude with a discussion of limitations and thoughts about future research.

Methods

To conduct our study, we examined nine US high technology companies' technology management mechanisms in four Asian Pacific countries. We relied on interviews to build case analyses so as (a) to gain an in-depth understanding of managerial actions and decision making, (b) to investigate from "within the subject of study" (Morgan/Smirch 1980), and (c) to develop theoretical premises (Eisenhardt 1989, Parkhe 1993).

Sample Selection

We studied firms from California's Silicon Valley in computer manufacturing and supporting industries because (a) we reasoned technology protection would be important for them and (b) we could find many firms in close proximity to each other to visit in person. We identified approximately 100 firms with operations in Asia by cross-referencing the CorpTech Directory of High-tech Firms (a listing of US High Technology firms – see CorpTech 1996) with the Bay Area 500 (a listing of the largest 500 San Francisco Bay Area firms, including both technology and non-technology firms – see Hoover 1994). We limited coverage to their Asian Pacific Rim expansions to minimize the number of operating environments.

We noted senior executives, such as chief executive officers (CEOs) or vice presidents (VPs) whose titles implied they had experience with or responsibility over their firms' Asian operations. Because turnover is high in Bay Area technology companies, we contacted each firm by phone to confirm that these executives were still in the same positions and, if not, who had experience and responsibility. We also requested a complete investor packet, which included the companies' most recent annual report, quarterly reports, and company press releases. We used this information to help prepare for each interview by learning more about each company's products, operations and industry, and, later, to provide additional data to compare and confirm interview data.

We mailed letters to our list of executives describing the study, requesting participation, and promising both anonymity and a final report. We phoned executives a week later to schedule meetings at their offices. We conducted the case interviews over a five-month period to allow some overlap of data analysis with data collection as suggested by Glaser and Strauss (1967).

We conducted interviews with 36 of the original 100 target companies. However, we include only a subset of nine cases for this study because these were the only companies among those we interviewed that (a) made a direct investment (either wholly owned or joint venture) in Asia (b) and transferred some technology to it. Six of the operations are in China and one each in Malaysia, Singapore, and Taiwan. Each company manufactures products encompassing sophisticated technology, and all own proprietary technology that is critical to their on-going success.

Interview Process and Analysis

We conducted interviews, either singularly or in author-pairs, at the company headquarters offices, where we also collected additional information not readily available publicly (e.g. lobby literature on new products, expansion plans, and new initiatives, as well as some internal company correspondence). Following Eisenhardt (1989), who contends that theory development through case studies should begin as close to a "no theory" genesis as possible, we relied primarily on open-ended questions to allow new insights to emerge without the restraint of pre-conceived ideas. For example, we asked respondents to reflect upon a recent foreign investment decision in Asia and to describe the most significant factors that affected that decision. We tried not to influence their answers at this juncture. After the executive's initial recitation (during which we occasionally prodded the respondent to continue), we refocused on those elements in the initial response that linked more directly to our study of technology management.

Following the recommendation of Bouchard (1976), we attempted to improve interviews' effectiveness and respondents' motivations by maintaining an inquiring stance, listening closely, and maximizing our appearance of neutrality and confidentiality. While we tried to allow for new executive insights to emerge during this process, we referred to a pre-constructed interview guide to help ensure we focused our interviews on our study's subject (e.g. why the companies entered the foreign markets, what technologies they transferred, what actions they have taken to protect technologies, etc.). After the open-ended discussion, we administered a short Likert-type survey, which used a forced number choice response (5 = strongly agree to 1 = strongly disagree). The survey allowed us to compare the open-ended responses to similarly worded questions with numerical responses. For example, if a respondent mentioned that transferred technology was tacit, we compared this opinion with a semantically differentiated response from our questionnaire. We encountered only one contradiction, which we clarified by re-contacting the respondent.

Immediately after each interview, we drafted summaries based on our hand written notes and recollections. In five cases we had multiple respondents. We compared these and found no inconsistencies. We completed within-case analyses of each interview that included the transcript, survey questionnaire, additional materials gathered from the company office, and previously assembled public information from annual reports, quarterly reports, and press releases (Yin 1994). Our objective was to create a deeper context for each case and to allow the validation of some of the issues discussed (Bourgeois/Eisenhardt 1988). Each author reviewed and coded each interview transcript (whether one or two authors conducted the interview) in a common agreed upon format to better permit cross case analysis.

We compared the coding of each case with respect to the nature (tacit/explicit) and importance (core/peripheral) of each company's technology and aspects of its methods of protecting its technology. The authors' initial coding of cases agreed in 8 of the 9 companies, an inter-rater reliability of 89%. We then discussed in more detail the different interpretations we had on the disagreed-upon case. This discussion, along with further research into the company, led to our eventual coding agreement.

We examined each case in comparison to related literature in an effort to allow novel theory to emerge from a fresh perspective of new data (Eisenhardt 1989). Finally, we compared the theoretical prescription of technology management methods with those of our company cases by using a pattern matching logic. The eventual identification of patterns within the case data base helped us enhance the internal validity of our findings (Trochim 1989, Yin 1994). We also compared the summed results among the cases so as to help explain our findings. And, per a suggestion by Henderson and Clark (1990), we organized a seminar for participants after we had organized our cases, where we obtained feedback and critique to help validate our data. We also mailed a draft of our findings to participants along with a request for critique and feedback.

Table 1. Description of Firms' Main Products and the Type and Nature of the Technologies They Transferred

Description	Firm 1	Firm 2	Firm 3	Firm 4
Main products description	Software & hardware data transfer devices.	Computers and related computing products.	Semiconductor wafer fabrication equipment.	Thin-film media for digital data storage.
Technology transferred to the foreign entity	Some product design technology.	How to operate modern PC assembly equipment.	Older component manufacturing technology.	Minor technology on one segment of manufacturing process.
Technology Core-Peripheral	Core (Product design technology)	Peripheral (Company's software operating system (OS), is core).	Peripheral (Older generation, not core chamber technology).	Peripheral (Sputtering – industry standard process).
Technology Tacit-Explicit	Tacit (Undocumented team-based design knowledge).	Explicit (Documented manager level instructions).	Tacit (Team-based manufacturing process knowledge).	Explicit (Documented manager level instructions).
Technology Independent-Dependent	Dependent (Segment of design knowledge).	Independent (Complete manufacturing knowledge, but not OS code).	Dependent (License technology tomanufacture; components produced are only used by the parent).	Dependent (Production from the subsidiary is only used by parent).
Foreign entity to which technology was transferred	Wholly-owned manufacturing subsidiary in Singapore.	Manufacturing joint venture with two partners in China.	Manufacturing joint venture in China.	Wholly-owned manufacturing subsidiary in Malaysia.

Theory and Findings

As discussed earlier, our interview questions were primarily based on supporting theory. However, we developed most of our viewpoints on alternative technology management methods (to explain companies' responses) after we completed our interviews. In the following, we integrate ex ante and ex post theories with information on companies' experiences, indicating whether we developed our viewpoints before or after we met with company representatives. Table 1 introduces our findings by indicating each company's main product, the nature of the technology that each company transferred, and each company's entry mode vehicle and destination. We discuss our findings in detail in the following sections.

Firm 5	Firm 6	Firm 7	Firm 8	Firm 9
Integrated circuits and related products.	Disk drives and related products.	Software and hardware of various computer systems.	Provide manufacture services for computer and electronic OEMs.	Inspection and measurement systems used by integrated circuit device manufacturers.
Technology for the manufacture of integrated circuit (IC) boards.	Very little technology in assembly and testing process.	Some software product design technologies.	Manufacture process technology.	Some product software design adaptation knowledge.
Peripheral (IC design is core technology).	Peripheral (Design is core technology).	Core (Software design is company's core technology).	Core (Efficient manufacture process is core element for firm's supply chain services).	Peripheral (Underlying software design is core technology).
Tacit (Team-based manf. process knowledge).	Explicit (Documented assembly instructions).	Tacit (Undocumented team-based development process).	Tacit (Team based manufacturing process knowledge).	Tacit (Undocumented unique s/w adaptation process).
Independent (IC boards can be used with other companies' ICs).	Dependent (Need design specifications to manufacture).	Dependent (Only segments of design technology are farmed out to subsidiary.)	Dependent (Manufacture process is only one element of total supply chain mgmt.	Dependent (Relies on parent product design and product supply).
Manufacturing JV in China.	Wholly-owned manufacturing subsidiaries in China.	Wholly-owned R&D center in China.	Wholly-owned manufacturing subsidiary in China.	Wholly-owned sales/service office in Taiwan.

Transactions Cost/Entry Mode

Transaction cost theory explains how management may limit the costs – namely, opportunistic costs by transaction partners, contractual and monitoring costs, and teaching costs – associated with transferring technologies across organizational boundaries into foreign markets (Coase 1937, Williamson 1975, Buckley/Casson 1976, Rugman 1981, Anderson/Gatignon 1986). In international technology transfers, the opportunistic costs include the economic losses caused by technology misappropriation from venture partners or rogue employees. The contractual and monitoring costs are the expenses to negotiate an agreement with a partner and enforce the partner's adherence to the agreement, such as on quality, honesty, and effort. Teaching costs include the costs of training people in other organizations to understand and use a technology. Based on transaction cost theory, the potential cost of opportunism is a function of the technology's value (Buckley/Casson 1976, Rugman 1981, Contractor 1990), while monitoring costs depend upon the company's level of control over the transaction activities. Finally, the cost of teaching a technology to other organizations is a function of the technology's tacitness (Kim/Hwang 1992, Kogut/Zander 1993). To minimize costs, transaction cost theory suggests companies should transfer technology within their organizational boundaries, i.e. to their wholly owned subsidiaries.

This perspective is consistent with the argument that views technologies and organizational knowledge as having the nature of public goods (Buckley/Casson 1976, Rugman 1981). According to this argument, once technologies are transferred, other companies may freely benefit from the technologies. Because of this, MNCs need to expand their organizational boundaries into foreign markets to exploit these technologies, and establishing a wholly owned subsidiary is a main avenue of expanding organizational boundaries overseas (Buckley/Casson 1976, Rugman 1981, Osborn/Baughn 1990).

However, having wholly owned subsidiaries may offer insufficient protection because companies must still transfer technologies to their subsidiary employees who may disclose them to competitors, especially if competitors hire them away from the subsidiaries. Therefore, we expect that MNCs use additional means to protect their technologies. Further, we expect them to use protective means other than ownership because governmental and resource constraints may necessitate ownership sharing (Peng 2000). Finally, while transaction cost theory seeks to explain the minimization of international transaction costs, MNCs may have objectives other than the minimization of these costs, such as value creation from an organizational capability perspective (Madhok 1997) and capability protection (Simonin 1999).

Because we included in our study only companies transferring technology that other firms might exploit, we expected and found that, ceteris paribus, all would have preferred wholly owned operations. However, six of the nine firms (those entering

China) faced Chinese governmental requirements either to share ownership with Chinese companies or satisfy Chinese authorities through negotiation that they would contribute sufficiently to Chinese economic objectives. Three of these six firms negotiated for wholly owned subsidiaries by agreeing either to increase technology transfer or to export more from China; the other three firms entered joint ventures.

For example, Firm 5, a manufacturer of integrated circuits, settled for a joint venture in China, but confided that, "... it is hard to protect intellectual property in China because the joint venture partner (30% owned by the Chinese government) learns and copies what it can". While Firm 1, a manufacturer of software and hardware data transfer devices, was able to establish a wholly owned subsidiary in Singapore, it acknowledged its technology was disseminated by its local labor force that later moved to other companies. The Firm 1 respondent said "... the Singapore government recognized this [that technology was disseminated], which is why it did not require a joint venture; rather, the government concentrated on building infrastructure, which attracted high-tech companies that would bring technology to local workers, who would eventually spread it throughout society". It becomes apparent from the experiences of these two firms, that while ownership structure is a desirable instrument to prevent technology misappropriation, it may be insufficient. Further, it is sometimes unavailable, and when available, not completely effective.

Value of Different Technologies

Researchers in the fields of strategy and technology management have examined technology transfer from a systems perspective. They have documented the value of and inter-relationships among different components within a technology system (Lawrence/Lorsch 1967, Henderson/Clark 1990) and have concluded that values of different technology components vary (Chesbrough/Teece 1996). Theorists have further distinguished between core and peripheral technologies. Core technologies are those that are crucial or critical to the companies' entire product or process system, and peripheral technologies are those that are old, nonproprietary, or non-critical to the companies' entire product or processing systems.[3] Transaction cost theory suggests that firms (a) transfer low value and explicit technologies to respectively reduce opportunistic and teaching costs (Contractor 1990) and (b) limit the transfer of core technologies to their wholly-owned operations (Daniels/Magill 1991).

Our preliminary results are consistent with transactions costs theory concerning the type of technology companies transfer to wholly-owned operations versus joint ventures. Three firms transferred core technologies, and in each case they transferred these technologies to their wholly-owned operations. Firm 1 transferred product design knowledge for its core product. Firm 7 transferred its core operating system design development knowledge, which was key to its competitive advantage in the creation of high-end computer systems. Firm 8 transferred its core efficient manufacturing service knowledge to its Chinese subsidiary. The remaining six firms transferred peripheral rather than core technology, three to wholly-owned operations and three to joint ventures. For example, Firm 2, a manufacturer of personal computers, transferred standard technology to test and operate personal computer assembly machines, which was peripheral to its core technology – its operating system for easy user interface.

Thus, we developed the following proposition:

Proposition 1. When transferring core technologies, companies prefer to take 100 percent ownership to prevent misappropriation of their transferred technology; however, this ownership may be neither a sufficient nor an available protection.

Tacitness as a Technology Protection Lever: Increasing the Cost/Difficulty of Technology Misappropriation

We found that companies used technology tacitness as a means of protecting against technology misappropriation in foreign markets. Although we developed the premise surrounding tacitness ex post, we'll discuss it before we illustrate examples of what companies did. We argue that the likelihood of technology misappropriation is reduced when the technology is difficult to learn.

Kim and Hwang (1992, p. 32) define tacit know-how as non-codifiable knowledge that is not embodied in physical items such as capital goods, equipment, and blueprints. Rather, it is the information that people and organizations must typically obtain via personal experience or exercise. Also referred to as 'know-how', tacit knowledge consists of the accumulated skill or expertise to perform a function effectively (von Hippel 1988). Kogut and Zander (1993) assert that tacit knowledge is more difficult to transmit than codified knowledge, particularly if transmission is between organizations. Relatedly, organizational research theorists have long argued that tacit organizational knowledge is more difficult to disseminate because organizational members lack codification to which they can refer (Nelson/Winter 1982, Hill/Ende 1994, Spender 1994, Szulanski 1996). Simonin (1999) found knowledge tacitness positively related to knowledge ambiguity and thus difficulty-of-knowledge-transfer between organizations. Schulz and Jobe (2001) treat codification as a continuum of abstractness, which roughly corresponds to a continuum between codifiable and tacit knowledge. The most abstract or codifiable are numbers, codes, and formulas. In the middle of the continuum are words, text, and reports. The least abstract or most tacit include knowledge stored in people and products.

Kogut and Zander (1992) raised the issue of technology tacitness as a factor affecting technology misappropriation, stating, "... there arises a fundamental paradox that codification and simplification of knowledge also induces the likelihood of imitation" (Kogut/Zander 1992, p. 384). They later stated, "In the attempt to speed the internal transfer of knowledge, the dilemma arises that capabilities which can be easily communicated within the firm are more likely to be easily imitated by competitors" (Zander/Kogut 1995, p. 76). Schulz and Jobe (2001, p. 141) agree with this notion, stating, "codification can facilitate the involuntary transfer of strategic know-how to competitors (e.g. leakage of databases, formulas, ..."). They build on this premise by asserting that the level of tacitness of organizational knowledge is an alternative strategy for organizations concerned about technology misappropriation. They explored the notion of a focused tacitness strategy which involves codifying only those parts of the technology system that are of the least value to the firm making the transfer. Therefore, firms may wish to pursue specific tacitness strategies for each of the components within their technology system, giving greatest care to those most valuable to them.

Following this, we reason that if a tacit technology is difficult to teach, it may also be difficult to misappropriate. Thus, technology tacitness may be an available lever to guard technology. We assert that an organization can create technology misappropriation barriers (increase the difficulty of appropriation) by increasing its technology's tacitness along two dimensions: first, by reducing codification, and, second, by increasing the breadth of context (number of complementary functions performed by distinct individuals or groups). First, the less a technology is codified, the more time and effort potential foreign competitors need to understand, codify, and appropriate it, particularly if these competitors must, in turn, pass on the knowledge to their own personnel. This gives MNCs more time to identify the misappropriation behavior and take suitable actions. Second, the more interrelated people necessary to complete the technology routine (Sophisticated technology is often embedded in an organizational routine or context carried out by multiple employees.), the more difficult for potential foreign competitors to gain access to the entire technology system. In other words, a company can increase the breadth of context of a technology by requiring interdependence among people completing a technology routine. Thus, no individual can complete a routine without support or assistance from others who understand complementary areas of the routine. This broader organizational context creates a barrier for foreign companies to misappropriate technologies by requiring them to get information from (such as by hiring away) multiple subsidiary employees.[4]

In essence, then, the tacit nature of a technology is a two edged sword. On one edge, tacitness constrains management's ability to transfer technology efficiently across organizational boundaries. On the other edge, it provides a lever that management can manipulate to constrain misappropriation by partners or rogue employees. Figure 1 illustrates that management can manipulate the relative tacitness of a technology through its two dimensions, codification and context. Specifically, management may purposefully reduce codification or documentation, and management may modify the manner in which it transfers a technology so that no single person understands the full context of its implementation. Thus, management may plan its international technology transfer by manipulating a technology's tacitness.

Six of the nine firms in our sample transferred tacit technologies to their foreign operations, of which three firms (#s 3, 5, and 8) transferred manufacturing process design technologies. These firms taught different subsidiary employees separate parts of the processes. Thus, no single person in the foreign operations could misappropriate the full process. For example, Firm 8 trained a team of 11 local engineers for its Chinese production facility. However, because the scope of the technology was so broad, the firm trained none of them in the full process. Therefore, the firm diminished the risk of opportunism because the team, rather than an individual, would need to defect for the technology package to pass to a competitor.

Firms 1, 7, and 9 transferred non-codified product development technology. The lack of codification constrains misappropriation because employees need a longer time to learn and impart the technology to another organization (Zander/Kogut 1995). For example, Firm 9 trained local engineers over time to adapt existing software to customers' specifications. The design adaptation was on a

Figure 1. Tacitness Lever and the Difficulty of Technology Misappropriation

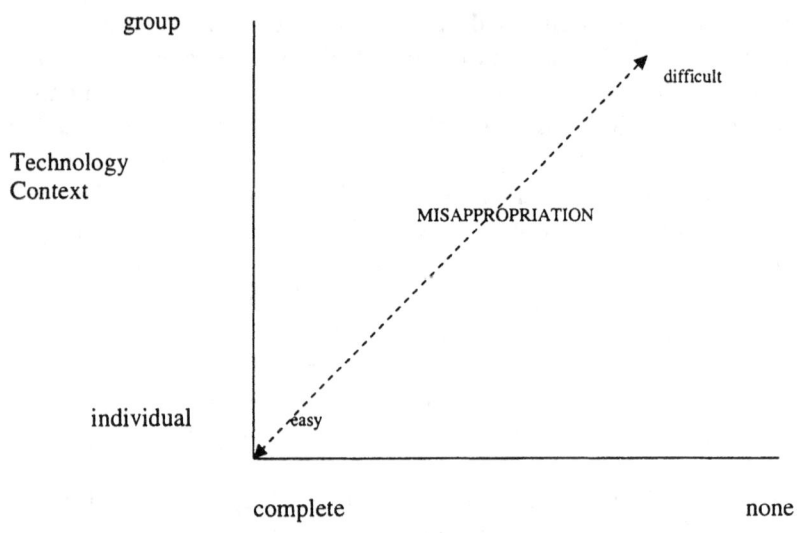

case-by-case basis and thus was not codified. Of course, a rogue employee could go off on his or her own to adapt software to a client's needs. However, this would likely create little competitive loss. The rogue employee would need to transfer the tacit adaptive skills to multiple software programmers for the competitive loss to be substantial, and this transfer would be long and arduous.

Whether firms deliberately designed their manufacturing and product development processes to protect against technology loss or simply designed processes to reduce costs and then transferred them is irrelevant because the end result is the same. In other words, companies reduce the risk of misappropriation of transferred technologies through tacitness. Further, although previous studies found MNCs more likely to transfer tacit technologies to their wholly owned than to their partially owned subsidiaries to reduce teaching costs (Kogut/Zander 1993), we found that MNCs transferred tacit technologies to two of the three joint ventures in our sample. This suggests that MNCs may be as concerned about diminishing technology misappropriation as about diminishing teaching costs associated with technology transfer to a joint venture.

Based on the above, we developed the following proposition:

Proposition 2. To decrease the likelihood of misappropriation of their transferred technologies, companies can increase the tacitness of their technologies by minimizing their codification and requiring distinct individuals to implement different parts of each technology.

Dependence as a Technology Protection Lever: Decreasing the Value/Motivation of Technology Misappropriation

As was the case with tacitness, we developed our premise of a dependence lever ex post, based on companies' responses. Basically, we argue that companies may reduce the value of technologies to potential misappropriators (and thus their motivation to misappropriate) by transferring dependent technologies.

Technology management literature has offered us useful insights on how to use a systems approach to reduce the value of a technology to potential appropriators, and, thus, lower the risks of misappropriation (Lawrence/Lorsch 1967, Henderson/Clark 1990). For example, Chesbrough and Teece (1996) categorize technologies as system (can be used only when combined with a specific set of complementary technologies) and autonomous (can be used independently of other technologies). Similarly, we argue that companies may transfer either independent or dependent technologies abroad. Companies can use the former alone for commercialization while they must combine the latter with complementary technologies to generate commercial value. Following this, we argue that potential appropriators will usually find independent technologies more valuable than dependent ones, regardless of how transferring companies (MNCs) value them.

Thus, MNCs may reduce technology misappropriation risks by transferring dependent technologies. By managing their technologies as a system, MNCs can create barriers for potential appropriators to generate economic rent. They can control complementary technologies without which dependent technologies have little commercial value to the foreign firms, thus diminishing foreign firms' motivation to misappropriate.

For example, firms can train each country's employees in specialized design functions so that each country's functions have to be combined with design knowledge from other countries or from headquarters. By making their technologies dependent, MNCs can reduce the value of the technology in any single country to foreign firms and thereby reduce the motivation for misappropriation behavior. This strategy is consistent with Hamel's (1991) premise that a firm may help protect its technology by breaking it into different pieces for each of its partners to handle separately.

Our dependent/independent argument extends the argument that MNCs should transfer low value technologies to reduce misappropriation risk. However, our argument focuses on the technology's value to the transferee, whereas the existing low value argument focuses on the value to the transferor. Of course, a transferred technology may be valuable to both, to neither, or may be asymmetric between transferors (MNCs) and transferees (foreign partners). Thus, MNCs can transfer technologies that are highly valuable to them, but of low value to foreign partners. One way of gaining this asymmetry is by transferring dependent technologies.

We found that our respondents do distinguish between independent technologies and dependent technologies. They primarily transfer dependent technologies to reduce international misappropriation risks. Seven of the nine firms in our study transferred dependent technology. For example, Firm 7, a manufacturer of high-end computer systems, established a Chinese technical center to develop, consult about, and sell sophisticated computing equipment to its customers. In order to gain permission to have a wholly owned subsidiary, the firm had to comply with the Chinese government's requirements to complete sophisticated development work and employ government appointed researchers in the development center.

Given these requirements, the firm realized that 100 percent ownership might not guard its technology sufficiently. Thus, it decided to conduct primary research on only a segment of its core operating system in China. The firm indicated that, "... the technology we transferred was embodied in the joint research with the Chinese engineers at the technical center ...". While the development work done in the Chinese subsidiary is important, it has little value unless combined with other development work the firm performs in the United States. Thus, the firm transferred only a dependent aspect of its core technology while accomplishing its strategic objective of closer contact with local customers while minimizing the risk of losing core technology through its transfer.

Similarly, Firm 1, a manufacturer of data transfer devices, transferred to its Singapore subsidiary a segment of core design technology that was useful only when combined with other product design segments. However, this transfer allowed the company to establish a low cost manufacturing subsidiary for its end products. Firms 1 and 7 both have wholly owned subsidiaries; however, they still protect their long-term competitiveness through technology-withholding strategies that make these subsidiaries dependent on headquarters.

Based on the above, we premise:

Proposition 3. To decrease the motivation and, thus, the likelihood of misappropriation of their transferred technologies, companies can increase the dependent nature of their technologies by making them more reliant on headquarters' controlled technologies.

Simultaneous Use of Multiple Technology Protection Levers

Although our sample is small, our findings suggest that companies are more likely to use multiple protection levers when transferring core technologies. Table 2 compares the number of levers each MNC used when transferring peripheral or core technologies. Only one of the six firms that transferred peripheral technologies used all three of the technology protection mechanisms (i.e. tacit, dependent, wholly owned subsidiary). However, all three firms that transferred core technologies used all three technology management levers. This suggests that MNCs believe a single lever is insufficient to prevent misappropriation of their core technologies. For example, in order to gain access to Chinese markets, Firm 7 had to transfer core technology and employ Chinese government selected engineers to do the development work. It transferred a tacit technology by requiring group development. It made the technology dependent on developments

Table 2. Transferring Core Technologies and Simultaneous Use of Technology Protection Levers

Technologies Transferred		Peripheral Technologies						Core Technologies		
Firm ID		Firm 2	Firm 3	Firm 4	Firm 5	Firm 6	Firm 9	Firm 1	Firm 7	Firm 8
Levers Used	Tacit	N	Y	N	Y	N	Y	Y	Y	Y
	Dependent	N	Y	Y	N	Y	Y	Y	Y	Y
	Wholly Owned Subsidiary	N	N	Y	N	Y	Y	Y	Y	Y
Total Number of Levers Used		0	2	2	1	2	3	3	3	3

(Y = Yes; N = No)

at US headquarters, and it acquired one hundred percent ownership of the operation. Similarly, Firm 1 transferred a dependent aspect of its tacit core product design technology to its wholly owned subsidiary in Singapore.

Using organizational theory and technology management literature, we argue that MNCs can use various levers to reduce technology misappropriation risks. These levers can substitute for or complement ownership structure or entry mode. Companies may use more than one protection lever because each lever protects differently. Thus a combination offers more protection. We hypothesize that MNCs are more likely to use both entry mode and non-entry mode devices to protect against misappropriation when technology loss can cause them a high economic loss. The tacit lever increases the difficulty for other companies to absorb and learn technologies; the dependence lever reduces other companies' capacity to generate economic rent from the technology they receive and thus lowers their motivation to misappropriate; the entry mode lever gives MNCs more control and legal authority over employees' access and use of their technologies in daily operations.

Based on the above, we propose that:

Proposition 4. The more crucial the technology (e.g., core technology) that companies transfer to foreign subsidiaries, the more likely they will use multiple protection levers.

Discussion and Theoretical Implications

This paper discusses the mechanisms MNCs use to protect their technologies when exploiting them in foreign markets. We argue that, in addition to foreign subsidiary ownership structure, MNCs can rely upon non-entry mode levers to protect their technologies. They can exert control over two critical conditions to reduce technology misappropriation risks. First, they can make misappropriation *more difficult* by increasing the tacitness of what they transfer. Second, they can *lower the motivation* for technology misappropriation by increasing the dependence of transferred technologies, which lowers their value to transferees. In either case, MNCs are more prone to use multiple protection levers when they transfer technologies that are highly valuable to them. Thus, non-ownership protection mechanisms are complements to ownership structure in international technology transfers.

Our arguments broaden the view of how transaction cost theory affects MNCs' behavior and strategies to protect technological advantages. For example, transaction cost theory holds that firms may prefer to transfer explicit technologies to reduce teaching costs. However, we argue that reducing teaching costs may not be the overriding consideration. This is, of course, consistent with much research showing that companies have multiple motives for sharing ownership abroad that may supersede concerns about minimizing transfer costs (Hill/Hwang/Kim 1990, Hagedoorn 1993, Madhok 1997, Teece 1998). Further, transferring tacit technologies, on the one hand, could require MNCs to incur higher coordination costs than if they transferred explicit technologies. But, transferring tacit technologies, on the other hand, should reduce the risk of having technologies misappropriated. Thus, even if transferring technology to their wholly owned subsidiaries, MNCs must weigh the transaction cost of teaching tacit technology against the potential cost of misappropriation. Here, a tacitness strategy helps keep a competitor from gaining access to a firm's resources, thereby providing a means to sustain competitive advantage (Barney 1986, 1991, Dierickx/Cool 1989).

Transaction cost theory holds that companies should transfer low value technologies to reduce opportunistic costs. However, *the value of a technology may be asymmetrical* (e.g. it may have a different value for the MNC than for its foreign partner). For example, MNCs can transfer technologies that are valuable to them without incurring high opportunistic costs if they make the technologies less valuable to foreign partners. By transferring dependent technologies, MNCs can reduce the value of technology to potential appropriators, thereby reducing the risk of loss.

Transaction cost theory argues that companies are likely to rely on wholly owned subsidiaries to minimize opportunism in international technology transfer. While we agree with that premise, we further argue that ownership may offer insufficient protection, causing companies to use non-ownership mechanisms to further protect their technologies in international markets. Table 3 provides a summary comparison between transaction cost arguments and our analysis.

Most prior research on technology misappropriation has focused on the opportunistic behavior by foreign partners (Contractor 1990, Kim/Hwang 1992). Our analysis goes beyond the domain of foreign partners because potential competitors (even if they are not partners) may gain information from employees in the foreign operations. By expanding the domain, we have focused on how to increase the difficulties and decrease the motivation for any potential competitor to engage successfully in opportunistic behavior.

Our discussion also extends our understanding of the use of companies' boundaries and ownership structures for technology protection. Rather than relying on the internalization of technologies within wholly owned foreign subsidiaries as the sole structural technology protection mechanism, we contend that companies may also use partially owned and non-owned assets in their global networks to host and protect components of their key technologies. For example, MNCs can control complementary technologies at headquarters or other parts of their global networks and transfer only dependent technologies to a specific foreign operation; thus, they may not need wholly owned subsidiaries to leverage and protect their transferred technologies. By viewing technology internalization

Table 3. Transaction Cost (TC) Theory and our Alternative Arguments

Transaction Cost Arguments	TC Predictions	Alternative (ALT) Arguments	ALT predictions
Reducing opportunistic costs	Transfer low value technologies	Criteria for valuing technologies could be different between MNCs and foreign partners.	MNCs can transfer high value (but dependent) technologies, thereby making them low value to foreign partners.
Reducing teaching costs	Transfer explicit technologies	The more difficult a technology is to learn, the more difficult it is to misappropriate.	MNCs may transfer tacit technologies to increase the barrier to misappropriate technologies.
Reducing monitoring costs	Use favorable entry mode (e.g., wholly owned subsidiaries) to increase control	Favorable entry modes are either unavailable to MNCs or are insufficient to protect technologies.	MNCs can use nonentry mode levers to protect technologies. When transferring important (core) technologies, MNCs are likely to simultaneously use multiple (entry mode as well as non-entry mode) technology protection levers
Overall Objective: **Reducing total transaction costs**		Overall Objective: **Protecting core technologies in international markets**	

in the broader context of their global networks rather than individual subsidiaries, MNCs may be better able to develop dynamic capabilities to respond to environmental changes through greater flexibility in strategizing, structuring, and managing their foreign assets (Teece/Pisano 1994). Eventually this greater flexibility may allow MNCs to develop additional competencies that expand and enhance their core capabilities (Grandstand/Patel/Pavitt 1997).

Our preceding discussion broadened our perspective and allowed us to develop a new framework to analyze the risk of international technology transfer. In contrast to existing research that focuses on technology transfers from MNCs' perspective, we propose a framework from the perspective of technology misappropriators (foreign firms). For foreign firms, the likelihood of technology misappropriation depends upon two conditions: the motivation and the difficulty of technology misappropriation.

We argue that, from the foreign partners' perspective, the value of the technology and punishment of misappropriation behavior are two important conditions affecting their motivation to misappropriate technology. This argument departs from prior research because we focus on the value and punishment to foreign partners (technology transferees), not MNCs. Much prior research takes the MNCs' (technology transferors') perspectives.

Similarly, organizational process and structure are the two important factors affecting the difficulty of technology misappropriation. Technology misappropriation is a type of knowledge transfer, thus misappropriators need organizational processes to learn and acquire the technology. If MNCs impede these processes, they can decrease the risk of misappropriation. We have discussed how they can do this by transferring tacit technology. They may also consider other organizational process barriers to prevent technology misappropriations. For example, they may design specific coordination processes or organizational procedures to control foreign partners' access to MNCs' technologies. Whereas transaction cost theory focuses on the costs of misappropriation for the companies transferring technology, the development of organizational process impediments focuses on costs for both the transferors and transferees.

In addition to organizational process, MNCs can also rely upon organizational structure to create barriers for foreign partners to misappropriate technologies. A wholly owned structure is one example of using structure to guard technologies. But MNCs can go far beyond the equity structure and use other aspects of organization structure to create barriers for foreign partners to misappropriate technologies. For example, they can closely manage reporting lines of communications and staff key positions with their own personnel, thereby limiting the observeability of product technology (Liebeskind 1996). Table 4 summarizes the framework of this argument.

Finally, this study also sheds insights on the strategy-structure relationships in international business by suggesting that strategies and structures may be either interrelated or independent from each other. For example, under certain circumstances, ownership structure (entry mode) is beyond organizational control because of foreign governmental mandates. Concomitantly, companies may treat ownership structure as a strategy to achieve certain organizational objectives. In sum, firms are potentially the best isolating mechanism for technology preservation and must be prepared to utilize all technology management levers available to preserve knowledge-based competitive advantage (Rumelt 1984).

Table 4. A Theoretical Framework on Managing International Technology Transfer Risks – Technology Transferee's Perspective

Two Conditions	Key Determinants	Examples
Motivation to misappropriate technologies	Value of technologies to foreign partners.	Dependent technology
	Punishment to foreign partners resulting from technology misappropriation.	Legal and economic punishment or losses
Barriers to misappropriate technologies	Organizational process barrier.	Tacit technology
	Organizational structure barrier.	Wholly owned subsidiary

Limitations and Future Research

We recognize that this study has limitations. Our research is exploratory. It has primarily developed some arguments and frameworks based on our attempts to explain the technology protection devices of nine US companies in Asia. Our sample size is very small and skewed toward operations in China (six cases). Further, two of our other three cases are in countries that share Chinese culture (Taiwan and Singapore). This problem may influence our findings. For example, we would be hard pressed to find another country that would require a foreign investor to hire government appointed engineers in its research department. Furthermore, China's traditional cultural and emerging market characteristics may influence how MNCs transfer and guard their technologies. These problems require us to exercise caution when examining the theoretical arguments of this paper.

We also recognize that high transaction costs may override potential costs of technology appropriation. The nature and maturity (Teece 1986) of the technology may also dictate whether companies can feasibly alter tacitness and dependence when transferring technology abroad. For instance, research-intensive companies are more likely to depend on tacit technologies than other companies (Osborn/Hagedoorn 1997), even though the latter may need to transfer and protect their technologies as well. Further, some technology cannot be easily divided into dependent and independent components. These constraints further illustrate the importance of examining multiple, rather than single, technology protection levers. Future researchers may try to analyze how these levers interact, how effective the different levers are, and what internal and external factors affect MNCs' choice of different technology protection levers.

Given the exploratory nature of our study, we relied on respondents to tell us (unprompted) about their technology protection strategies. As such, we did not probe them about their possible use of and experience with other protective devices mentioned in past research. These protective devices include strategies to build trust among partners, legal tactics (patents, licensing to one's own subsidiary, and contracts with employees not to divulge competitive information), and administrative structures (division of control over different joint venture functions and employing back-to-back joint ventures). Future researchers might itemize the full array of protective levers and compare their importance, effectiveness, and cost under different operating scenarios.

Our paper examined technology transfers from the viewpoint of home-country companies. Clearly, host country companies differ in various aspects (Cohen/Levinthal 1990, George et al. 2001) and may affect whether and how they appropriate the technology. Future research may focus on both home and host country companies when analyzing international technology transfer issues. Additionally, we did not address a number of factors that may influence technology misappropriation. These include potential misappropriators' absorptive capacity (Cohen/Levinthal 1990, George et al. 2001) and intent to learn (Hamel 1991).

Host country companies (transferees) may also incur costs when they misappropriate technologies, such as through legal sanctions or loss of reputation. A potential fruitful extension of our research would be to add these potential costs to the analysis of potential misappropriators. In other words, what levers might they use to simultaneously misappropriate and reduce potential costs of doing so?

We have discussed non-ownership mechanisms that protect against technology appropriation without regard to the effects their use may have on other aspects of companies' operating structures and performance. For example, as companies use these mechanisms, they may need to shift more control from their subsidiaries to corporate or regional headquarters. This shift may have the effect of limiting the innovative capacity of joint venture operations and may increase coordinating costs. Thus, analysis of systemic changes may provide a useful avenue for future research.

The companies in our study were all basically engaged in one-way technology transfers, which is not surprising inasmuch as all transferors were companies from the United States (a large developer and net-exporter of technology), and all host countries depend primarily on imported technology for production and export of high tech products (International Bank for Reconstruction and Development 2002). Yet, many technology collaborations, especially those where both partners are from technologically advanced countries, involve technological contributions from more than one partner, especially in joint R&D situations (Hagedoorn/Narula 1996). The suitability of different protective levers in these circumstances offers another avenue for research. For example, protective levers may reduce abilities to capture the value of each partner's potential contribution (Osborn/Baughn 1990).

The aforementioned limitations dictate that our findings on international technology transfer management strategies are suggestive rather than definitive. As such, more research is necessary to systematically test and extend our arguments. However, we are hopeful that this study may serve to inspire future researchers to take a much broader perspective in analyzing technology protection in international business.

Endnotes

1 (The three authors made equal contributions to this paper and are listed in alphabetical order.) The authors gratefully acknowledge the vital critique and direction of the co-editors of this edition, Dr. David Brock and Dr. Julian Birkinshaw, as well as that of the anonymous reviewers. Thank you.
2 We define technology as knowledge embodied in products or in any process that transforms inputs into outputs, irrespective of whether that technology was developed internal or external to the firm (Teece 1986, Narula 2001).
3 Alternative technology classifications have been offered by other scholars. Please see Grandstand et al. (1997), Nagarajan and Mitchell (1998), and Narula (2001) for further explication.
4 Liebeskind (1996) recommends a similar notion, disaggregation of job design from joint development to inter-reliant individual development.

References

Anderson, E./Gatignon, H., Modes of Foreign Entry: A Transaction Cost Analysis and Propositions, *Journal of International Business Studies*, 17, Fall 1986, pp. 1–26.
Arrow, K., Economic Welfare and the Allocation of Resources for Invention, in Nelson R. (ed.), *The Rate and Direction of Inventive Activity*, Princeton, NJ: National Bureau of Economic Research 1962, pp. 609–625.
Barney, J. B., Strategic Factor Markets: Expectations, Luck and Business Strategy, *Management Science*, 32, 10, 1986, pp. 1231–1241.
Barney, J. B., Firm Resources and Sustained Competitive Advantage, *Journal of Management*, 17 1, 1991, pp. 99–120.
Bartlett, C. A., MNCs: Get Off the Reorganization Merry-Go-Round., *Harvard Business Review*, 61, 2, 1983, pp. 138–146.
Bouchard, T. J. Jr., Field Research Methods: Interviewing, Questionnaires, Participant Observation, Systematic Observation, Unobtrusive Measures, in Dunnette, M. D. (eds.), *Handbook of Industrial and Organizational Psychology*, Chicago, IL: Rand McNally College Publishing Company 1976, pp. 363–413.
Bourgeois, J. J./Eisenhardt, K. M., Strategy Decision Processes in High Velocity Environments: Four Cases in the Microcomputer Industry, *Management Science*, 34, 1988, pp. 816–835.
Buckley, P. J./Casson, M., *The Future of the Multinational Enterprise*, London: Macmillan 1976.
Chandler, A., *Strategy and Structure*, Cambridge, MA: MIT Press 1962.
Chesbrough, H. W./Teece, D. J., When is Virtual Virtuous? Organizing for Innovation, *Harvard Business Review*, January–February 1996, pp. 65–73.
Coase, R. H., The Nature of the Firm, *Economica*, 4, 1937, pp. 386–405.
Cohen, W. M./Levinthal, D. A., Absorptive Capacity: A New Perspective on Learning and Innovation, *Administrative Science Quarterly*, 35, 1, 1990, pp. 128–152.
Contractor, F.J., Contractual and Cooperative Forms of International Business: Towards a Unified Theory of Modal Choice, *Management International Review*, 30, 1990, pp. 31–54.
CorpTech Directory of Technology Companies, 11th edition, 3, MA: Information Services, Inc. 1996.
Daniels, J. D./Magill, S. L., The Utilization of International Joint Ventures by United States Firms in High Technology Industries, *Journal of High Technology Management Research*, 2, 1, 1991, pp. 113–131.
Davis, P. S./Desai, A. S./Francis, J. D., Mode of Entry: An Isomorphism Perspective, *Journal of International Business Studies*, 30, 2, 2000, pp. 239–258.
Dierickx, I./Cool, K., Asset Stock Accumulation and Sustainability of Competitive Advantage, *Management Science*, 35, 1989, pp. 1504–1513.

Dosi, G. C./Freeman, R./Nelson, G./Silverberg/Soete, L., *Technical Change and Economic Theory*, London: Pinter 1988.
Eisenhardt, K. M., Building Theories from Case Study Research, *Academy of Management Review*, 14, 1989, pp. 532-550.
George, G./Zahra, S. A./Wheatley, K. K./Khan, R., The Effects of Alliance Portfolio Characteristics and Absorptive Capacity on Performance: A Study of Biotechnology Firms, *Journal of High Technology Management Research*, 12, 2001, pp. 205-226.
Glaser, B./Strauss, A., The *Discovery of Grounded Theory: Strategies for Qualitative Research*, Chicago, IL: Aldine 1967.
Grandstand, O./Patel, P./Pavitt, K., Multi-Technology Corporations: Why they have 'Distributed' Rather than 'Distinctive Core' Competencies, *California Management Review*, 39, 4, Summer 1997, pp. 8-25.
Hagedoorn, J., Understanding the Rationale of Strategic Technology Partnering: Interorganizational Modes of Cooperation and Sectoral Differences, *Strategic Management Journal*, 14, 1993, pp. 371-385.
Hagedoorn J./Narula, R, Choosing Modes of Governance for Strategic Technology Partnering: International and Sectoral Differences, *Journal of International Business Studies*, 27, 1996, pp. 265-284.
Hall D./Saias M., Strategy Follow Structure, *Strategic Management Journal*, 1, 1980, pp. 149-163.
Hamel, G., Competition for Competence and Interpartner Learning within International Strategic Alliances, *Strategic Management Journal*, 12, 1991, pp. 83-103.
Henderson, R./Clark, K., Architectural Innovation: The Reconfiguration of Existing Product Technologies and the Failure of Established Firms, *Administratively Science Quarterly*, 35, 1990, pp. 9-30.
Hill, C. W./Hwang, P./Kim, W. C., An Eclectic Theory of the Choice of International Entry Mode, *Strategic Management Journal*, 11, 1990, pp. 117-128.
Hill, L. E./Ende, E. T., Towards a Personal Knowledge of Economic History: Reflections on our Intellectual Heritage from the Polanyi Brothers, *American Journal of Economics and Sociology*, 53, 1, 1994, pp. 17-26.
Hoover, G., *The Bay Area 500: Hoover's Guide to the Top San Francisco Area Companies*, Austin, TX: The Reference Press 1994.
Hymer, S., *The International Operations of National Firms: A Study of Direct Foreign Investment*, MIT: Ph.D. Dissertation 1960.
International Bank for Reconstruction and Development, Science and Technology, *World Development Indicators for 2000*, Washington: International Bank for Reconstruction and Development 2002, p. 300.
Isobe, T./Makino, S./Montgomery, D., Resource Commitment, Entry Timing, and Market Performance of Foreign Direct Investments in Emerging Economies: The Case of Japanese International Joint Ventures in China, *Academy of Management Journal*, 43, 3, 2000, pp. 468-484.
Khanna, T./Gulati, R./Nohria, N., The Dynamics of Learning Alliances: Competition, Cooperation and Relative Scope, *Strategic Management Journal*, 19, 3, 1998, pp. 193-210.
Kim, W. C./Hwang, P., Global Strategy and Multinational's Entry Mode Choice, *Journal of International Business Studies*, First Quarter 1992, pp. 29-52.
Kogut, B./Zander, U., Knowledge of the Firm, Combinative Capabilities, and the Replication of Technology, *Organization Science*, 3, 3, 1992, pp. 383-397.
Kogut, B./Zander, U., Knowledge of the Firm and the Evolutionary Theory of the Multinational Corporation, *Journal of International Business Studies*, Fourth Quarter 1993, pp. 625-45.
Lawrence, P. R./Lorsch, J. W., *Organization and Environment: Managing Differentiation and Integration*, Boston: Harvard Business School Press 1967.
Liebeskind, J. P., Knowledge, Strategy, and the Theory of the Firm, *Strategic Management Journal*, 17, Winter Special Issue 1996, pp. 77-91.
Madhok, A., Cost, Value and Foreign Market Entry Mode: The Transaction and the Firm, *Strategic Management Journal*, 18, 1997, pp. 39-61.
Miller, D., Configurations of Strategy and Structure: Towards a Synthesis, *Strategic Management Journal*, 7, 1986, pp. 233-249.
Morgan, G./Smirch, L., The Case for Qualitative Research, *Academy of Management Review*, 5, 4, 1980, pp. 491-500.

Mowery, D. C./Oxley, J. E./Silverman, B. S., Strategic Alliances and Interfirm Knowledge Transfer, *Strategic Management Journal*, 17, Winter Special Issue 1996, pp. 77–91.

Nagarajan, A./Mitchell, W., Evolutionary Diffusion: Internal and External Methods Used to Acquire Encompassing, Complementary, and Incremental Technological Changes in the Lithotripsy Industry, *Strategic Management Journal*, 19, 1998, pp. 1063–1077.

Narula, R., Choosing Between Internal and Non-internal R&D Activities: Some Technological and Economic Factors, *Technology Analysis and Strategic Management*, 13, 3, 2001, pp. 365–387.

Nelson, R. R./Winter S. G., *An Evolutionary Theory of Economic Change*, Cambridge: Belknap 1982.

Osborn, R./Baughn, C., Forms of Inter-Organizational Governance for Multinational Alliances, *Academy of Management Journal*, 33, 1990, pp. 503–519.

Osborn, R./Hagedoorn, J., The Institutionalization and Evolutionary Dynamics of Interorganizational Alliances and Networks, *Academy of Management Journal*, 40, 1997, pp. 261–278.

Parkhe, A., Messy Research, Methodological Predisposition, and Theory Development in International Joint Venture, *Academy of Management Review*, 18, 1993, pp. 227–268.

Peng, M. W., Controlling the Foreign Agent: How Governments Deal with Multinationals in a Transition Economy, *Management International Review*, 40, 2, 2000, pp. 141–65.

Pitts, R./Daniels, J. D., Aftermath of the Matrix Mania, *Columbia Journal of World Business*, 19, 2, 1984, pp. 48–54.

Porter, M., *Competitive Strategy*, New York Free Press: 1980

Rugman, A. M., *Inside the Multinationals: The Economics of Internal Markets*, London: Croom Helm 1981.

Rumelt, R. P., Towards a Strategic Theory of the Firm, in Lamb, R. B. (ed.), *Competitive Strategic Management*, Englewood Cliffs, NJ: Prentice-Hall 1984 pp. 556–570.

Schulz, M./Jobe, L. A., Codification and Tacitness as Knowledge Management Strategies: An Empirical Exploration, *Journal of High Technology Management Research*, 12, 2001, pp. 139–165.

Simonin, B. L., Ambiguity and the Process of Knowledge Transfer in Strategic Alliances, *Strategic Management Journal*, 20, 1999, pp. 595–623.

Spender, J. C., Organizational Knowledge, Collective Practice and Penrose Rents, *International Business Review*, 3, 4, 1994, pp. 353–367.

Szulanski, G., Exploring Internal Stickiness: Impediments to the Transfer of Best Practices Within the Firm, *Strategic Management Journal*, 17, Winter Special Issue 1996, pp. 27–43.

Teece, D. J., Profiting from Technological Innovation: Implications for Integration, Collaboration, Licensing and Public Policy, *Research Policy*, 15, 1986, pp. 285–305.

Teece, D. J./Pisano, G., The Dynamic Capabilities of Firms: An Introduction, *Industrial and Corporate Change*, 3, 3, 1994, pp. 537–556.

Teece, D. J., Firm Organization, Industrial Structure and Technological Innovation, *Journal of Economic Behavior and Organization*, 31, 1996, pp. 193–224.

Teece, D. J., Capturing Value from Knowledge Assets: The New Economy, Markets for Know-How, and Intangible Assets, *California Management Review*, 40, 3, Spring 1998, pp. 55–79.

Trochim, W., Outcome Pattern Matching and Program Theory, *Evaluation and Program Planning*, 2, 1989, pp. 355–366.

von Hippel, E., *The Sources of Innovation*, New York: Oxford University Press 1988.

Williamson, O. L., *Markets and Hierarchies: Analysis and Antitrust Implications*, New York: Free Press 1975.

Yin, R. K., *Case Study Research: Design and Methods*, 2nd edition, Thousand Oaks: Sage Publications 1994.

Zander, U./Kogut, B., Knowledge and the Speed of the Transfer and Imitation of Organizational Capabilities: An Empirical Test, *Organization Science*, 6, 1, 1995, pp. 76–92.

Management
International Review
© Gabler Verlag 2004

EDITORIAL OBJECTIVES

MANAGEMENT INTERNATIONAL REVIEW presents insights and analyses which reflect basic and topical advances in the key areas of International Management. Its target audience includes scholars and executives in business and administration.

EDITORIAL POLICY

MANAGEMENT INTERNATIONAL REVIEW is a refereed journal which aims at the advancement and dissemination of international applied research in the fields of Management and Business. The scope of the journal comprises International Business, Transnational Corporations, Intercultural Management, Strategic Management, and Business Policy.

MANAGEMENT INTERNATIONAL REVIEW stresses the interaction between theory and practice of management by way of publishing articles, research notes, reports and comments which concentrate on the application of existing and potential research for business and other organizations. Papers are invited and given priority which are based on rigorous methodology, suggest models capable to solve practical problems. Also papers are welcome which advise as to whether and to what extent models can be translated and applied by the practising manager. Work which has passed the practical test of successful application is of special interest to MIR. It is hoped that besides its academic objectives the journal will serve some useful purpose for the practical world, and also help bridging the gap between academic and business management.

PUBLISHING · SUBSCRIPTION · ADVERTISEMENTS

Published quarterly, fixed annual subscription rate for foreign countries: Individual subscription 114 Euro (approx. US $ 129.–), institutional subscription 228 Euro (approx. US $ 258.–), single copy 62 Euro – (approx. US $ 64.–). Fixed annual subscription rate for Germany: Individual subscription 104 Euro –, institutional subscription 218 Euro. Payment on receipt of invoice. Subscriptions are entered on a calendar basis only (Jan.–Dec.). Cancellations must be filed by referring to the subscription number six weeks before closing date (subscription invoice); there will be no confirmation. There may be 1 to 4 supplementary issues per year. Each supplementary issue will be sent to subscribers with a separate invoice allowing 25% deduction on the regular price. Subscribers have the right to return the issue within one month to the distribution company. – Subscription office: VVA, post-box 7777, D-33310 Gütersloh, Germany, Tel. 0049/(0)5241-801968/802891, Fax 80 96 20. Distribution: Kristiane Alesch, Tel. 0049/(0)611/7878-359. Advertising office: Thomas Werner, Tel. 0049/(0)611/7878-138. Editorial Department: Susanne Kramer, Tel. 0049/(0) 611/7878-234, e-mail: Susanne.Kramer@gwv-fachverlage.de. Annelie Meisenheimer, Tel. 0049/(0)611/7878-232. Production: Frieder Kumm, Tel. 0049/(0)611/7878-175, Fax 7878-400. Internet: Publisher http://www.gabler.de; Editor http://www.uni-hohenheim.de./~mir; Managing Director Dr. Hans-Dieter Haenel; Publishing Director Dr. Heinz Weinheimer; Senior Publishing Editor Claudia Splittgerber; Sales Manager Gabriel Göttlinger; Production Manager Reinhard van den Hövel. Produced by Druckhaus „Thomas Müntzer" GmbH, Bad Langensalza – Contributions published in this journal are protected by copyright.

© Betriebswirtschaftlicher Verlag Dr. Th. Gabler/GWV Fachverlage GmbH, Wiesbaden 2004. Gabler Verlag is a company of Springer Science+Business Media.

No part of this publication may be reproduced, stored in a retrieval system or transmitted in any form or by any means: electronic, magnetic tape, mechanical, photocopying, recording or otherwise, without permission in writing from the publisher. There is no liability for manuscripts and review literature which were submitted without invitation.

ISSN 0938-8249

Have you already visited our **mir** homepage?

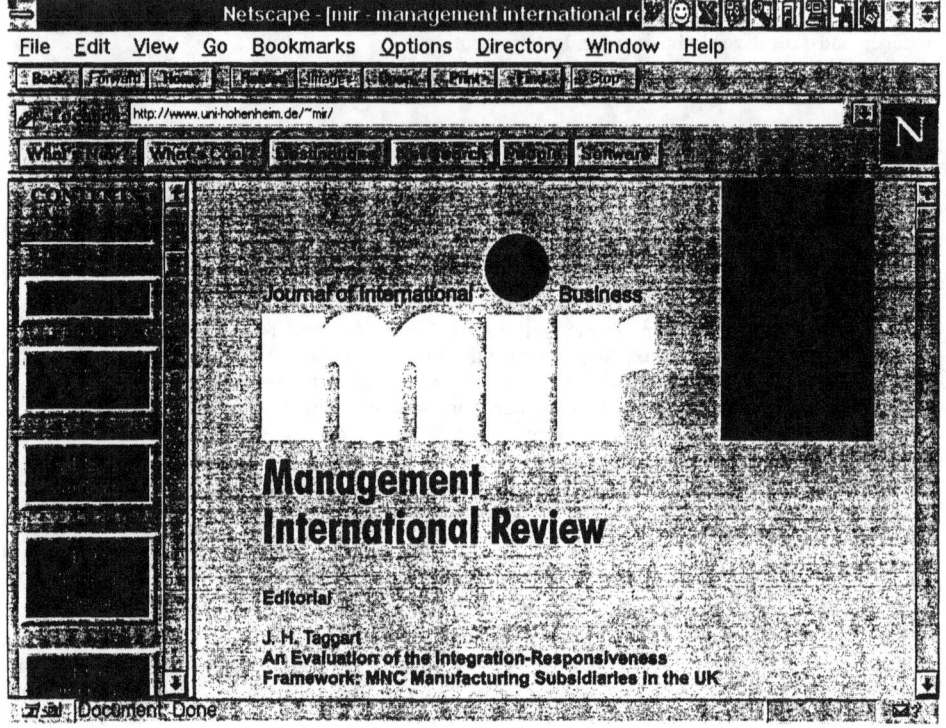

If not, then it is high time you did!

http://www.uni-hohenheim.de/~mir

ISBN 3-409-12544-2
VVA 126/02544

GPSR Compliance
The European Union's (EU) General Product Safety Regulation (GPSR) is a set of rules that requires consumer products to be safe and our obligations to ensure this.

If you have any concerns about our products, you can contact us on

ProductSafety@springernature.com

In case Publisher is established outside the EU, the EU authorized representative is:

Springer Nature Customer Service Center GmbH
Europaplatz 3
69115 Heidelberg, Germany

www.ingramcontent.com/pod-product-compliance
Lightning Source LLC
LaVergne TN
LVHW011944070526
838202LV00054B/4793